Active Directory Domain Services 2008

HOW-TO

SAMS | 800 East 96th Street, Indianapolis, Indiana 46240 USA

Active Directory Domain Services 2008 How-To

Copyright © 2009 by Pearson Education, Inc.

ISBN-13: 978-0-672-33045-2
ISBN-10: 0-672-33045-8

Library of Congress Cataloging-in-Publication Data
Policelli, John.
Active directory 2008 how-to / John Policelli.
  p. cm.
ISBN-13: 978-0-672-33045-2
ISBN-10: 0-672-33045-8
1. Directory services (Computer network technology)   2. Microsoft Windows.   I. Title.
TK5105.595.P65 2009
005.7'1376–dc22

                                    2009011935

Printed in the United States of America

First Printing

Trademarks

Warning and Disclaimer

Bulk Sales

Sams Publishing offers excellent discounts on this book when ordered in quantity for bulk purchases or special sales. For more information, please contact

U.S. Corporate and Government Sales
1-800-382-3419
corpsales@pearsontechgroup.com

For sales outside of the U.S., please contact

International Sales
international@pearson.com

Editor-in-Chief
Karen Gettman

Executive Editor
Neil Rowe

Development Editor
Mark Renfrow

Managing Editor
Patrick Kanouse

Project Editor
Mandie Frank

Copy Editor
Megan Wade

Indexer
Ken Johnson

Proofreader
Leslie Joseph

Technical Editor
Todd Meister

Publishing Coordinator
Cindy Teeters

Designer
Gary Adair

Compositor
Bronkella Publishing LLC

Contents at a Glance

Table of Contents

9 Manage Group Policy   **327**

About the Author

John Policelli (Microsoft MVP for Directory Services, MCTS, MCSA, ITSM, iNet+, Network+, and A+) is a solutions-focused IT consultant with more than a decade of combined success in architecture, security, strategic planning, and disaster recovery planning. John has designed and implemented dozens of complex directory service, e-messaging, web, networking, and security enterprise solutions.

John has spent the past nine years focused on identity and access management and providing thought leadership for some of the largest installations of Active Directory in Canada. He has been involved as an author, a technical reviewer, and a subject matter expert for more than 50 training, exam writing, press, and whitepaper projects related to Windows Server 2008 Identity and Access Management, networking, and collaboration. John maintains a blog at http://policelli.com/blog.

Dedication

I dedicate this book to my parents, Rina and Anthony, and my brother, Dino. Thank you for your constant belief in me and for guiding me through life.

Acknowledgments

I would like to thank my beautiful wife Maria for her unconditional love and support, and for being my motivation to succeed.

Although my name appears on the cover of this book, there is a team of individuals at Pearson who worked diligently to evolve this book from the initial concept through to the final product. I would like to thank Neil Rowe for the publishing opportunity and the ongoing guidance throughout the various stages of the writing and publishing process. I would like to thank Mandie Frank, Mark Renfrow, Megan Wade, and Todd Meister for their invaluable assistance and hard work through the publishing process. I would also like to thank all of those from Pearson who worked on the publishing process, but who I did not get to meet.

We Want to Hear from You!

As the reader of this book, *you* are our most important critic and commentator. We value your opinion and want to know what we're doing right, what we could do better, what areas you'd like to see us publish in, and any other words of wisdom you're willing to pass our way.

You can email or write me directly to let me know what you did or didn't like about this book—as well as what we can do to make our books stronger.

Please note that I cannot help you with technical problems related to the topic of this book, and that due to the high volume of mail I receive, I might not be able to reply to every message.

When you write, please be sure to include this book's title and author as well as your name and phone or email address. I will carefully review your comments and share them with the author and editors who worked on the book.

E-mail: consumer@samspublishing.com

Mail: Neil Rowe
         Executive Editor
         Sams Publishing
         800 East 96th Street
         Indianapolis, IN 46240 USA

Reader Services

Visit our website and register this book at www.informit.com/title/9780672330452 for convenient access to any updates, downloads, or errata that might be available for this book.

INTRODUCTION

Overview of This Book

Active Directory has been on the market for roughly a decade now. Prior to Windows Server 2008, the changes in Active Directory functionality had been relatively minuscule in comparison to the changes introduced in Windows Server 2008. Windows Server 2008 is the first Windows Server operating system release to introduce such significant changes to Active Directory functionality since its inception in Windows 2000 Server. Now is likely the most important time for IT professionals to familiarize themselves with the new Active Directory Domain Services (AD DS) in Windows Server 2008.

IT professionals have access to more resources today than ever before. An infinite number of websites, blogs, newsgroups, magazines, and books claim to provide you with the latest and greatest Active Directory information. With the information overload we are experiencing today, it is a task in itself to decipher the profuse amount of information and find exactly what you are looking for.

Look no further! IT professionals can turn to this book first, to get reliable, easy-to-implement solutions they can trust—and use immediately. This completely up-to-date book brings together tested, step-by-step procedures for planning, installing, customizing, and managing AD DS in any production environment. This hands-on how-to guide walks you through performing approximately 200 tasks, with clear and accurate steps and diagrams for each one.

How-To Benefit from This Book

We've designed this book to be easy to read from cover to cover. This book will provide you with the ability to gain a full understanding of Active Directory Domain Services in Windows Sever 2008, while breaking down the subject matter into 13 easy-to-navigate chapters. They include

- ► Introduction to Active Directory Domain Services
- ► Prepare for Active Directory Domain Services Installation
- ► Install and Uninstall Active Directory Domain Services
- ► Manage Trusts and Functional Levels
- ► Manage Operations Master Roles and Global Catalog Servers
- ► Manage Sites and Replication

- Manage the Active Directory Domain Services Schema
- Manage Active Directory Domain Services Data
- Manage Group Policy
- Manage Password Replication Policies
- Manage Fine-Grained Password and Account Lockout Policies
- Manage Active Directory Domain Services Backup and Recovery
- Manage Active Directory Domain Services Auditing

Within each of these chapters are subheadings that focus on the primary elements of administering that portion of AD DS.

Beneath the subheadings are Scenario/Problem introductions. These serve as mini-starting points for the administrator to consider. At times, the information provided helps you deal with a specific problem you might be facing; however, typically a scenario is described that enables you to determine whether this direction is necessary for your particular organization.

How-To Continue Expanding Your Knowledge

Certainly there are more books, articles, and sites you can and should consider in expanding your knowledge of Windows Server 2008 Active Directory Domain Services, especially because it will no doubt continue to evolve and change as more and more features, fixes, and enhancements are added by Microsoft. How does one stay on top of the flood of information?

Well, several sites are invaluable. They include the following:

- **The Active Directory Domain Services Microsoft TechNet Library (http://technet.microsoft.com/en-ca/library/cc770946.aspx)**—This has to be one of the most valuable online resources for Windows Server 2008 AD DS information. Here you will find getting started guides, the AD DS planning and architecture guide, the AD DS deployment guide, the AD DS operations guide, and the AD DS Installed Help.

- **What's New in AD DS in Windows Server 2008 Microsoft document (http://technet.microsoft.com/en-us/library/cc755093.aspx)**—This document provides a great overview of each of the new AD DS features in Windows Server 2008, as well as links to more granular information on each new feature.

- **Ask the Directory Services Team Blog (http://blogs.technet.com/askds)**—This is Microsoft's official Enterprise Platform Support DS blog.

- **Discussions in Active Directory (http://www.microsoft.com/communities/newsgroups/en-us/default.aspx?dg=microsoft.public.windows.server.active_directory)**—This is Microsoft's Active Directory newsgroup.

In addition, several blog sites from Active Directory MVPs, Microsoft employees, and Active Directory gurus are worth investigating, including the following:

- ▶ http://blogs.dirteam.com (Dirteam.com/ActiveDir.org)
- ▶ http://www.identityblog.com (Kim Cameron)
- ▶ http://blogs.technet.com/ad (Tim Springston)
- ▶ http://blog.joeware.net (Joe Richards)
- ▶ http://www.gilkirkpatrick.com/Blog (Gil Kirkpatrick)
- ▶ http://www.open-a-socket.com (Tony Murray)
- ▶ http://briandesmond.com/blog (Brian Desmond)

These are just a handful of the ones I personally enjoy, although you will easily find many more. Choose the ones you feel are most helpful to you.

Last, but certainly not least, you are welcome to visit my website for free AD DS education: http://www.policelli.com. It includes a link to my blog, articles I've written, a variety of publications, and so forth.

CHAPTER 1

Introduction to Active Directory Domain Services

Active Directory has changed significantly in Windows Server 2008. Windows Server 2008 includes a number of new features for the Active Directory Domain Services server role. The minimum and recommended system requirements for Active Directory Domain Services in Windows Server 2008 have also changed.

This chapter starts with an overview of the Active Directory Domain Services server role in Windows Server 2008. Thereafter, details on the new Active Directory Domain Services features are covered. Lastly, the system requirements for Windows Server 2008 and the steps to install Windows Server 2008 are covered in this chapter.

Active Directory Domain Services (AD DS) is Microsoft's implementation of a directory service that provides centralized authentication and authorization services. AD DS in Windows Server 2008 provides a powerful directory service to centrally store and manage security principals, such as users, groups, and computers, and it offers centralized and secure access to network resources.

AD DS is one of the most important server roles in Windows Server 2008. It provides the basis for authentication and authorization for virtually all other server roles in Windows Server 2008 and is the foundation for Microsoft's Identity and Access Solutions. Additionally, a number of enterprise products, including Exchange Server and Windows SharePoint Services, require AD DS.

What's New in Windows Server 2008 Active Directory Domain Services

Active Directory Domain Services in Windows Server 2008 provides a number of enhancements over previous versions, including these:

▶ **Auditing**—AD DS auditing has been enhanced significantly in Windows Server 2008. The enhancements provide more granular auditing capabilities through four new auditing categories: Directory Services Access, Directory Services Changes, Directory Services Replication, and Detailed Directory Services Replication. Additionally, auditing now provides the capability to log old and new values of an attribute when a successful change is made to that attribute.

▶ **Fine-Grained Password Policies**—AD DS in Windows Server 2008 now provides the capability to create different password and account lockout policies for different sets of users in a domain. User and group password and account lockout policies are defined and applied via a Password Setting Object (PSO). A PSO has attributes for all the settings that can be defined in the Default Domain Policy, except Kerberos settings. PSOs can be applied to both users and groups.

▶ **Read-Only Domain Controllers**—AD DS in Windows Server 2008 introduces a new type of domain controller called a read-only domain controller (RODC). RODCs contain a read-only copy of the AD DS database. RODCs are covered in more detail in Chapter 6, "Manage Sites and Replication."

▶ **Restartable Active Directory Domain Services**—AD DS in Windows Server 2008 can now be stopped and restarted through MMC snap-ins and the command line. The restartable AD DS service reduces the time required to perform certain maintenance and restore operations. Additionally, other services running on the server remain available to satisfy client requests while AD DS is stopped.

▶ **AD DS Database Mounting Tool**—AD DS in Windows Server 2008 comes with a AD DS database mounting tool, which provides a means to compare data as it exists in snapshots or backups taken at different times. The AD DS database mounting eliminates the need to restore multiple backups to compare the AD data that they contain and provides the capability to examine any change made to data stored in AD DS.

Windows Server 2008 System Requirements

The published system requirements for Windows Server 2008 are summarized in Table 1.1.

Table 1.1 **Windows Server 2008 System Requirements**

Component	Requirement
Processor	**Minimum**: 1GHz (for x86 processors) or 1.4GHz (for x64 processors) **Recommended**: 2GHz or faster **NOTE**: An Intel Itanium 2 processor is required for Windows Server 2008 for Itanium-Based Systems.
Memory	**Minimum**: 512MB **Recommended**: 2GB or more **Maximum (32-bit systems)**: 4GB (for Windows Server 2008 Standard) or 64GB (for Windows Server 2008 Enterprise or Windows Server 2008 Datacenter) **Maximum (64-bit systems)**: 32GB (for Windows Server 2008 Standard) or 2 TB (for Windows Server 2008 Enterprise, Windows Server 2008 Datacenter, or Windows Server 2008 for Itanium-Based Systems) **NOTE**: Computers with more than 16GB of RAM require more disk space for paging, hibernation, and dump files.
Disk space	**Minimum**: 10GB **Recommended**: 40GB or more **NOTE**: Computers with more than 16GB of RAM require more disk space for paging, hibernation, and dump files. DVD-ROM drive Super VGA (800 x 600) or higher-resolution monitor Keyboard and Microsoft mouse (or other compatible pointing device)

Installing Windows Server 2008

The procedure that follows provides the steps necessary to install Windows Server 2008. These steps cover a full installation of Windows Server 2008:

1. Insert the Windows Server 2008 installation media into the DVD drive.

2. Reboot the computer.

3. When prompted for an installation language and other regional options, make your selection and click Next.

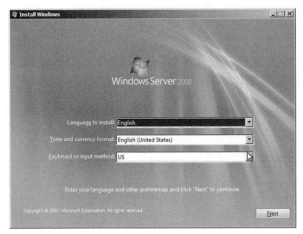

FIGURE 1.1
Language and other preferences.

4. Click Install Now to begin the installation process.

FIGURE 1.2
Install Now.

5. On the Select the Operating System You Want to Install page, select Windows Server 2008 Enterprise (Full Installation) and click Next.

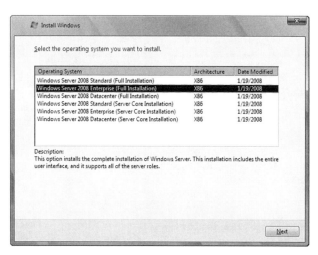

FIGURE 1.3
Select the operating system you want to install.

6. Read and accept the license terms by selecting the check box; then click Next.

7. On the Which Type of Installation Do You Want? page, select Custom (Advanced).

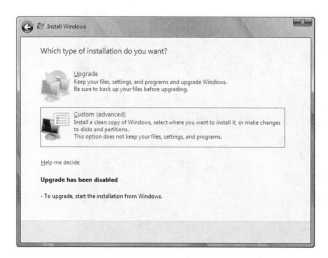

FIGURE 1.4
Which type of installation do you want?

8. On the Where Do You Want to Install Windows? click Drive Options, click New, and verify the size of the drive. Then click Apply, and then click Next.

9. The installation of Windows Server 2008 begins.

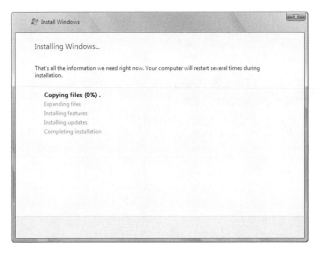

FIGURE 1.5
Installing Windows.

10. When the installation process is complete, the server reboots and you are prompted to change the user's password before logging on for the first time, as shown in Figure 1.6.

FIGURE 1.6
Initial password change.

11. Click OK to change the password for the Administrator account.

12. Enter a password of Today01! in the New Password field.

13. Reenter the password Today01! in the Confirm Password field and click the arrow, as shown in Figure 1.7.

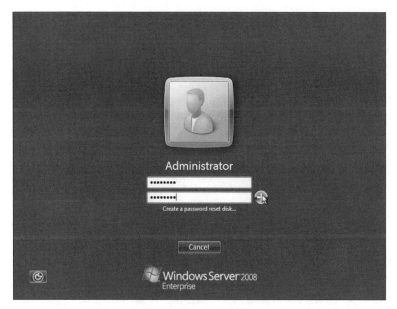

FIGURE 1.7
The Change Password Window.

14. Click OK on the password change confirmation page.

    Windows creates the profile for the Administrator account. After the profile is created, the Initial Configuration Tasks window appears, as shown in Figure 1.8.

15. On the Initial Configuration Tasks page, check the option Do Not Show This Window at Logon; then click Close.

    After the Initial Configuration Tasks page is closed, Server Manager opens automatically (see Figure 1.9).

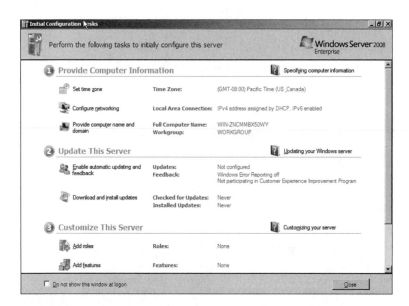

FIGURE 1.8
Initial configuration tasks.

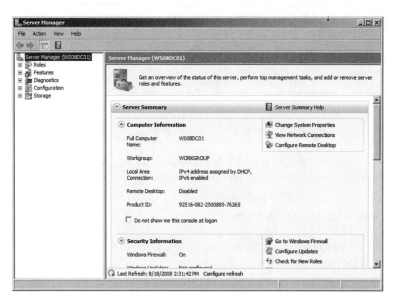

FIGURE 1.9
Server Manager.

16. On the Server Manager page, select the option Do Not Show Me This Console at Logon; then close Server Manager.

The installation of Windows Server 2008 is now complete.

CHAPTER 2

Prepare for Active Directory Domain Services Installation

Windows Server 2008 can be installed into an existing Windows 2000 Server or Windows Server 2003 Active Directory Domain Services (AD DS) forest. You must take certain steps to prepare for AD DS installation when your environment contains an existing forest.

The forest itself must be prepared for Windows Server 2008 AD DS. Thereafter, each domain that will contain domain controllers running Windows Server 2008 also needs to be prepared. Lastly, if you plan to deploy read-only domain controllers (RODCs) into the forest, additional preparation is required.

This chapter describes the steps necessary to prepare for Active Directory Domain Services installation.

Prepare an Existing Forest for Windows Server 2008 Active Directory Domain Services

Scenario/Problem: If your environment consists of an existing Windows 2000 Server or Windows Server 2003 Active Directory Domain Services forest, you must prepare the existing forest for Windows Server 2008 before you can add a domain controller that has Windows Server 2008 installed. Preparing an existing forest consists of updating the AD DS schema.

Solution: The schema update consists of extending the existing AD DS schema to include the attributes and classes that are new in Windows Server 2008. The Windows Server 2008 installation media includes the ADPrep command-line tool, which is used to prepare an existing forest for Windows Server 2008 AD DS. The schema update must be completed on the domain controller that holds the schema master operations master role.

To find the domain controller that holds the schema master operations master role, type the following command into a command prompt window:

```
netdom query fsmo
```

NOTE The Netdom command-line tool is not installed with Windows Server 2000 or Windows Server 2003. Netdom can be installed from the Windows Support tools for these operating systems. The Netdom command-line tool is installed with the Windows Server 2008 operating system by default.

Figure 2.1 shows the output of the Netdom command-line tool.

To complete this task, you must use an AD DS account that has membership in the following AD DS groups:

- ▶ Enterprise Admins

- ▶ Schema Admins

- ▶ Domain Admins in the forest root domain

FIGURE 2.1
Using the Netdom command-line tool to find the schema master operations master role holder.

To prepare an existing forest for Windows Server 2008 Active Directory Domain Services, perform the following steps:

1. Log on to the schema master.

2. Insert the Windows Server 2008 DVD into the DVD drive.

3. Click Start and select Command Prompt.

4. Type the following command, and then press Enter:

   D:\sources\adprep\adprep /forestprep

   (where D: is your DVD drive's drive letter.)

5. As shown in Figure 2.2, adprep.exe presents a warning that indicates that all Windows 2000 domain controllers in the forest must have Service Pack 4 installed. If you meet this minimum requirement, type **C** and press Enter.

FIGURE 2.2
Forest prep completed successfully.

After the forest update is complete, you will receive a message that states `Adprep successfully updated the forest-wide information`.

You can also use a number of methods to ensure the schema update was successful.

Start by examining the log file created by adprep; to accomplish this, follow these steps:

1. Select Start, Run.

2. In the Run dialog box, type `%windir%\Debug\adprep\logs`. Then click OK.

3. Open the folder that corresponds to the date and time that `adprep.exe` was run. For example, if the `adprep` command was run at 4:32:02 p.m. on August 18, 2008, the folder name will be `20080818163202`.

4. Examine the `adprep.log` file.

You can also verify the schema version is in fact version 44 after that completion of adprep by performing the following steps:

1. Select Start, Run.

2. In the Run dialog box, type `adsiedit.msc`; then click OK. The ADSI Edit console opens, as shown in Figure 2.3.

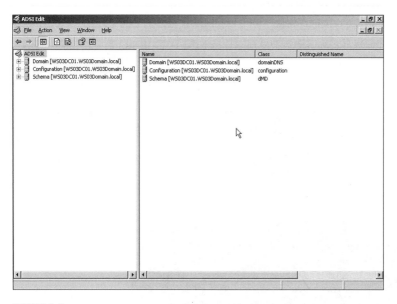

FIGURE 2.3
ADSI Edit Console.

3. Select the Schema node in the console tree on the left.

4. Right-click the schema container in the details pane, and select Properties. The Attribute Editor for the schema object opens, as shown in Figure 2.4.

FIGURE 2.4
Schema Object Attribute Editor.

5. Scroll down to the `objectVersion` attribute and ensure the value is 44, as shown in Figure 2.5.

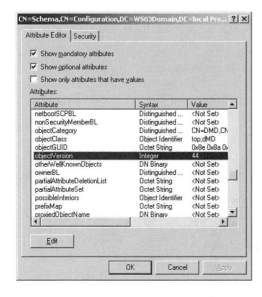

FIGURE 2.5
objectVersion.

Prepare an Existing Domain for Windows Server 2008 Active Directory Domain Services

Scenario/Problem: After the existing forest has been prepared for Windows Server 2008 AD DS, you need to prepare each domain in the forest that will contain Windows Server 2008 domain controllers. Preparing existing domains for Windows Server 2008 AD DS consists of applying permission changes to AD DS.

Solution: Each existing domain that will contain one or more Windows Server 2008 domain controllers must be prepared. The Windows Server 2008 installation media includes the adprep command-line tool, which is used to prepare an existing domain for Windows Server 2008 AD DS. The domain update must be completed on the domain controller that holds the infrastructure master operations master role.

To find the domain controller that holds the infrastructure master operations master role, type the following command into a command prompt window:

`netdom query /domain:DomainName fsmo`

(where *DomainName* is the name of the domain you are trying to determine the infrastructure master role holder for).

To complete this task, you must use an AD DS account that has membership in the following AD DS group:

▶ Domain Admins in the domain you are preparing

To prepare an existing domain for Windows Server 2008 Active Directory Domain Services, perform the following steps:

1. Log on to the infrastructure master.

2. Insert the Windows Server 2008 DVD into the DVD drive.

3. Click Start and select Command Prompt.

4. Type the following command, and then press Enter:

   `D:\sources\adprep\adprep /domainprep /gpprep`

   (where D: is your DVD drive's drive letter).

After the domain update is complete, you will receive a message that states Adprep successfully updated the domain-wide information, as shown in Figure 2.6.

The changes made by the domain update are also logged in the %windir%\Debug\ adprep\logs directory.

The domain prep process creates a new object in the System container in the domain. This new container is used to store fine-grained password policies.

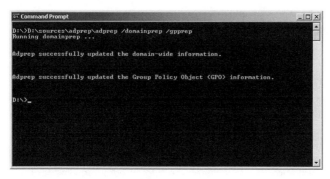

FIGURE 2.6
Domain prep completed successfully.

One additional method of verifying the completion of the domain prep process is to ensure the new container has been created. You can use the steps that follow to verify the successful completion of the domain prep process.

1. Select Start, Administrative Tools, Active Directory Users and Computers.

2. In the Active Directory Users and Computers console, go to View and select Advanced Features.

3. Expand the domain in the console tree and select the System container.

As shown in Figure 2.7, a container called Password Settings Container exists in the details pane; it was created by the domain prep process.

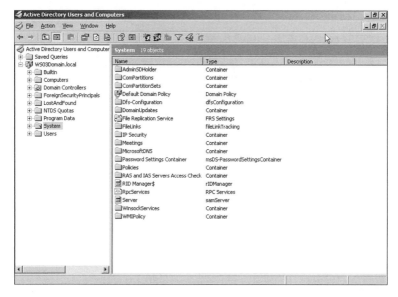

FIGURE 2.7
Password Settings Container.

Prepare an Existing Domain for a Read-Only Domain Controller

Scenario/Problem: If you plan to deploy read-only domain controllers into your forest, you must first prepare the forest for RODCs. This is required before you can add any RODCs to your forest.

Solution: Each forest that will contain one or more RODCs must be prepared. The Windows Server 2008 installation media includes the adprep command-line tool, which is used to prepare the forest for Windows Server 2008 RODCs. The RODC can be run on any member server.

To complete this task, you must use an AD DS account that has membership in the following AD DS group:

▶ Enterprise Admins

To prepare an existing domain for a read-only domain controller, perform the following steps:

1. Log on to any computer in the forest.

2. Insert the Windows Server 2008 DVD into the DVD drive.

3. Click Start, right-click Command prompt, and then click Run as Administrator.

4. Type the following command, and then press Enter:

   `D:\sources\adprep\adprep /rodcprep`

   (where D: is your DVD drive's drive letter).

5. The RODC prep process will complete, and you will receive a message that states *Adprep completed without errors.* All partitions are updated. See the ADPrep.log in directory...for more information, as shown in Figure 2.8.

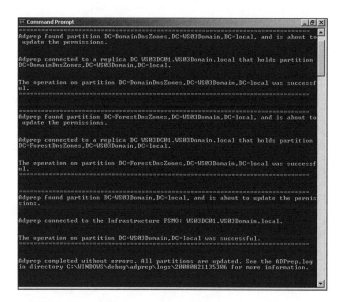

FIGURE 2.8
RODC prep completed successfully.

CHAPTER 3

Install and Uninstall Active Directory Domain Services

Active Directory Domain Services (AD DS) was introduced with the release of Windows 2000 Server and has been included in each subsequent release of the server operating system from Microsoft. The majority of companies have at least one AD DS forest deployed. However, some companies continue to deploy new AD DS forests for various reasons.

This chapter describes the steps required to install and uninstall Active Directory Domain Services.

Install a New Windows Server 2008 Forest

Scenario/Problem: In some cases, you will deploy a new Windows Server 2008 Active Directory Domain Service forest instead of adding domain controllers (DCs) to an existing forest. Although the installation of a new Windows Server 2008 AD DS forest does not require any of the preparation steps that were performed in Chapter 2, "Prepare for Active Directory Domain Services Installation," you still need to perform the installation following specific steps.

Solution: Installing a new Windows Server 2008 forest consists of promoting a Windows Server 2008 server to a domain controller. Thereafter, additional DCs and domains can be added to the new forest. The installation of a new Windows Server 2008 forest can be performed by using the Windows interface, the command line, and an answer file.

Install a New Forest by Using the Windows Interface

To install a new forest by using the Windows interface, perform the following steps using a local account that has membership in the following local group:

▶ Administrators

1. Log on to the server you want to promote to a domain controller.

2. Click Start and then click Server Manager.

3. In Roles Summary, click Add Roles.

4. On the Before You Begin page, click Next.

5. On the Select Server Roles page, shown in Figure 3.1, click the Active Directory Domain Services check box; then click Next.

6. On the Active Directory Domain Services page, click Next.

7. On the Confirm Installation Selections page, click Install.

8. On the Installation Results page, shown in Figure shown in Figure 3.2, verify that the installation succeeded and then click Close this wizard and launch the Active Directory Domain Services Installation Wizard (dcpromo.exe).

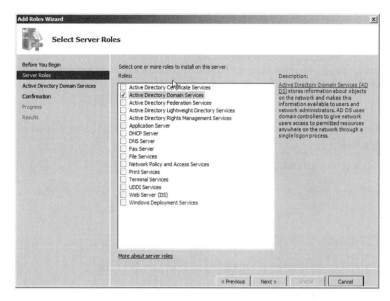

FIGURE 3.1
The Select Server Roles page.

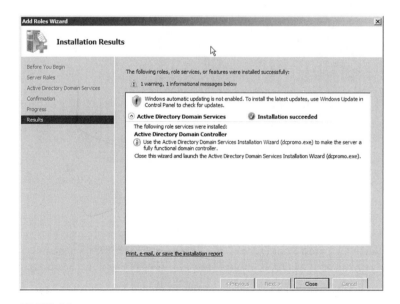

FIGURE 3.2
The Installation Results page.

TIP It is a best practice to assign a static IP address as opposed to a dynamic IP address on a domain controller. If you have not assigned a static IP address, now is the best time to do so. If you proceed with the steps that follow without assigning a static IP address, you will be presented with a warning during the AD DS installation process. You can accept the warning and proceed with the installation if desired.

9. On the Welcome to the Active Directory Domain Services Installation Wizard page, click Next.

10. On the Operating System Compatibility page, click Next.

11. On the Choose a Deployment Configuration page, shown in Figure 3.3, click Create a new domain in a new forest; then click Next.

FIGURE 3.3
The Choose a Deployment Configuration page.

12. On the Name the Forest Root Domain page, shown in Figure 3.4, type the fully qualified domain name (FQDN) for the forest root domain and then click Next.

13. On the Set Forest Functional Level page, shown in Figure 3.5, select the forest functional level that meets your requirements and click Next.

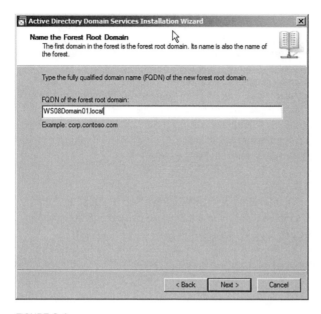

FIGURE 3.4
The Name the Forest Root Domain page.

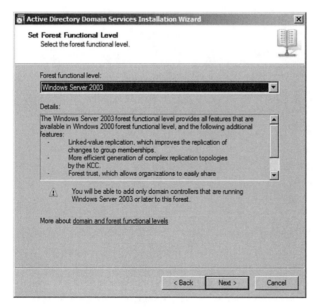

FIGURE 3.5
The Set Forest Functional Level page.

> **NOTE** Active Directory Domain Services functional levels control the available domain or forest advanced features. For example, a number of the new features introduced in Windows Server 2008 require a domain functional level of Windows Server 2008. Functional levels also control the operating systems that you can run on domain controllers. If your domain functional level is set to Windows Server 2008, you cannot have domain controllers that have Windows Server 2003 installed. Lastly, once you set or raise a functional level, you cannot change the functional level to a lower level.
>
> For more information on AD DS functional levels, go to http://technet.microsoft.com/en-us/library/cc754918.aspx.

14. If you set a forest functional level other than Windows Server 2008, the Set Domain Functional Level page displays, as shown in Figure 3.6. Select the domain functional level that meets your requirements and click Next.

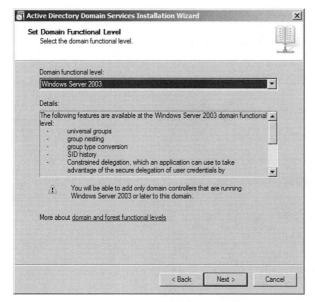

FIGURE 3.6
The Set Domain Functional Level page.

15. On the Additional Domain Controller Options page, shown in Figure 3.7, DNS Server is selected by default, which allows the DNS infrastructure to be created by the installation process. If you plan to use AD-Integrated DNS, click Next. If you plan to use an existing DNS infrastructure and do not want the domain controller to be a DNS server, clear the DNS Server check box and click Next.

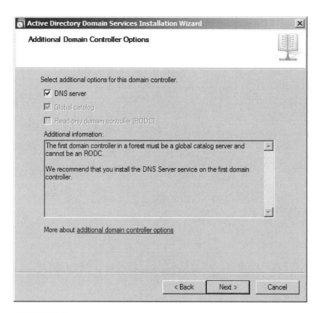

FIGURE 3.7
The Additional Domain Controller Options page.

16. If the wizard cannot create a delegation for the DNS server, it displays a message to indicate that you can create the delegation manually, as shown in Figure 3.8. To continue, click Yes.

FIGURE 3.8
The manual DNS Delegation Message.

17. On the Location for Database, Log Files, and SYSVOL page, shown in Figure 3.9, type the volume and folder locations for the database file, the directory service log files, and the SYSVOL files; then click Next.

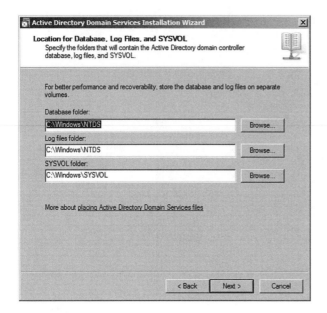

FIGURE 3.9
The Location for Database, Log Files, and SYSVOL page.

18. On the Directory Services Restore Mode Administrator Password page, shown
    in Figure 3.10, type and confirm the restore mode password and then click Next.

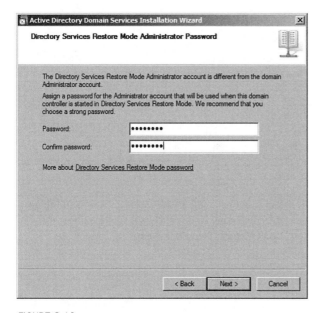

FIGURE 3.10
The Directory Services Restore Mode Administrator Password page.

19. On the Summary page, shown in Figure 3.11, click Next after you review your selections.

TIP You can click the Export button to export the selections you made to an answer file, which can be used later for an unattended installation.

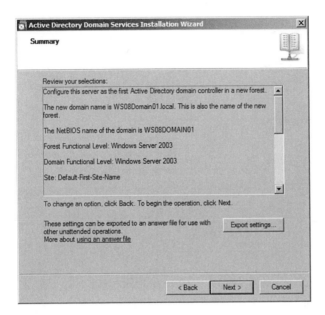

FIGURE 3.11
The Summary page.

The Active Directory Domain Services installation process starts, as shown in Figure 3.12.

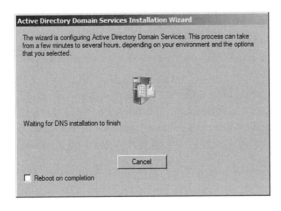

FIGURE 3.12
The Active Directory Domain
Services Installation page.

20. After the installation is complete, the Completing the Active Directory Domain Services Installation Wizard page appears, as shown in Figure 3.13. Ensure the installation was successful and click Finish.

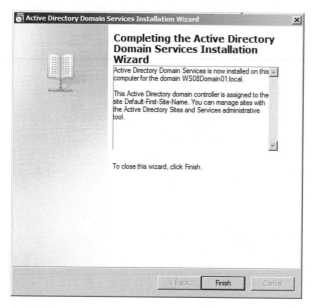

FIGURE 3.13
The Completing the Active Directory Domain Services Installation Wizard page.

21. When prompted to restart, click Restart Now.

22. To validate the installation process, click Start, click Run, type **C:\Windows\Debug**, and click OK.

23. Open the DCPROMO.log file and analyze the results in the file.

Install a New Forest by Using the Command Line

Active Directory Domain Services can also be installed by using the command line. This is particularly useful when installing AD DS on a server that has a Server Core installation of Windows Server 2008.

The installation options when using the command line are the same as those used when installing AD DS using an unattended installation. When installing AD DS by using the command line, you type the installation options and parameters into the command line as opposed to an answer file, which is used for an unattended installation.

Table 3.1 lists the installation parameters used in the steps that follow and the corresponding action of each parameter.

TABLE 3.1   Installing a New Forest by Using the Command Line Installation Parameters

Installation Parameter	Corresponding Action
InstallDns:yes	DNS server will be installed.
dnsOnNetwork:No	DNS server will be installed.
replicaOrNewDomain:domain	A new domain will be created.
newDomain:forest	A new forest will be created.
newDomainDnsName:WS08Domain02.local	FQDN of the new domain.
DomainNetbiosName:WS08Domain02	NetBIOS name of the new domain.
databasePath:"c:\Windows\ntds"	Database path.
logPath:"c:\Windows\ntds"	Log file path.
sysvolpath:"c:\Windows\sysvol"	SYSVOL path.
safeModeAdminPassword:Today01!	DSRM Administrator password.
forestLevel:2	Forest functional level will be set to Windows Server 2003.
domainLevel:2	Domain functional level will be set to Windows Server 2003.
rebootOnCompletion:yes	Server will be rebooted after completion.

> **TIP**   For a complete list of installation options and parameters, go to http://technet.microsoft.com/en-us/library/cc733048.aspx.

To install a new forest by using the command line, perform the following steps using a local account that has membership in the following local group:

▶ Administrators

1. Log on to the server you want to promote to a domain controller.
2. Click Start and then click Command Prompt.
3. Type the following into the command prompt window, as shown in Figure 3.14, and then press Enter:

```
dcpromo /unattend /InstallDns:yes /dnsOnNetwork:no
/replicaOrNewDomain:domain /newDomain:forest
/newDomainDnsName:WS08Domain02.local
/DomainNetbiosName:WS08Domain02 /databasePath:"c:\Windows\ntds"
/logPath:"c:\Windows\ntds" /sysvolpath:"c:\Windows\sysvol"
/safeModeAdminPassword:Today01! /forestLevel:2 /domainLevel:2
/rebootOnCompletion:yes
```

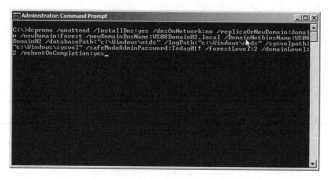

FIGURE 3.14
Installing a new forest using the command line.

The dcpromo process begins by determining whether the AD DS binaries are installed. If the binaries are not installed, dcpromo installs them, as shown in Figure 3.15.

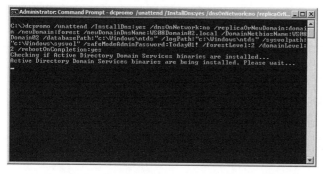

FIGURE 3.15
Installing AD DS services binaries.

4. After the AD DS binaries have been installed, a summary of the installation options is presented in the command prompt window, as shown in Figure 3.16. Then the AD DS installation process begins.

5. The status of the AD DS installing is updated in the command prompt window, as shown in Figure 3.17.

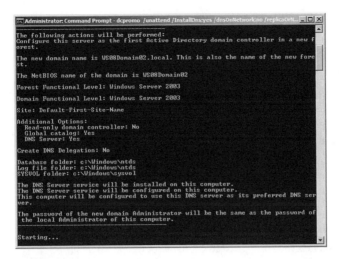

FIGURE 3.16
Installing AD DS.

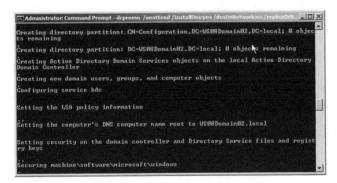

FIGURE 3.17
The installation's progress.

6. When the installation process is complete, the server reboots automatically if the /rebootOnCompletion option was used in the command line. If the /rebootOnCompletion option was not used in the command line, you are prompted to restart the server.

7. To validate the installation process, click Start, click Run, type **C:\Windows\Debug**, and click OK.

8. Open the DCPROMO.log file and analyze the results in the file.

Install a New Forest by Using an Answer File

Active Directory Domain Services can also be installed using an answer file. This is useful when installing AD DS on a server that has a Server Core installation of Windows Server 2008.

Table 3.2 lists the installation parameters used in the steps that follow and the corresponding action of each parameter.

TABLE 3.2   Installing a New Forest by Using Answer File Installation Parameters

Installation Parameter	Corresponding Action
InstallDNS=yes	DNS server will be installed.
NewDomain=forest	A new forest will be created.
NewDomainDNSName=WS08Domain03.local	FQDN of the new domain.
DomainNetBiosName=WS08Domain03	NetBIOS name of the new domain.
ReplicaOrNewDomain=domain	A new domain will be created.
ForestLevel=3	Forest functional level will be set to Windows Server 2008.
DomainLevel=3	Domain functional level will be set to Windows Server 2008.
DatabasePath="c:\Windows\ntds"	Database path.
LogPath="c:\Windows\ntds"	Log file path.
RebootOnCompletion=yes	Server will be rebooted after completion.
SYSVOLPath=c:\Windows\sysvol"	SYSVOL path.
SafeModeAdminPassword=Today01!	DSRM Administrator password.

> **TIP**   For a complete list of installation options and parameters, go to http://technet.microsoft.com/en-us/library/cc733048.aspx.

In order to install a new forest by using an answer file, perform the following steps using a local account that has membership in the following local group:

▶ Administrators

1. Log on to the server you want to promote to a domain controller.
2. Click Start, click Run, type **notepad**, and click OK.
3. On the first line, type **[DCINSTALL]**, and then press ENTER.

4. Type the following entries, one entry on each line, as shown in Figure 3.18:

```
InstallDNS=yes
NewDomain=forest
NewDomainDNSName=WS08Domain03.local
DomainNetBiosName=WS08Domain03
ReplicaOrNewDomain=domain
ForestLevel=3
DomainLevel=3
DatabasePath="c:\Windows\ntds"
LogPath="c:\Windows\ntds"
RebootOnCompletion=yes
SYSVOLPath="c:\Windows\sysvol"
SafeModeAdminPassword=Today01!
```

FIGURE 3.18
The answer file.

5. Save the answer file as `C:\DCAnswer.txt`.

6. Click Start and then click Command Prompt.

7. Type the following into the command prompt window, as shown in Figure 3.19, and then press Enter:

`dcpromo /unattend:"C:\DCAnswer.txt"`

The dcpromo process begins by determining whether the AD DS binaries are installed. If the binaries are not installed, dcpromo installs them.

8. After the AD DS binaries have been installed, a summary of the installation options is presented in the command prompt window; then the AD DS installation process begins. The status of the AD DS installing is updated in the command prompt window.

FIGURE 3.19
Installing a new forest by using an answer file.

9. When the installation process is complete, the server reboots automatically if the /rebootOnCompletion option was used in the answer file. If the /rebootOnCompletion was not used in the answer file, you are prompted to restart the server.

10. To validate the installation process, click Start, click Run, type **C:\Windows\Debug**, and click OK.

11. Open the DCPROMO.log file and analyze the results in the file.

Install a New Windows Server 2008 Child Domain

Scenario/Problem: You require additional domains within your AD DS forest. If the new domain is to share a contiguous namespace with one or more domains, you need to create a new child domain.

Solution: Installing a new Windows Server 2008 child domain consists of selecting the option to create a new child domain during the promotion of a domain controller. The installation of a new Windows Server 2008 child domain can be performed using the Windows interface, the command line, and an answer file.

TIP If you are installing a new Windows Server 2008 child domain into an existing Windows Server 2008 forest, you do not have to prepare the forest before you begin the installation. However, if you are installing a new Windows Server 2008 child domain into an existing Windows 2000 Server or Windows Server 2003 forest, you must first prepare the forest by performing the steps in Chapter 2.

Install a Child Domain by Using the Windows Interface

To install a child domain by using the Windows interface, perform the following steps using an AD DS account that has membership in the following AD DS group:

▶ Enterprise Administrators

1. Log on to the server you want to promote to a domain controller.
2. Click Start and then click Server Manager.
3. In Roles Summary, click Add Roles.
4. On the Before You Begin page, click Next.
5. On the Select Server Roles page, click the Active Directory Domain Services check box; then click Next.
6. On the Active Directory Domain Services page, click Next.
7. On the Confirm Installation Selections page, shown in Figure 3.20, click Install.

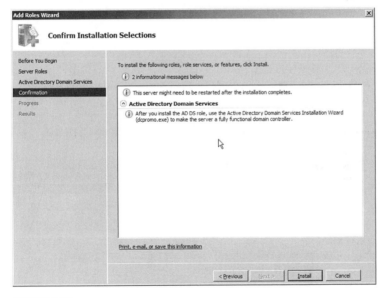

FIGURE 3.20
The Confirm Installation Selections page.

8. On the Installation Results page, shown in Figure 3.21, verify that the installation succeeded and then click Close this wizard and launch the Active Directory Domain Services Installation Wizard (dcpromo.exe).

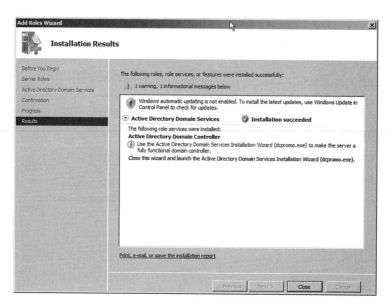

FIGURE 3.21
The Installation Results page.

9. On the Welcome to the Active Directory Domain Services Installation Wizard page, shown in Figure 3.22, click Next.

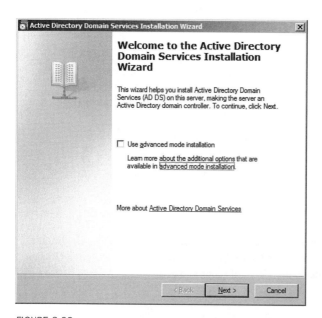

FIGURE 3.22
The Welcome to the Active Directory Domain Services Installation Wizard page.

10. On the Operating System Compatibility page, shown in Figure 3.23, click Next.

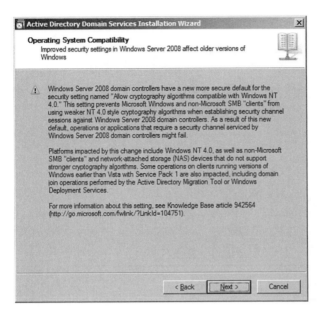

FIGURE 3.23
The Operating System Compatibility page.

11. On the Choose a Deployment Configuration page, select Existing forest, select Create a new domain in an existing forest, and click Next.

12. On the Network Credentials page, shown in Figure 3.24, type the DNS name of the domain you want to join. Under Specify the account credentials to use to perform the installation, click Alternate Credentials; then click Set. On the Windows Security dialog box, enter the username and password for an account that has the permission to add the domain to the forest, and then click OK. Click Next to proceed.

13. On the Name the New Domain page, shown in Figure 3.25, type the FQDN of the parent domain and the Single-label DNS name of the child domain. Then click Next.

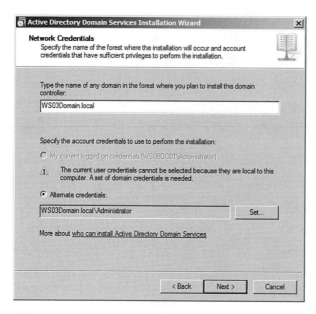

FIGURE 3.24
The Network Credentials page.

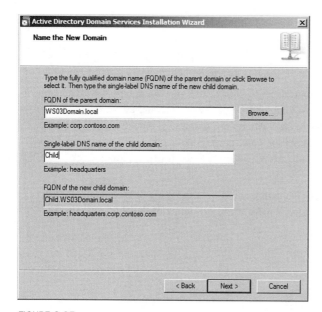

FIGURE 3.25
The Name the New Domain page.

14. On the Set Domain Functional Level page, Select the domain functional level that meets your requirements and click Next.

15. On the Select a Site page, shown in Figure 3.26, select the site to which you want the domain controller to belong and click Next.

FIGURE 3.26
The Select a Site page.

16. On the Additional Domain Controller Options page, select the desired additional options for the domain controller and click Next.

17. On the Location for Database, Log Files, and SYSVOL page, type the volume and folder locations for the database file, the directory service log files, and the SYSVOL files; then click Next.

18. On the Directory Services Restore Mode Administrator Password page, type and confirm the restore mode password and then click Next.

19. On the Summary page, click Next after you review your selections.

The Active Directory Domain Services installation process starts, as shown in Figure 3.27.

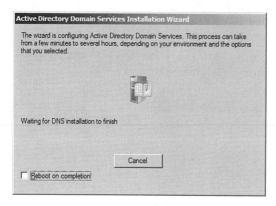

FIGURE 3.27

The Active Directory Domain Services Installation Wizard screen.

20. After the installation is complete, the Completing the Active Directory Domain Services Installation Wizard page appears. Ensure the installation was successful and click Finish.

21. When prompted to restart, click Restart Now.

22. To validate the installation process, click Start, click Run, type **C:\Windows\Debug**, and click OK.

23. Open the DCPROMO.log file and analyze the results in the file.

Install a Child Domain by Using the Command Line

Table 3.3 lists the installation parameters used in the steps that follow and the corresponding action of each parameter.

TABLE 3.3   **Installing a Child Domain by the Command Line Installation Parameters**

Installation Parameter	Corresponding Action
/InstallDns:yes	DNS server will be installed.
/ParentDomainDNSName:WS03Domain.local	Name of the parent domain to which this domain will be added.
/replicaOrNewDomain:domain	A new domain will be created.
/newDomain:child	The new domain will be a child domain.
/newDomainDnsName:child02.WS03Domain.local	FQDN of the new child domain.
/childName:child02	Name of the new child domain.
/DomainNetbiosName:child02	NetBIOS name of the new child domain.
/databasePath:"c:\Windows\ntds"	Database path.

TABLE 3.3   **Installing a Child Domain by the Command Line Installation Parameters**   (continued)

Installation Parameter	Corresponding Action
/logPath:"c:\Windows\ntds"	Log file path.
/sysvolpath:"c:\Windows\sysvol"	SYSVOL path.
/safeModeAdminPassword:Today01!	DSRM Administrator password.
/forestLevel:2	Forest functional level will be set to Windows Server 2003.
/domainLevel:2	Domain functional level will be set to Windows Server 2003.
/rebootOnCompletion:no	Server will not be rebooted after completion.
/userName:WS03Domain\Administrator	The username that will be used to promote the server to a domain controller.
/userDomain:WS03Domain	The domain of the user account that will be used to promote the server to a domain controller.
/password:Today01!	The password of the user that will be used to promote the server to a domain controller.

> **TIP**   For a complete list of installation options and parameters, go to
> http://technet.microsoft.com/en-us/library/cc733048.aspx.

To install a child domain by using the command line, perform the following steps using an AD DS account that has membership in the following AD DS group:

- ▶ Enterprise Administrators

1. Log on to the server you want to promote to a domain controller.
2. Click Start and then click Command Prompt.
3. Type the following into the command prompt window and then press Enter:

```
dcpromo /unattend /InstallDns:yes
/ParentDomainDNSName:WS03Domain.local
/replicaOrNewDomain:domain /newDomain:child
/newDomainDnsName:child02.WS03Domain.local /childName:child02
/DomainNetbiosName:child02 /databasePath:"c:\Windows\ntds"
/logPath:"c:\Windows\ntds" /sysvolpath:"c:\Windows\sysvol"
/safeModeAdminPassword:Today01! /forestLevel:2 /domainLevel:2
/rebootOnCompletion:no /userName:WS03Domain\Administrator
/userDomain:WS03Domain /password:Today01!
```

The dcpromo process begins by determining whether the AD DS binaries are installed. If the binaries are not installed, dcpromo installs them.

4. After the AD DS binaries have been installed, a summary of the installation options is presented in the command prompt window; then the AD DS installation process begins.

5. The status of the AD DS installing is updated in the command prompt window.

6. When the installation process is complete, the server reboots automatically if the /rebootOnCompletion option was used in the command line. If the /rebootOnCompletion was not used in the command line, you are prompted to restart the server, as shown in Figure 3.28.

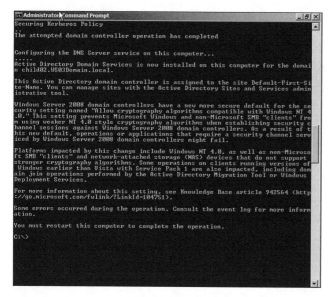

FIGURE 3.28
Installation complete.

The installation is complete.

7. To validate the installation process, click Start, click Run, type **C:\Windows\Debug**, and click OK.

8. Open the DCPROMO.log file and analyze the results in the file.

Install a Child Domain by Using an Answer File

Table 3.4 lists the installation parameters used in the steps that follow and the corresponding action of each parameter.

TABLE 3.4   Installing a Child Domain by Using Answer File Installation Parameters

Installation Parameter	Corresponding Action
`ParentDomainDNSName=WS03Domain.local`	Name of parent domain to which this domain will be added.
`UserName=WS03Domain\Administrator`	The username that will be used to promote the server to a domain controller.
`UserDomain:WS03Domain`	The domain of the user account that will be used to promote the server to a domain controller.
`Password=Today01!`	The password of the user that will be used to promote the server to a domain controller.
`NewDomain=child`	The new domain will be a child domain.
`ChildName=Child03`	The new domain will be a child domain.
`DomainNetBiosName=Child03`	NetBIOS name of the new child domain.
`ReplicaOrNewDomain=domain`	Forest functional level will be set to Windows Server 2003.
`DomainLevel=2`	Domain functional level will be set to Windows Server 2003.
`DatabasePath="c:\Windows\ntds"`	Database path.
`LogPath="c:\Windows\ntds"`	Log file path.
`SYSVOLPath="c:\Windows\sysvol"`	SYSVOL path.
`InstallDNS=yes`	DNS server will be installed.
`SafeModeAdminPassword=Today01!`	DSRM Administrator password.
`RebootOnCompletion=no`	Server will not be rebooted after completion.

> **TIP**   For a complete list of installation options and parameters, go to http://technet.microsoft.com/en-us/library/cc733048.aspx.

To install a child domain by using an answer file, perform the following steps using an AD DS account that has membership in the following AD DS group:

▶ Enterprise Administrators

1. Log on to the server you want to promote to a domain controller.

2. Click Start, click Run, type **notepad**, and click OK.

3. On the first line, type **[DCINSTALL]**; then press ENTER.

4. Type the following entries, one entry on each line, as shown in Figure 3.29:

```
ParentDomainDNSName=WS03Domain.local
UserName=WS03Domain\Administrator
UserDomain=WS03Domain
Password=Today01!
NewDomain=child
ChildName=Child03
DomainNetBiosName=Child03
ReplicaOrNewDomain=domain
DomainLevel=2
DatabasePath="c:\Windows\ntds"
LogPath="c:\Windows\ntds"
SYSVOLPath="c:\Windows\sysvol"
InstallDNS=yes
SafeModeAdminPassword=Today01!
RebootOnCompletion=no
```

FIGURE 3.29
The answer file.

5. Save the answer file as C:\DCAnswer.txt.

6. Click Start and then click Command Prompt.

7. Type the following into the command prompt window, as shown in Figure 3.30, and then press Enter:

```
dcpromo /unattend:"C:\DCAnswer.txt"
```

The dcpromo process begins by determining whether the AD DS binaries are installed. If the binaries are not installed, dcpromo installs them.

8. After the AD DS binaries have been installed, a summary of the installation options is presented in the command prompt window; then the AD DS installation process begins. The status of the AD DS installing is updated in the command prompt window, as shown in Figure 3.31.

FIGURE 3.30
Installing a new child domain using an answer file.

FIGURE 3.31
The status of installing AD DS.

9. When the installation process is complete, the server reboots automatically if the /rebootOnCompletion option was used in the answer file. If the /rebootOnCompletion was not used in the answer file, you are prompted to restart the server.

10. To validate the installation process, click Start, click Run, type in **C:\Windows\Debug**, and click OK.

11. Open the DCPROMO.log file and analyze the results in the file.

Install a New Windows Server 2008 Domain Tree

Scenario/Problem: When you create a new domain in a forest and the domain DNS namespace is not related to the other domains in the forest, you need to create a new domain tree.

Solution: Installing a new Windows Server 2008 domain tree consists of selecting the option to create a new domain tree during the promotion of a DC. The installation of a new Windows Server 2008 domain tree can be performed using the Windows interface, the command line, and an answer file.

TIP If you are installing a new Windows Server 2008 domain tree in an existing Windows Server 2008 forest, you do not have to prepare the forest before you begin the installation. However, if you are installing a new Windows Server 2008 domain tree in an existing Windows 2000 Server or Windows Server 2003 forest, you must first prepare the forest by performing the steps in Chapter 2.

Install a Domain Tree by Using the Windows Interface

To install a domain tree by using the Windows interface, perform the following steps using an AD DS account that has membership in the following AD DS group:

▶ Enterprise Administrators

1. Log on to the server you want to promote to a domain controller.
2. Click Start, click Run, type **dcpromo**, and click OK.
3. The AD DS server role is installed, as shown in Figure 3.32.

TIP The AD DS server role can be installed by using the dcpromo command.

4. On the Welcome to the Active Directory Domain Services Installation Wizard page, select the Use Advanced Mode Installation option and click Next.
5. On the Operating System Compatibility page, click Next.
6. On the Choose a Deployment Configuration page, select Existing forest, select Create a new domain in an existing forest, select the Create a new domain tree root instead of a new child domain check box, and then click Next.
7. On the Network Credentials page, type the DNS name of the domain you want to join. Under Specify the account credentials to use to perform the installation, click Alternate credentials, and then click Set. On the Windows Security dialog box, enter the username and password for an account that has the permission to add the domain to the forest; then click OK. Click Next to proceed.

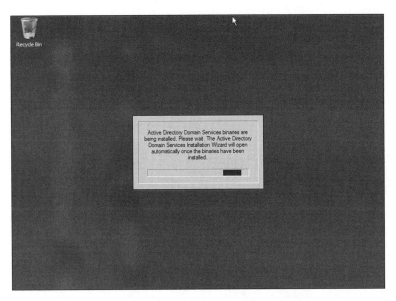

FIGURE 3.32
Installing AD DS server role using dcpromo.

8. On the Name the New Domain Tree Root page, shown in Figure 3.33, type the FQDN of the new domain tree and click Next.

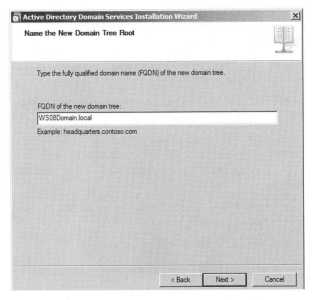

FIGURE 3.33
The Name the New Domain Tree Root page.

9. On the Domain NetBIOS Name page, shown in Figure 3.34, enter the NetBIOS name for the new domain tree and click Next.

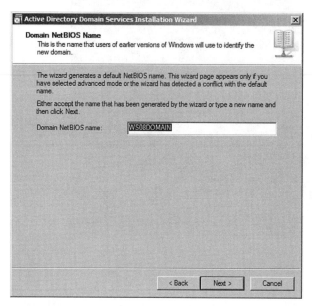

FIGURE 3.34
The Domain NetBIOS Name page.

10. On the Set Domain Functional Level page, select the domain functional level that meets your requirements and click Next.

11. On the Select a Site page, select the site to which you want the domain controller to belong and click Next.

12. On the Additional Domain Controller Options page, select the desired additional options, such as DNS server and/or Global catalog, for the domain controller and click Next.

13. On the Location for Database, Log Files, and SYSVOL page, type the volume and folder locations for the database file, the directory service log files, and the SYSVOL files; then click Next.

14. On the Directory Services Restore Mode Administrator Password page, type and confirm the restore mode password. Then click Next.

15. On the Summary page, click Next after you review your selections.

The Active Directory Domain Services installation process starts, as shown in Figure 3.35.

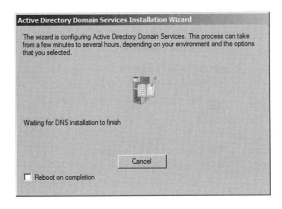

FIGURE 3.35
The Active Directory Domain
Services Installation Wizard page.

16. After the installation is complete, the Completing the Active Directory Domain
    Services Installation Wizard page appears. Ensure the installation was successful
    and click Finish.

17. When prompted to restart, click Restart Now.

18. To validate the installation process, click Start, click Run, type
    C:\Windows\Debug, and click OK.

19. Open the DCPROMO.log file and analyze the results in the file.

Install a Domain Tree by Using the Command Line

Table 3.5 lists the installation parameters used in the steps that follow and the corresponding action of each parameter.

TABLE 3.5   **Installing a Domain Tree by Using the Command Line Installation
Parameters**

Installation Parameter	Corresponding Action
/InstallDns:yes	DNS server will be installed.
/ParentDomainDNSName:WS03Domain.local	Name of the forest root domain to which this domain tree will be added.
/replicaOrNewDomain:domain	A new domain will be created.
/newDomain:tree	The new domain will be a new domain tree.
/newDomainDnsName:WS08DomainB.local	FQDN of the new domain tree.
/DomainNetbiosName:WS08DomainB	NetBIOS name of the new domain tree.
/databasePath:"c:\Windows\ntds"	Database path.
/logPath:"c:\Windows\ntds"	Log file path.
/sysvolpath:"c:\Windows\sysvol"	SYSVOL path.
/safeModeAdminPassword:Today01!	DSRM Administrator password.

continues

TABLE 3.5   **Installing a Domain Tree by Using the Command Line Installation
Parameters**   (continued)

Installation Parameter	Corresponding Action
/forestLevel:2	Forest functional level will be set to Windows Server 2003.
/domainLevel:2	Domain functional level will be set to Windows Server 2003.
/rebootOnCompletion:no	Server will not be rebooted after completion.
/userName:WS03Domain\Administrator	The username that will be used to promote the server to a domain controller.
/userDomain:WS03Domain	The domain of the user account that will be used to promote the server to a domain controller.
/password:Today01!	The password of the user that will be used to promote the server to a domain controller.

> **TIP**   For a complete list of installation options and parameters, go to
> http://technet.microsoft.com/en-us/library/cc733048.aspx.

To install child domain tree by using the command line, perform the following steps
using an AD DS account that has membership in the following AD DS group:

▶ Enterprise Administrators

1. Log on to the server you want to promote to a domain controller.
2. Click Start and then click Command Prompt.
3. Type the following into the command prompt window, as shown in Figure 3.36,
   and then press Enter:

```
dcpromo /unattend /InstallDns:yes
/ParentDomainDNSName:WS03Domain.local
/replicaOrNewDomain:domain /newDomain:tree
/newDomainDnsName:WS08DomainB.local /DomainNetbiosName:WS08DomainB
/databasePath:"c:\Windows\ntds" /logPath:"c:\Windows\ntds"
/sysvolpath:"c:\Windows\sysvol" /safeModeAdminPassword:Today01!
/forestLevel:2 /domainLevel:2 /rebootOnCompletion:no
/userName:WS03Domain\Administrator /userDomain:WS03Domain
/password:Today01!
```

FIGURE 3.36
Installing a new domain tree using the command line.

The dcpromo process begins by determining whether the AD DS binaries are installed. If the binaries are not installed, dcpromo installs them.

4. After the AD DS binaries have been installed, a summary of the installation options is presented in the command prompt window; then the AD DS installation process begins.

5. The status of the AD DS installing is updated in the command prompt window.

6. When the installation process is complete, the server reboots automatically if the /rebootOnCompletion option was used in the command line. If the /rebootOnCompletion was not used in the command line, you are prompted to restart the server.

7. To validate the installation process, click Start, click Run, type **C:\Windows\Debug**, and click OK.

8. Open the DCPROMO.log file and analyze the results in the file.

Install a Domain Tree by Using an Answer File

Table 3.6 lists the installation parameters used in the steps that follow and the corresponding action of each parameter.

TABLE 3.6   **Installing a Domain Tree by Using Answer File Installation Parameters**

Installation Parameter	Corresponding Action
InstallDns=yes	DNS server will be installed.
ParentDomainDNSName=WS03Domain.local	Name of the forest root domain to which this domain tree will be added.
replicaOrNewDomain=domain	A new domain will be created.
newDomain=tree	The new domain will be a new domain tree.

continues

TABLE 3.6   **Installing a Domain Tree by Using Answer File Installation Parameters**   (continued)

Installation Parameter	Corresponding Action
newDomainDnsName=WS08DomainC.local	FQDN of new domain tree.
DomainNetbiosName=WS08DomainC	NetBIOS name of the new domain tree.
databasePath="c:\Windows\ntds"	Database path.
logPath="c:\Windows\ntds"	Log file path.
Sysvolpath="c:\Windows\sysvol"	SYSVOL path.
safeModeAdminPassword=Today01!	DSRM Administrator password.
forestLevel=2	Forest functional level will be set to Windows Server 2003.
domainLevel=2	Domain functional level will be set to Windows Server 2003.
rebootOnCompletion=no	Server will not be rebooted after completion.
userName=WS03Domain\Administrator	The username that will be used to promote the server to a domain controller.
userDomain=WS03Domain	The domain of the user account that will be used to promote the server to a domain controller.
Password=Today01!	The password of the user that will be used to promote the server to a domain controller.

TIP   For a complete list of installation options and parameters, go to http://technet.microsoft.com/en-us/library/cc733048.aspx.

To install child domain tree by using an answer file, perform the following steps using an AD DS account that has membership in the following AD DS group:

▶ Enterprise Administrators

1. Log on to the server you want to promote to a domain controller.

2. Click Start, click Run, type **notepad**, and click OK.

3. On the first line, type **[DCINSTALL]**; then press ENTER.

4. Type the following entries, one entry on each line:

```
InstallDns=yes
ParentDomainDNSName=WS03Domain.local
replicaOrNewDomain=domain
newDomain=tree
newDomainDnsName=WS08DomainC.local
```

```
DomainNetbiosName=WS08DomainC
databasePath="c:\Windows\ntds"
logPath="c:\Windows\ntds"
sysvolpath="c:\Windows\sysvol"
safeModeAdminPassword=Today01!
forestLevel=2
domainLevel=2
rebootOnCompletion=no
userName=WS03Domain\Administrator
userDomain=WS03Domain
password=Today01!
```

5. Save the answer file as `C:\DCAnswer.txt`.

6. Click Start and then click Command Prompt.

7. Type the following into the command prompt window, as shown in Figure 3.37, and then press ENTER:

   dcpromo /unattend:"C:\DCAnswer.txt"

FIGURE 3.37
Installing a domain tree using an answer file.

The dcpromo process begins by determining whether the AD DS binaries are installed. If the binaries are not installed, dcpromo installs them.

8. After the AD DS binaries have been installed, a summary of the installation options is presented in the command prompt window. Then the AD DS installation process begins. The status of the AD DS installing is updated in the command prompt window.

9. When the installation process is complete, the server reboots automatically if the /rebootOnCompletion option was used in the answer file. If the /rebootOnCompletion was not used in the answer file, you are prompted to restart the server.

10. To validate the installation process, click Start, click Run, type `C:\Windows\Debug`, and click OK.

11. Open the DCPROMO.log file and analyze the results in the file.

Install an Additional Windows Server 2008 Domain Controller

Scenario/Problem: To provide adequate fault tolerance and optimize authentication, you require a minimum of two DCs.

Solution: Installing an additional Windows Server 2008 DC consists of promoting a member server to a DC in an existing domain. The installation of an additional Windows Server 2008 DC can be performed using the Windows interface, the command line, and an answer file.

TIP If you are installing an additional Windows Server 2008 DC in an existing Windows Server 2008 forest, you do not have to prepare the forest before you begin the installation. However, if you are installing an additional Windows Server 2008 DC in an existing Windows 2000 Server or Windows Server 2003 forest, you must first prepare the forest; then you must prepare the domain in which the DC will reside. This can be done by performing the steps in Chapter 2.

Install an Additional Domain Controller by Using the Windows Interface

To install an additional DC by using the Windows interface, perform the following steps using an AD DS account that has membership in the following AD DS group:

▶ Domain Admins for the domain for which you want to add a writable domain controller.

1. Log on to the server you want to promote to a domain controller.

2. Click Start, Run, type in **dcpromo**, and click OK.

3. The dcpromo process begins by determining whether the AD DS binaries are installed. If the binaries are not installed, dcpromo installs them.

4. After the dcpromo process installs the Active Directory Domain Services server role, the Welcome to the Active Directory Domain Services Installation Wizard page appears. Click Next.

5. On the Operating System Compatibility page, click Next.

6. On the Choose a Deployment Configuration page, select Existing forest, select Add a domain controller to an existing forest, and click Next.

7. On the Network Credentials page, enter the DNS name of the domain to which you want to add the domain controller. Under Specify the account credentials to use to perform the installation, click Alternate credentials, and then click Set. On the Windows Security dialog box, enter the username and password for an account that has the permission to add the domain to the forest, and then click OK. Click Next to proceed.

8. On the Select a Domain page, shown in Figure 3.38, select the domain to which you want to add the domain controller and click Next.

FIGURE 3.38
The Select a Domain page.

9. On the Select a Site page, select the site to which you want the domain controller to belong and click Next.

10. On the Additional Domain Controller Options page, select the desired additional options, such as DNS server and/or Global catalog, for the domain controller and click Next.

11. On the Location for Database, Log Files, and SYSVOL page, type the volume and folder locations for the database file, the directory service log files, and the SYSVOL files; then click Next.

12. On the Directory Services Restore Mode Administrator Password page, type and confirm the restore mode password. Then click Next.

13. On the Summary page, click Next after you review your selections.

The Active Directory Domain Services installation process starts.

14. After the installation is complete, the Completing the Active Directory Domain Services Installation Wizard page appears. Ensure the installation was successful and click Finish.

15. When prompted to restart, click Restart Now.

16. To validate the installation process, click Start, click Run, type **C:\Windows\Debug**, and click OK.

17. Open the DCPROMO.log file and analyze the results in the file.

Install an Additional Domain Controller by Using the Command Line

Table 3.7 lists the installation parameters used in the steps that follow and the corresponding action of each parameter.

TABLE 3.7   **Installing an Additional DC by Using the Command Line Installation Parameters**

Installation Parameter	Corresponding Action
`InstallDns:yes`	DNS server will be installed.
`confirmGC:yes`	Specifies the domain controller is a global catalog server.
`replicaOrNewDomain:replica`	An additional domain controller will be added to the domain.
`replicaDomainDNSName:WS03Domain.local`	The DNS name of the domain that the domain controller will be added to.
`databasePath:"c:\windows\ntds"`	Database path.
`logPath:"c:\windows\ntds"`	Log file path.
`sysvolpath:"c:\windows\sysvol"`	SYSVOL path.
`safeModeAdminPassword:Today01!`	DSRM Administrator password.
`rebootOnCompletion:no`	Server will not be rebooted after completion.
`userName:WS03Domain\Administrator`	The username that will be used to promote the server to a domain controller.
`userDomain:WS03Domain`	The domain of the user account that will be used to promote the server to a domain controller.
`password:Today01!`	The password of the user that will be used to promote the server to a domain controller.

> **TIP** For a complete list of installation options and parameters, go to
> http://technet.microsoft.com/en-us/library/cc733048.aspx.

To install an additional DC by using the command line, perform the following using an
AD DS account that has membership in the following AD DS group:

▶ Domain Admins for the domain for which you want to add a writable domain
controller.

1. Log on to the server you want to promote to a domain controller.

2. Click Start and then click Command Prompt.

3. Type the following into the command prompt window, as shown in Figure 3.39,
and then press ENTER:

```
dcpromo /unattend /InstallDns:yes /confirmGC:yes
/replicaOrNewDomain:replica /replicaDomainDNSName:WS03Domain.local
/databasePath:"c:\windows\ntds" /logPath:"c:\windows\ntds"
/sysvolpath:"c:\windows\sysvol" /safeModeAdminPassword:Today01!
/rebootOnCompletion:yes
```

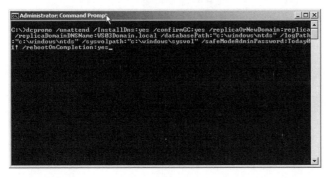

FIGURE 3.39
Installing an additional DC using the command line.

The dcpromo process begins by determining whether the AD DS binaries are
installed. If the binaries are not installed, dcpromo installs them.

4. After the AD DS binaries have been installed, a summary of the installation
options is presented in the command prompt window; then the AD DS installation process begins.

5. The status of the AD DS installing is updated in the command prompt window.

6. When the installation process is complete, the server reboots automatically if the
/rebootOnCompletion option was used in the command line. If the
/rebootOnCompletion was not used in the command line, you are prompted to
restart the server.

7. To validate the installation process, click Start, click Run, type **C:\Windows\Debug**, and click OK.

8. Open the DCPROMO.log file and analyze the results in the file.

Install an Additional Domain Controller by Using an Answer File

Table 3.8 lists the installation parameters used in the steps that follow and the corresponding action of each parameter.

TABLE 3.8   **Installing an Additional DC by Using Answer File Installation Parameters**

Installation Parameter	Corresponding Action
InstallDns=yes	DNS server will be installed.
confirmGC=yes	Specifies the domain controller is a global catalog server.
replicaOrNewDomain=replica	An additional domain controller will be added to the domain.
replicaDomainDNSName=WS03Domain.local	The DNS name of the domain to which the domain controller will be added.
databasePath="c:\windows\ntds"	Database path.
logPath="c:\windows\ntds"	Log file path.
sysvolpath="c:\windows\sysvol"	SYSVOL path.
safeModeAdminPassword=Today01!	DSRM Administrator password.
rebootOnCompletion=no	Server will not be rebooted after completion.
userName=WS03Domain\Administrator	The username that will be used to promote the server to a domain controller.
userDomain=WS03Domain	The domain of the user account that will be used to promote the server to a domain controller.
password=Today01!	The password of the user that will be used to promote the server to a domain controller.

> **TIP**   For a complete list of installation options and parameters, go to http://technet.microsoft.com/en-us/library/cc733048.aspx.

To install an additional DC by using an answer file, perform the following using an AD DS account that has membership in the following AD DS group:

▶ Domain Admins for the domain for which you want to add a writable domain controller.

1. Log on to the server you want to promote to a domain controller.

2. Click Start, click Run, type **notepad**, and click OK.

3. On the first line, type **[DCINSTALL]** and then press ENTER.

4. Type the following entries, one entry on each line, as shown in Figure 3.40:

```
InstallDns=yes
confirmGC=yes
replicaOrNewDomain=replica
replicaDomainDNSName=WS03Domain.local
databasePath="c:\windows\ntds"
logPath="c:\windows\ntds"
sysvolpath="c:\windows\sysvol"
safeModeAdminPassword=Today01!
rebootOnCompletion=no
UserName=WS03Domain\Administrator
UserDomain=WS03Domain
Password=Today01!
```

5. Save the answer file as C:\DCAnswer.txt.

6. Click Start and then click Command Prompt.

7. Type the following into the command prompt window, as shown in Figure 3.40, and then press ENTER:

```
dcpromo /unattend:"C:\DCAnswer.txt"
```

FIGURE 3.40
Installing an additional DC by using an answer file.

The dcpromo process begins by determining whether the AD DS binaries are installed. If the binaries are not installed, dcpromo installs them.

8. After the AD DS binaries have been installed, a summary of the installation options is presented in the command prompt window; then the AD DS installation process begins. The status of the AD DS installing is updated in the command prompt window.

9. When the installation process is complete, the server reboots automatically if the /rebootOnCompletion option was used in the answer file. If the /rebootOnCompletion was not used in the answer file, you are prompted to restart the server.

10. To validate the installation process, click Start, click Run, type **C:\Windows\Debug**, and click OK.

11. Open the DCPROMO.log file and analyze the results in the file.

Perform a Staged Installation of a Read-Only Domain Controller

Scenario/Problem: You need to deploy a Read-only domain controllers (RODC) in a branch office. You plan to delegate the installation of AD DS on the RODCs to someone physically located in the branch office.

Solution: A staged installation of an RODC consists of two stages. The first stage of the installation creates an account for the RODC in AD DS. The second stage of the installation attaches the server to the account that was created in the first stage. The first stage requires elevated permissions in AD DS. However, the second stage can be performed by someone you delegate the ability to attach the server to the account.

Stage 1: Create an RODC Account in AD DS

To create an RODC account in AD DS, perform the following steps using an AD DS account that has membership in the following AD DS group:

▶ Domain Admins for the domain for which you want to add a RODC.

1. Click Start, click Administrative Tools, and then click Active Directory Users and Computers.

2. Right-click the Domain Controllers Organizational Unit (OU) and select Pre-create Read-only Domain Controller account, as shown in Figure 3.41.

3. On the Welcome to the Active Directory Domain Services page, shown in Figure 3.42, click Next.

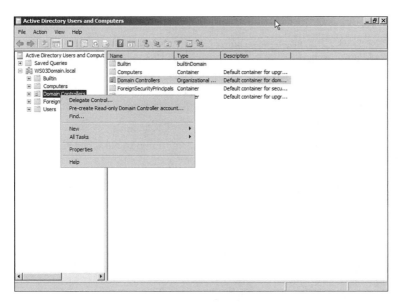

FIGURE 3.41
Selecting Pre-create Read-only Domain Controller account.

FIGURE 3.42
The Welcome to the Active Directory Domain Services page.

4. On the Operating System Compatibility page, click Next.

5. On the Network Credentials page, under Specify the account credentials to use to perform the installation, click My current logged on credentials or click Alternate credentials. If you select Alternate credentials, click Set and in the Windows Security dialog box, provide the user name and password for an account that can install the additional DC. When you are finished providing credentials, click Next.

6. On the Specify the Computer Name page, shown in Figure 3.43, enter the name of the server that will be the RODC; then click Next.

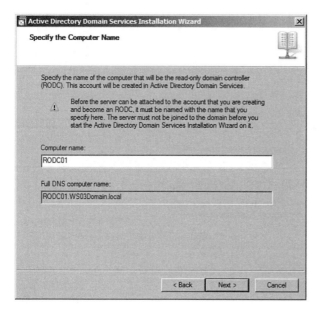

FIGURE 3.43
The Specify the Computer Name page.

7. On the Select a Site page, select the site to which you want the domain controller to belong and click Next.

8. On the Additional Domain Controller Options page, select the desired additional options, such as DNS server and/or Global catalog, for the domain controller and click Next.

9. On the Delegation of RODC Installation and Administration page, shown in Figure 3.44, enter the group or user that can attach the server to the RODC account and click Next.

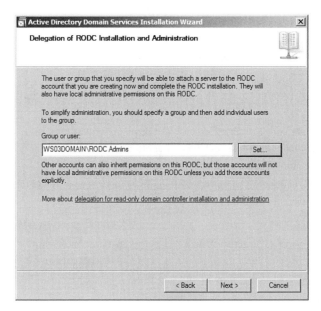

FIGURE 3.44
The Delegation of RODC Installation and Administration page.

10. On the Summary page, click Next.

11. On the Completing the Active Directory Domain Services Installation Wizard page, click Finish.

Stage 2: Attach Server to RODC Account

To attach a server to an RODC account, perform the following steps using an AD DS account that has been delegated the permission to attach the server to the RODC account in stage 1, outlined previously, and with membership in the following local group:

- Administrators

1. Log on to the server you want to attach to the RODC account using an account that has been delegated the permission to attach the server to the RODC account in stage 1.

2. Click Start, click Command Prompt.

3. In the Command Prompt window, type **dcpromo /UseExistingAccount:Attach** and press ENTER.

   The dcpromo process begins by determining whether the AD DS binaries are installed. If the binaries are not installed, dcpromo installs them.

4. On the Welcome to the Active Directory Domain Services Installation Wizard page, click Next.

5. On the Network Credentials page, click Next.

6. On the Select Domain Controller Account page, confirm that the wizard has found an existing RODC account that matches the name of the server; then click Next.

7. On the Location for Database, Log Files, and SYSVOL page, type or browse to the volume and folder locations for the database file, the directory service log files, and the system volume (SYSVOL) files. Then click Next.

8. On the Directory Services Restore Mode Administrator Password page, type and confirm the restore mode password and click Next.

9. On the Summary page, click Next.

10. On the Completing the Active Directory Domain Services Installation Wizard page, click Finish.

11. To validate the installation process, click Start, click Run, type **C:\Windows\Debug**, and click OK.

12. Open the DCPROMO.log file and analyze the results in the file.

Install AD DS from Restored Backup Media

Scenario/Problem: You need to minimize network traffic during the installation of Active Directory Domain Services.

Solution: Install AD DS from restored backup media.

Create Installation Media

To create AD DS installation media, perform the following steps using an account that has the permissions to log on to a DC interactively and be able to make a backup.

1. Log on to the domain controller you will use to create the media.

2. Click Start, and click Command Prompt.

3. In the command prompt window, type **ntdsutil** and press ENTER.

4. At the ntdsutil prompt, type **activate instance ntds** and press ENTER.

5. At the ntdsutil prompt, type **ifm** and press ENTER.

6. At the `ifm:` prompt, shown in Figure 3.45, type the command for the type of installation media that you want to create; then press ENTER. To create the media for an RODC, type **Create rodc C:\Folder**, where C:\Folder is the path to store the media. To create the media for a full (writable), type **Create full C:\Folder**, where C:\Folder is the path to store the media. Press ENTER when complete.

FIGURE 3.45
IFM prompt.

7. ntdsutil creates the installation media, as shown in Figure 3.46.

FIGURE 3.46
Create ifm installation media.

8. When the installation media has been created successfully, you are returned to the `ifm:` prompt, as shown in Figure 3.47.

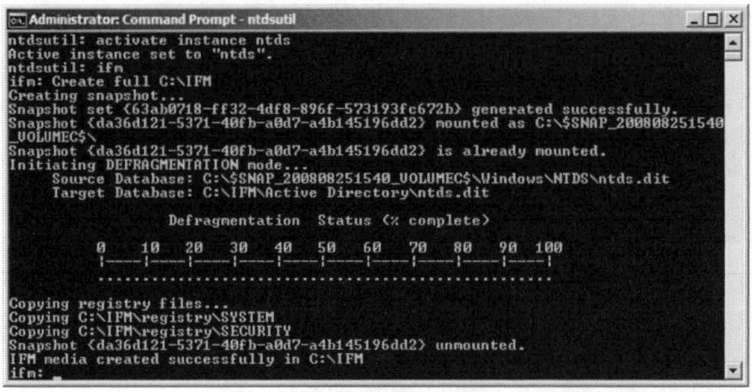

FIGURE 3.47
The IFM created successfully.

9. Type **Q** to exit the `ifm:` prompt.

10. Type **Q** to exit `ntdsutil`.

11. Close the command prompt window.

Install AD DS from Media

To install AD DS from media, perform the following steps using an account that has the permissions to log on to a DC interactively and be able to make a backup.

1. Log on to the domain controller you will install AD DS on.

2. Click Start, click Run, type **dcpromo**, and click OK.

3. The dcpromo process begins by determining whether the AD DS binaries are installed. If the binaries are not installed, dcpromo installs them.

4. On the Welcome to the Active Directory Domain Services Installation Wizard page, select Use advanced mode installation and click Next.

5. On the Operating System Compatibility page, click Next.

6. On the Choose a Deployment Configuration page, select Existing forest, select Add a domain controller to an existing domain, and click Next.

7. On the Network Credentials page, type the DNS name of the domain you want to join. Under Specify the account credentials to use to perform the installation, click Alternate credentials, and then click Set. On the Windows Security dialog box, enter the user name and password for an account that has the permission to add the domain to the forest; then click OK. Click Next to proceed.

8. On the Select a Domain page, select the domain to which you want to add the domain controller and click Next.

9. On the Select a Site page, select the site to which you want the domain controller to belong and click Next.

10. On the Additional Domain Controller Options page, select the desired additional options for the domain controller and click Next.

11. On the Install from Media page, shown in Figure 3.48, select Replicate data from media at the following location, type the location of the installation media that was previously created, and click Next.

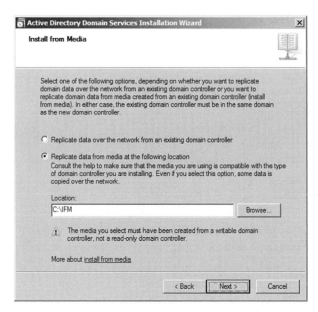

FIGURE 3.48
The Install from Media page.

12. On the Source Domain Controller page, shown in Figure 3.49, select a source domain controller for the installation partner or select Let the wizard choose an appropriate domain controller; then click Next.

13. On the Location for Database, Log Files, and SYSVOL page, type the volume and folder locations for the database file, the directory service log files, and the SYSVOL files; then click Next.

14. On the Directory Services Restore Mode Administrator Password page, type and confirm the restore mode password and click Next.

15. On the Summary page, click Next after you review your selections.

The Active Directory Domain Services installation process starts.

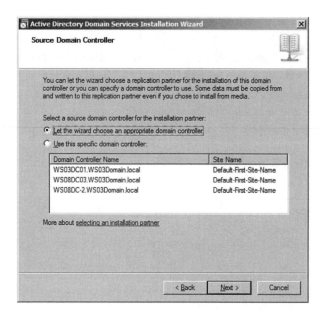

FIGURE 3.49
The Source Domain Controller page.

16. After the installation is complete, the Completing the Active Directory Domain Services Installation Wizard page appears. Ensure the installation was successful and click Finish.

17. When prompted to restart, click Restart Now.

18. To validate the installation process, click Start, click Run, type C:\Windows\Debug, and click OK.

19. Open the DCPROMO.log file and analyze the results in the file.

Remove a Domain Controller from a Domain

Scenario/Problem: A domain controller that is located in one of your offices is no longer required.

Solution: Remove the domain controller from the domain.

To remove a domain controller from a domain, perform the following steps using an AD DS account that has membership in the following AD DS group:

▸ Domain Admins

1. Log on to the domain controller you want to remove from the domain.

2. Click Start, click Run, type **dcpromo**, and click OK.

3. On the Welcome to the Active Directory Domain Services Installation Wizard page, click Next.

4. If the domain controller is a global catalog server, a message appears to warn you about the effect of removing a global catalog server from the environment, as shown in Figure 3.50. Click OK to continue.

FIGURE 3.50
Global catalog warning.

5. On the Delete the Domain page, make no selection if this is not the last domain controller in the domain. If you do want to delete the domain, select the option to delete the domain and click Next.

6. On the Administrator Password page, type and confirm a secure password for the local Administrator account; then click Next.

7. On the Summary page, click Next.

8. The Active Directory Domain Services Installation Wizard deletes AD DS from the server.

9. On the Completing the Active Directory Domain Services Installation Wizard page, click Finish. Then reboot the server.

Forcing the Removal of a Windows Server 2008 Domain Controller

Scenario/Problem: You are forced into a situation where you cannot gracefully uninstall Active Directory Domain Services from a DC.

Solution: In Windows Server 2008, you can forcefully remove a DC when it is started in Directory Services Restore Mode. Typically, you force the removal of a DC only if the DC has no connectivity with other DCs.

Because the DC cannot contact other DCs during the operation, the AD DS forest metadata is not automatically updated as it is when a DC is removed normally. Instead, you must manually update the forest metadata after you remove the DC.

To force the removal of a Windows Server 2008 DC, perform the following steps:

1. Log on to the server using the Directory Services Restore Mode Administrator account.

2. Click Start, click Run, type **dcpromo /forceremoval**, and press ENTER.

3. On the Welcome to the Active Directory Domain Services Installation Wizard page, click Next.

4. On the Force the Removal of Active Directory Domain Services page, click Next.

5. On the Administrator Password page, type and confirm a password for the local Administrator account; then click Next.

6. On the Summary page, click Next.

7. Restart the server after the removal is complete.

Performing Metadata Cleanup

Scenario/Problem: You forced the removal of a DC, but data is lingering in AD DS. You need to remove this lingering data.

Solution: To remove lingering objects from AD DS after a forceful removal of a DC, you must perform metadata cleanup.

To perform a metadata cleanup, perform the following steps:

1. Log on to a writable domain controller.

2. Click Start, click Administrative Tools, and click Active Directory Users and Computers.

3. In the Active Directory Users and Computers console, select the Domain Controllers Organizational Unit (OU).

4. Right-click the domain controller you want to remove from the metadata, and select Delete.

5. On the dialog box to confirm the computer object deletion, shown in Figure 3.51, click Yes.

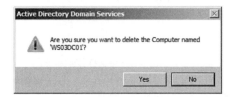

FIGURE 3.51
Confirming computer deletion.

6. On the Deleting Domain Controller dialog box, shown in Figure 3.55, select the option This Domain Controller is permanently offline and can no longer be demoted using the Active Directory Domain Services Installation Wizard (DCPROMO). Then click Delete.

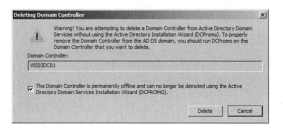

FIGURE 3.55
The Deleting Domain Controller dialog box.

7. If the domain controller was also a global catalog server, you receive an additional prompt asking whether you want to continue, as shown in Figure 3.56; click Yes.

FIGURE 3.56
Global catalog deletion confirmation.

8. If the domain controller holds any operations master roles, an additional prompt displays. Click OK to move the roles to the server(s) DCPROMO recommends, or click Cancel and move the roles manually.

9. The Active Directory Domain Users and Computers console cleans all metadata for the DC.

Rename a Domain Controller

Scenario/Problem: The name of a DC is taken from the name of the member server during the installation of AD DS. In some cases, you might need to change the name of the DC after AD DS has been installed.

Solution: The netdom command-line tool can be used to rename a Windows Server 2008 DC.

To rename a domain controller, perform the following steps using an AD DS account that has membership in one of the following AD DS groups:

- ▶ Domain Admins
- ▶ Enterprise Admins

1. Log on to the domain controller you want to rename.

2. Click Start and click Command Prompt.

3. In the Command Prompt window, type **netdom computername CurrentComputerName /add:NewComputerName**, where CurrentComputerName is the current FQDN name and NewComputerName is the new FQDN name. Then press ENTER.

4. Ensure the computer account updates and DNS registrations are completed. In the Command Prompt window, type **netdom computername CurrentComputerName /makeprimary:NewComputerName**, where CurrentComputerName is the current FQDN name and NewComputerName is the new FQDN name. Then press ENTER.

5. In the Command Prompt window, type **netdom computername NewComputerName /remove:OldComputerName**, where CurrentComputerName is the current FQDN name and NewComputerName is the new FQDN name. Then press ENTER.

CHAPTER 4

Manage Trusts and Functional Levels

The security boundaries of Active Directory Domain Services (AD DS) domains and forests can be extended by using *trusts*. Trust relationships enable you to establish a communication path so a computer in one domain or forest can communicate with a computer in another domain or forest. Through these trust relationships, users in the trusted domain or forest can access resources in the trusting domain or forest. Trust relationships can also be used to make authentication more efficient.

Domain and forest functional levels control which advanced features in the domain or forest are available. Domain and forest functional levels are dependent on the operating system installed on domain controllers in your environment.

This chapter describes the steps required to manage trusts and functional levels.

Create Forest Trusts

Scenario/Problem: By default, AD DS authentication is limited to the domains within a forest. You might need to provide users in your forest with the ability to access resources in another AD DS forest. Additionally, users in another forest might need to access resources in your forest.

Solution: Forest trusts are used to provide users access to resources in another forest. Forest trusts can be two-way or one-way. A *two-way* trust allows users from either forest to access resources in the other forest. Furthermore, domains in each forest trust domains in the other forest implicitly. A *one-way* trust allows users in the trusted forest to access resources in the trusting forest.

The steps to create forest trusts differ depending on the direction of the trust being created. The sections that follow detail the steps to create forest trusts.

Create a Two-way Forest Trust

To complete this task, you must use an AD DS account that has membership in one of the following AD DS groups:

▶ Domain Admins in the forest root domain

▶ Enterprise Admins

To create a two-way forest trust, perform the following steps:

1. Log on to a domain controller or a member computer that has Windows Server 2008 Remote Server Administration Tools (RSAT) installed.

2. Click Start, click Administrative Tools, and then click Active Directory Domains and Trusts.

3. In the console tree, right-click the domain node for the forest root domain; then click Properties.

4. Click the Trusts tab, as shown in Figure 4.1.

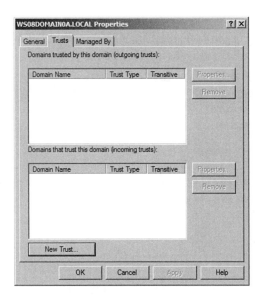

FIGURE 4.1
Trusts Tab.

5. Click New Trust.

6. On the Welcome to the New Trust Wizard page, click Next.

7. On the Trust Name page, as shown in Figure 4.2, type the DNS name of the other forest; then click Next.

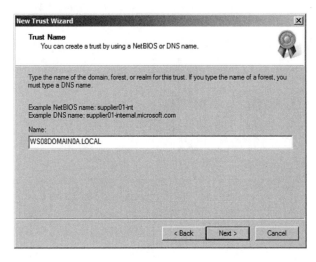

FIGURE 4.2
Trust Name page.

8. On the Trust Type page, select Forest Trust, and click Next.

9. On the Direction of Trust page, as shown in Figure 4.3, select Two-way, and click Next.

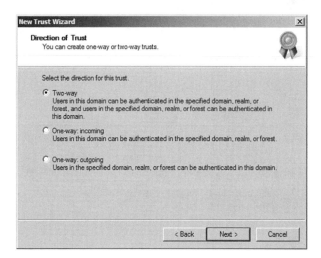

FIGURE 4.3
Direction of Trust page.

10. On the Sides of Trust page, as shown in Figure 4.4, select This domain only or Both this domain and the specified domain. Then click Next (see Figure 4.4).

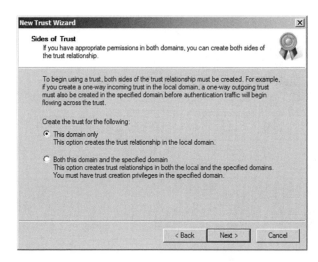

FIGURE 4.4
Sides of Trust page.

11. If you selected Both this domain and the specified domain in Step 10, the User Name and Password page displays. Enter a user name and password for an account in the other forest that has the necessary permissions to create the forest trust and then click Next, as shown in Figure 4.5.

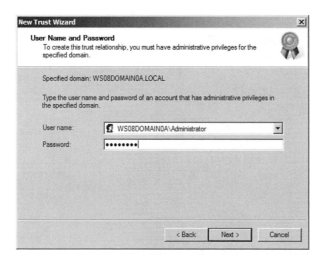

FIGURE 4.5
User Name and Password page.

12. If you selected Both this domain and the specified domain in Step 10, the Outgoing Trust Authentication Level—Local Forest page displays. On the Outgoing Trust Authentication Level—Local Forest page, shown in Figure 4.6, select Forest-wide authentication or Selective authentication. Then click Next.

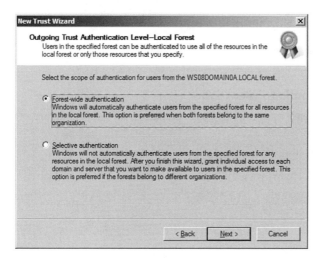

FIGURE 4.6
Outgoing Trust Authentication Level—Local Forest page.

13. If you selected Both this domain and the specified domain in Step 10, the Outgoing Trust Authentication Level—Specified Forest page displays. On the Outgoing Trust Authentication Level—Specified Forest page, shown in Figure 4.7, select Forest-wide authentication or Selective authentication. Then click Next.

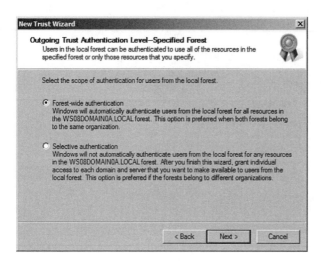

FIGURE 4.7
Outgoing Trust Authentication Level—Specified Forest page.

14. On the Trust Selections Complete page, click Next.

15. If you are presented with the Confirm Outgoing Trust page, click No, do not confirm the outgoing trust, and then click Next.

16. If you are presented with the Confirm Incoming Trust page, click No, do not confirm the incoming trust, and then click Next.

17. On the New Trust Wizard page, click Finish.

Create a One-way Incoming Forest Trust

To complete this task, you must use an AD DS account that has membership in one of the following AD DS groups:

▶ Domain Admins in the forest root domain

▶ Enterprise Admins

To create a one-way incoming forest trust, perform the following steps:

1. Log on to a domain controller or a member computer that has Windows Server 2008 Remote Server Administration Tools installed.

2. Click Start, click Administrative Tools, and then click Active Directory Domains and Trusts.

3. In the console tree, right-click the domain node for the forest root domain; then click Properties.

4. Click the Trusts tab.

5. Click New Trust.

6. On the Welcome to the New Trust Wizard page, click Next.

7. On the Trust Name page, shown in Figure 4.8, type the DNS name of the other forest and then click Next.

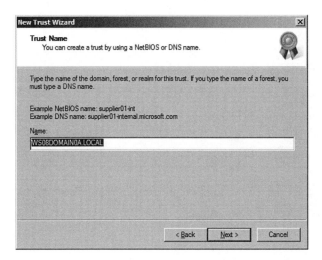

FIGURE 4.8
Trust Name page.

8. On the Trust Type page, select Forest Trust and click Next.

9. On the Direction of Trust page, shown in Figure 4.10, select One-way: shown in Figure 4.9, incoming and click Next.

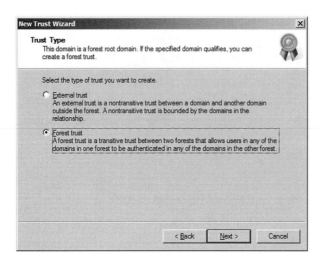

FIGURE 4.9
Trust Type page.

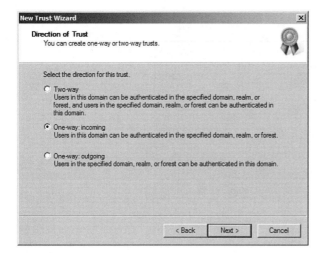

FIGURE 4.10
Direction of Trust page.

10. On the Sides of Trust page, shown in Figure 4.11, select This domain only or Both this domain and the specified domain; then click Next.

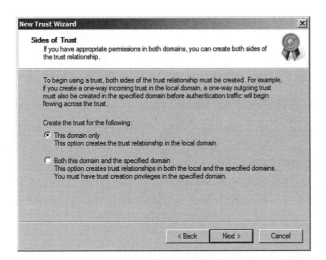

FIGURE 4.11
Sides of Trust page.

11. If you selected Both this domain and the specified domain in Step 10, the User
    Name and Password page displays, as shown in Figure 4.12. Enter a user name
    and password for an account in the other forest that has the necessary permis-
    sions to create the forest trust. Then click Next.

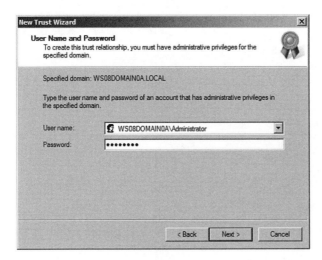

FIGURE 4.12
User Name and Password page.

12. If you selected Both this domain and the specified domain in Step 10, the Outgoing Trust Authentication Level—Specified Forest page displays, as shown in Figure 4.13. On the Outgoing Trust Authentication Level—Specified Forest page, select Forest-wide authentication or Selective authentication, and click Next.

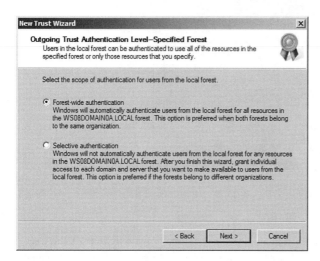

FIGURE 4.13
Outgoing Trust Authentication Level—Specified Forest page.

13. On the Trust Selections Complete page, click Next, as shown in Figure 4.14.

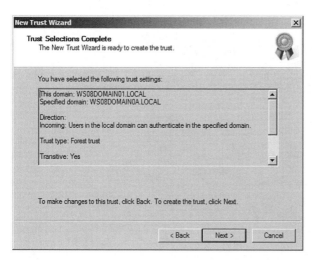

FIGURE 4.14
Trust Selections Complete page.

14. If you are presented with the Confirm Outgoing Trust page, click No, do not confirm the outgoing trust, and then click Next.

15. If you are presented with the Confirm Incoming Trust page, click No, do not confirm the incoming trust, and then click Next.

16. On the New Trust Wizard page, click Finish.

Create a One-Way Outgoing Forest Trust

To complete this task, you must use an AD DS account that has membership in one of the following AD DS groups:

▶ Domain Admins in the forest root domain

▶ Enterprise Admins

To create a one-way outgoing forest trust, perform the following steps:

1. Log on to a domain controller or a member computer that has Windows Server 2008 Remote Server Administration Tools installed.

2. Click Start, click Administrative Tools, and then click Active Directory Domains and Trusts.

3. In the console tree, right-click the domain node for the forest root domain; then click Properties.

4. Click the Trusts tab.

5. Click New Trust.

6. On the Welcome to the New Trust Wizard page, click Next.

7. On the Trust Name page, type the DNS name of the other forest, and then click Next, as shown in Figure 4.15.

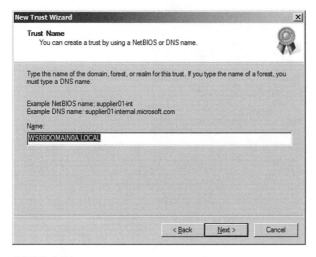

FIGURE 4.15
Trust Name page.

8. On the Trust Type page, select Forest trust shown in Figure 4.16, and click Next.

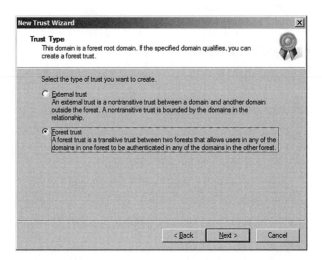

FIGURE 4.16
Trust Type page.

9. On the Direction of Trust page, select One-way: outgoing and click Next, as shown in Figure 4.17.

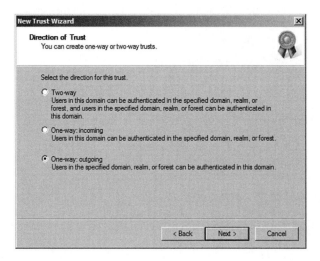

FIGURE 4.17
Direction of Trust page.

10. On the Sides of Trust page, shown in Figure 4.18, select This domain only or Both this domain and the specified domain; then click Next.

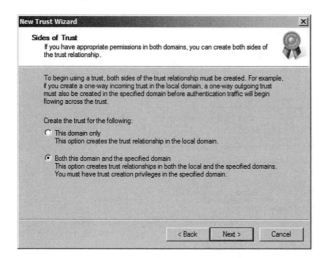

FIGURE 4.18
Sides of Trust page.

11. If you selected Both this domain and the specified domain in Step 10, the User Name and Password page displays, as shown in Figure 4.19. Enter a user name and password for an account in the other forest that has the necessary permissions to create the forest trust, and click Next.

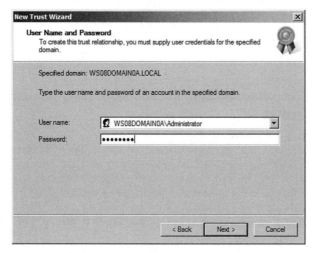

FIGURE 4.19
User Name and Password page.

12. If you selected Both this domain and the specified domain in Step 10, the Outgoing Trust Authentication Level—Local Forest page displays, as shown in Figure 4.20. On the Outgoing Trust Authentication Level—Local Forest page, select Forest-wide authentication or Selective authentication and click Next.

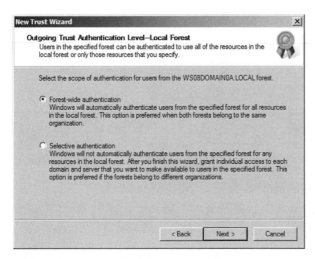

FIGURE 4.20
Outgoing Trust Authentication Level—Local Forest page.

13. On the Trust Selections Complete page, click Next.

14. If you are presented with the Confirm Outgoing Trust page, click No, do not confirm the outgoing trust, and then click Next.

15. If you are presented with the Confirm Incoming Trust page, click No, do not confirm the incoming trust, and then click Next.

16. On the New Trust Wizard page, click Finish.

Create External Trusts

Scenario/Problem: Forest trusts are forest-wide, which provides users in all the domains in one forest with the capability to access resources in all the domains in the other forest. In some cases, you might need to provide users in one domain in your forest with the capability to access resources in a domain in another forest.

Solution: External trusts are used to provide users in one domain in a forest access to resources in one domain in another forest. Domain trusts can be two-way or one-way. A two-way trust allows users from either domain to access resources in the other domain. A one-way trust allows users in the trusted domain to access resources in the trusting domain.

The steps to create external trusts differ depending on the direction of the trust being created. The sections that follow detail the steps to create external trusts.

Create a Two-Way External Trust

To complete this task, you must use an AD DS account that has membership in one of the following AD DS groups:

- ▶ Domain Admins in the forest root domain
- ▶ Enterprise Admins

To create a two-way external trust, perform the following steps:

1. Log on to a domain controller or a member computer that has Windows Server 2008 Remote Server Administration Tools installed.

2. Click Start, click Administrative Tools, and then click Active Directory Domains and Trusts.

3. In the console tree, right-click the domain node for the forest root domain; then click Properties.

4. Click the Trusts tab.

5. Click New Trust.

6. On the Welcome to the New Trust Wizard page, click Next.

7. On the Trust Name page, type the DNS name of the other forest and click Next, as shown in Figure 4.21.

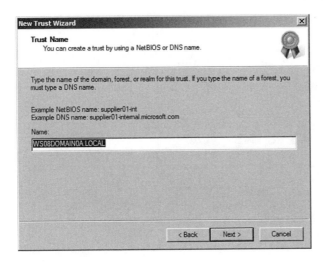

FIGURE 4.21
Trust Name page.

8. On the Trust Type page, select External Trust and click Next.

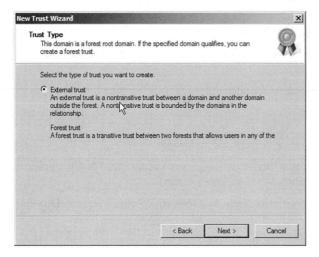

FIGURE 4.22
Trust Type page.

9. On the Direction of Trust page, shown in Figure 4.23, select Two-way and click Next.

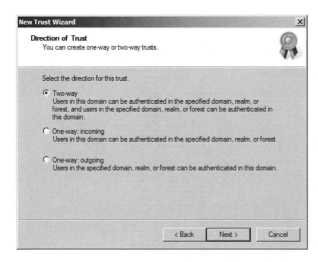

FIGURE 4.23
Direction of Trust page.

10. On the Sides of Trust page, shown in Figure 4.24, select This domain only or Both this domain and the specified domain; then click Next.

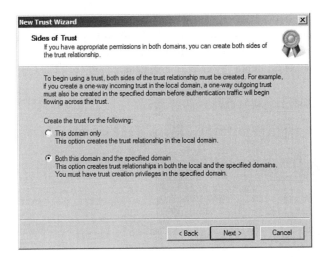

FIGURE 4.24
Sides of Trust page.

11. If you selected Both this domain and the specified domain in Step 10, the User Name and Password page displays, as shown in Figure 4.25. Enter a user name and password for an account in the other forest that has the necessary permissions to create the forest trust, and click Next.

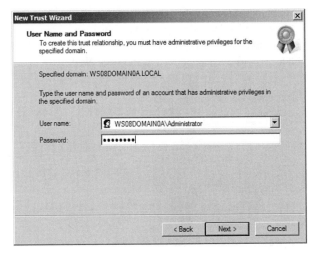

FIGURE 4.25
User Name and Password page.

12. If you selected Both this domain and the specified domain in Step 10, the Outgoing Trust Authentication Level—Local Domain page displays, as shown in Figure 4.26. On the Outgoing Trust Authentication Level—Local Domain page, select Domain-wide authentication or Selective authentication and click Next.

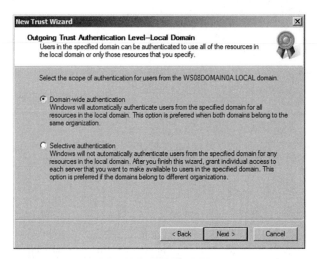

FIGURE 4.26
Outgoing Trust Authentication Level—Local Domain page.

13. If you selected Both this domain and the specified domain in step 10, the Outgoing Trust Authentication Level—Specified Domain page displays, as shown in Figure 4.27. On the Outgoing Trust Authentication Level—Specified Domain page, select Domain-wide authentication or Selective authentication and click Next.

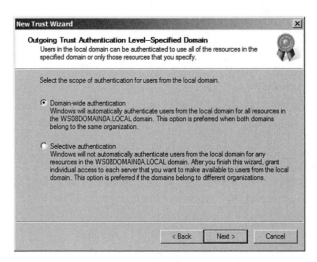

FIGURE 4.27
Outgoing Trust Authentication Level—Specified Domain page.

14. On the Trust Selections Complete page, click Next.

15. If you are presented with the Confirm Outgoing Trust page, click No, do not confirm the outgoing trust, and then click Next.

16. If you are presented with the Confirm Incoming Trust page, click No, do not confirm the incoming trust, and then click Next.

17. On the New Trust Wizard page, click Finish.

Create a One-Way Incoming Forest Trust

To complete this task, you must use an AD DS account that has membership in one of the following AD DS groups:

▶ Domain Admins in the forest root domain

▶ Enterprise Admins

To create a one-way incoming forest trust, perform the following steps:

1. Log on to a domain controller or a member computer that has Windows Server 2008 Remote Server Administration Tools installed.

2. Click Start, click Administrative Tools, and then click Active Directory Domains and Trusts.

3. In the console tree, right-click the domain node for the forest root domain; then click Properties.

4. Click the Trusts tab.

5. Click New Trust.

6. On the Welcome to the New Trust Wizard page, click Next.

7. On the Trust Name page, shown in Figure 4.28, type the DNS name of the other forest and then click Next.

8. On the Trust Type page, shown in Figure 4.29, select External Trust and click Next.

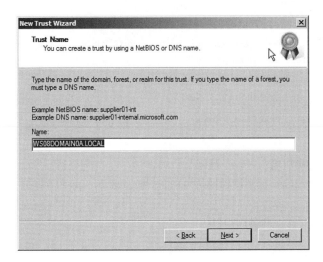

FIGURE 4.28
Trust Name page.

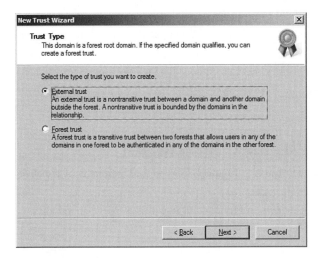

FIGURE 4.29
Trust Type page.

9. On the Direction of Trust page, select One-way: incoming and click Next, as shown in Figure 4.30.

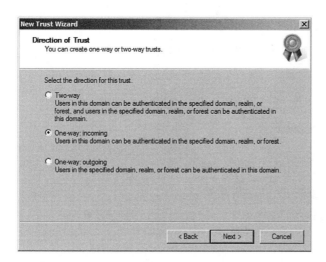

FIGURE 4.30
Direction of Trust page.

10. On the Sides of Trust page, shown in Figure 4.31, select This domain only or Both this domain and the specified domain and click Next.

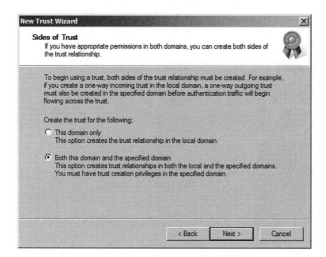

FIGURE 4.31
Sides of Trust page.

11. If you selected Both this domain and the specified domain in Step 10, the User Name and Password page displays, as shown in Figure 4.32. Enter a user name and password for an account in the other forest that has the necessary permissions to create the forest trust and click Next.

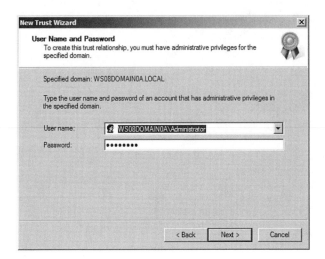

FIGURE 4.32
User Name and Password page.

12. If you selected Both this domain and the specified domain in Step 10, the Outgoing Trust Authentication Level—Specified Domain page displays, as shown in Figure 4.33. On the Outgoing Trust Authentication Level—Specified Domain page, select Domain-wide authentication or Selective authentication and click Next.

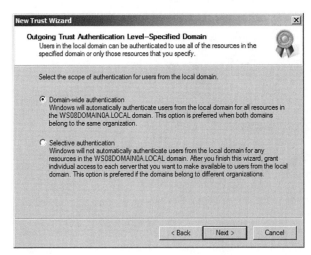

FIGURE 4.33
Outgoing Trust Authentication Level—Specified Domain page.

13. On the Trust Selections Complete page, click Next.

14. If you are presented with the Confirm Outgoing Trust page, click No, do not confirm the outgoing trust, and then click Next.

15. If you are presented with the Confirm Incoming Trust page, click No, do not confirm the incoming trust, and then click Next.

16. On the New Trust Wizard page, click Finish.

Create a One-Way Outgoing Forest Trust

To complete this task, you must use an AD DS account that has membership in one of the following AD DS groups:

▷ Domain Admins in the forest root domain

▷ Enterprise Admins

To create a one-way outgoing forest trust, perform the following steps:

1. Log on to a domain controller or a member computer that has Windows Server 2008 Remote Server Administration Tools installed.

2. Click Start, click Administrative Tools, and then click Active Directory Domains and Trusts.

3. In the console tree, right-click the domain node for the forest root domain; then click Properties.

4. Click the Trusts tab.

5. Click New Trust.

6. On the Welcome to the New Trust Wizard page, click Next.

7. On the Trust Name page, shown in Figure 4.34, type the DNS name of the other forest and then click Next.

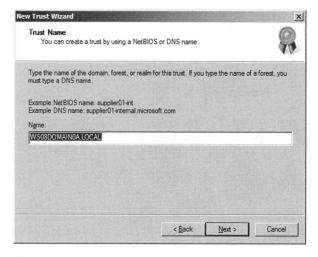

FIGURE 4.34
Trust Name page.

8. On the Trust Type page, select External Trust and click Next, as shown in Figure 4.35.

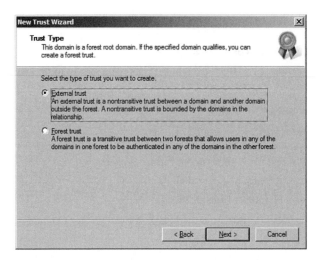

FIGURE 4.35
Trust Type page.

9. On the Direction of Trust page, shown in Figure 4.36, select One-way: outgoing and click Next.

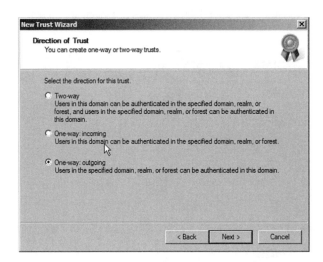

FIGURE 4.36
Direction of Trust page.

10. On the Sides of Trust page, shown in Figure 4.37, select This domain only or Both this domain and the specified domain and click Next.

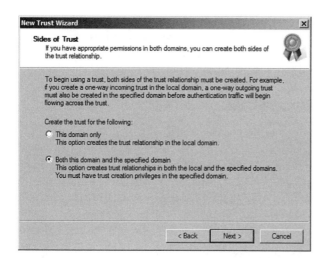

FIGURE 4.37
Sides of Trust page.

11. If you selected Both this domain and the specified domain in Step 10, the User
    Name and Password page displays, as shown in Figure 4.38. Enter a user name
    and password for an account in the other forest that has the necessary permis-
    sions to create the forest trust and click Next.

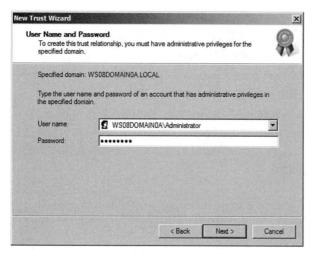

FIGURE 4.38
User Name and Password page.

12. If you selected Both this domain and the specified domain in Step 10, the
    Outgoing Trust Authentication Level—Local Domain page displays, as shown in
    Figure 4.39. On the Outgoing Trust Authentication Level—Local Domain page,
    select Domain-wide authentication or Selective authentication and click Next.

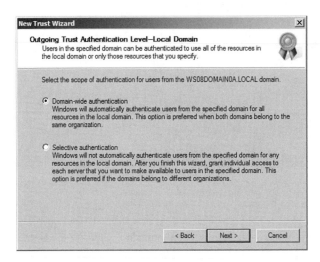

FIGURE 4.39
Outgoing Trust Authentication Level—Local Domain page.

13. On the Trust Selections Complete page, click Next.

14. If you are presented with the Confirm Outgoing Trust page, click No, do not
    confirm the outgoing trust, and then click Next.

15. If you are presented with the Confirm Incoming Trust page, click No, do not
    confirm the incoming trust, and then click Next.

16. On the New Trust Wizard page, click Finish.

Create Realm Trusts

Scenario/Problem: You might need to provide users from a domain in your
forest with the capability to access resources in a non-Windows Kerberos version
5 (V5) realm. You might also need to provide users from a non-Windows
Kerberos version 5 (V5) realm with the capability to access resources in a
domain in your forest.

Solution: *Realm* trusts are used to provide cross-platform interoperability with security services that are based on other versions of the Kerberos V5 protocol. Realm trusts can be two-way or one-way. A two-way realm trust allows users in the domain in your forest and the realm to access resources in either domain or realm. A one-way realm trust allows users in your domain to access resources in the realm, or users in the realm to access resources in your domain.

The steps to create realm trusts differ depending on the direction of the trust being created. The sections that follow detail the steps to create realm trusts.

To complete this task, you must use an AD DS account that has membership in one of the following AD DS groups:

▶ Domain Admins in the forest root domain

▶ Enterprise Admins

To create a realm trust, perform the following steps:

1. Log on to a domain controller or a member computer that has Windows Server 2008 Remote Server Administration Tools installed.

2. Click Start, click Administrative Tools, and then click Active Directory Domains and Trusts.

3. In the console tree, right-click the domain node for the forest root domain; then click Properties.

4. Click the Trusts tab.

5. Click New Trust.

6. On the Welcome to the New Trust Wizard page, click Next.

7. On the Trust Name page, shown in Figure 4.40, type the DNS name of the other forest and then click Next.

8. On the Trust Type page, select Realm trust and click Next, as shown in Figure 4.41.

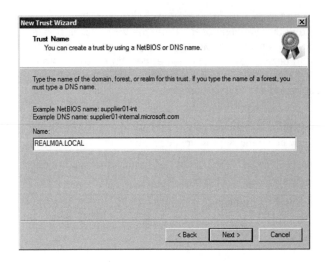

FIGURE 4.40
Trust Name page.

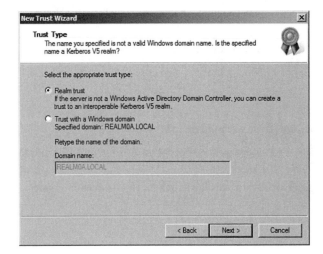

FIGURE 4.41
Trust Type page.

9. On the Transitivity of Trust page, shown in Figure 4.42, select Nontransitive or Transitive and click Next.

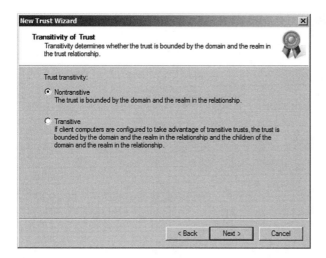

FIGURE 4.42
Transitivity of Trust page.

10. On the Direction of Trust page, shown in Figure 4.43, select Two-way, One-way: incoming, or One-way: outgoing, and click Next.

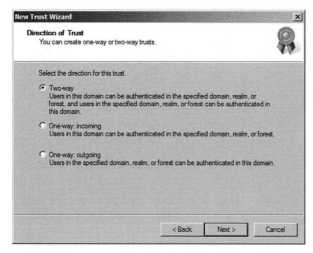

FIGURE 4.43
Direction of Trust page.

11. On the Trust Password page, shown in Figure 4.44, enter and confirm a password to be used for the creation of the trust; then click Next.

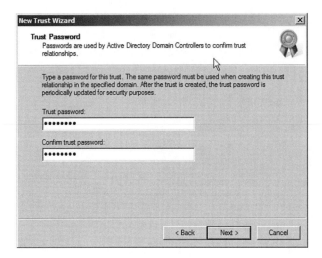

FIGURE 4.44
Trust Password page.

12. On the Trust Selections Complete page, click Next.

13. On the New Trust Wizard page, click Finish.

Create Shortcut Trusts

Scenario/Problem: When your Active Directory Domain Services forest consists of multiple domain trees, authentication requests must first travel a trust path between domain trees for users in one domain tree to access resources in another domain tree. In a large AD DS environment, this can take time. This can be a burden if many users in a domain regularly log onto other domains in a forest.

Solution: *Shortcut* trusts are used to make the authentication process more effi-cient when authentication requests cross different domain trees. Shortcut trusts can be two-way or one-way and are always transitive. A one-way shortcut trust improves the time it takes to authenticate across domain trees, but only in one direction. A two-way shortcut trust improves authentication across domain trees, and it does so in both directions.

The steps to create shortcut trusts differ depending on the direction of the trust being created. The sections that follow detail the steps to create shortcut trusts.

To complete this task, you must use an AD DS account that has membership in one of the following AD DS groups:

- Domain Admins in the forest root domain
- Enterprise Admins

To create a shortcut trust, perform the following steps:

1. Log on to a domain controller or a member computer that has Windows Server 2008 Remote Server Administration Tools installed.

2. Click Start, click Administrative Tools, and then click Active Directory Domains and Trusts.

3. In the console tree, right-click the domain node for the forest root domain; then click Properties.

4. Click the Trusts tab.

5. Click New Trust.

6. On the Welcome to the New Trust Wizard page, click Next.

7. On the Trust Name page, type the DNS name or NetBIOS name of the domain with which you want to create a shortcut trust; then click Next.

8. On the Direction of Trust page, select Two-way, One-way: incoming, or One-way: outgoing. Then click Next.

9. On the Trust Selections Complete page, click Next.

10. If you are presented with the Confirm Outgoing Trust page, click No, do not confirm the outgoing trust, and then click Next.

11. If you are presented with the Confirm Incoming Trust page, click No, do not confirm the incoming trust, and then click Next.

12. On the New Trust Wizard page, click Finish.

Change the Routing Status of a Name Suffix

Scenario/Problem: Name suffixes include user principal name (UPN) suffixes, service principal name (SPN) suffixes, and Domain Name System (DNS) forest or domain tree names. When you create a forest trust, all unique name suffixes are routed by default. In some cases, you might want to control authentication requests over a forest trust.

Solution: *Name suffix routing* allows you to control authentication requests that take place between forests that are joined by a forest trust. By using the Active Directory Domains and Trusts console, you can change the routing status of a name suffix.

To complete this task, you must use an AD DS account that has membership in the following AD DS group:

▶ Domain Admins

To change the routing status of a name suffix, perform the following steps:

1. Log on to a domain controller or a member computer that has Windows Server 2008 Remote Server Administration Tools installed.

2. Click Start, click Administrative Tools, and then click Active Directory Domains and Trusts.

3. In the console tree, right-click the domain node for the forest root domain; then click Properties.

4. Click the Trusts tab.

5. Select an outgoing or incoming trust and click Properties. The properties page for forest trust is shown in Figure 4.45.

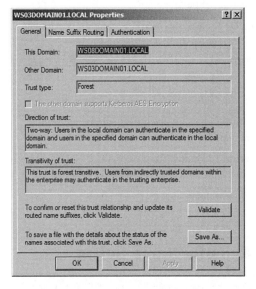

FIGURE 4.45
The Trust Properties General tab.

6. On the Trust Properties page, click the Name Suffix Routing tab, as shown in Figure 4.46.

7. Click the name suffix you want to modify, and select Edit.

8. On the Edit Name Suffix page, click the suffix you want to modify and click Enable or Disable.

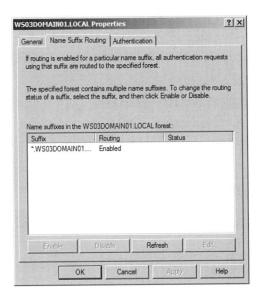

FIGURE 4.46
The Name Suffix Routing tab.

Enable or Disable an Existing Name Suffix from Routing

Scenario/Problem: Name suffixes include UPN suffixes, SPN suffixes, and DNS forest or domain tree names. When you create a forest trust, all unique name suffixes are routed by default. In some cases, you might want to control authentication requests over a forest trust.

Solution: Name suffix routing allows you to control authentication requests that take place between forests joined by a forest trust. By using the Active Directory Domains and Trusts console, you can enable or disable an existing name suffix from routing.

To complete this task, you must use an AD DS account that has membership in the following AD DS group:

▶ Domain Admins

To Enable or Disable an Existing Name Suffix from Routing, perform the following steps:

1. Log on to a domain controller or a member computer that has Windows Server 2008 Remote Server Administration Tools installed.

2. Click Start, click Administrative Tools, and then click Active Directory Domains and Trusts.

3. In the console tree, right-click the domain node for the forest root domain; then click Properties.

4. Click the Trusts tab.

5. Select an outgoing or incoming trust and click Properties.

6. On the Trust Properties page, click the Name Suffix Routing tab.

7. To enable a name suffix, click the suffix you want to enable as shown in Figure 4.47, and click Enable. To disable a name suffix, click the suffix you want to disable and click Disable.

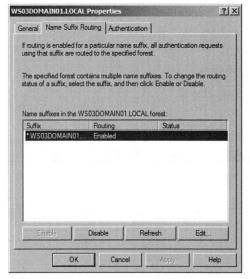

FIGURE 4.47
Enabling or disabling name suffixes.

TIP   If the Enable button appears dimmed, the name suffix is already enabled. If the Disable button appears dimmed, the name suffix is already disabled.

Exclude Name Suffixes from Routing to a Local Forest

Scenario/Problem: Name suffixes include UPN suffixes, SPN suffixes, and DNS forest or domain tree names. When you create a forest trust, all unique name suffixes are routed by default. In some cases, you might want to control authentication requests over a forest trust.

Solution: Name suffix routing allows you to control authentication requests that take place between forests joined by a forest trust. By using the Active Directory Domains and Trusts console, you can exclude name suffixes from routing to a local forest.

To complete this task, you must use an AD DS account that has membership in the following AD DS group:

▶ Domain Admins

To exclude name suffixes from routing to a local forest, perform the following steps:

1. Log on to a domain controller or a member computer that has Windows Server 2008 Remote Server Administration Tools installed.

2. Click Start, click Administrative Tools, and then click Active Directory Domains and Trusts.

3. In the console tree, right-click the domain node for the forest root domain; then click Properties.

4. Click the Trusts tab.

5. Select an outgoing or incoming trust, and click Properties.

6. On the Trust Properties page, click the Name Suffix Routing tab.

7. Click the name suffix you want to modify, as shown in Figure 4.48, and select Edit.

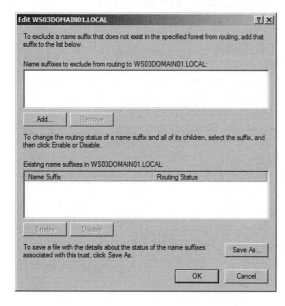

FIGURE 4.48
Excluding name suffixes from routing to a local forest.

8. In Name Suffixes to Exclude from Routing to page, click Add.

9. On the Add Excluded Name Suffix page, shown in Figure 4.49, type a DNS name suffix that is subordinate to the unique name suffix; then click OK.

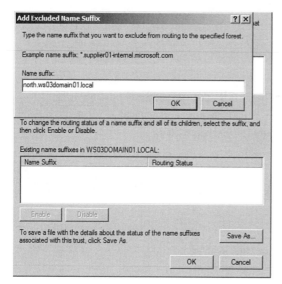

Add Excluded Name Suffix

Type the name suffix that you want to exclude from routing to the specified forest.

Example name suffix: *.supplier01-internal.microsoft.com

Name suffix:
north.ws03domain01.local

OK   Cancel

To change the routing status of a name suffix and all of its children, select the suffix, and then click Enable or Disable.

Existing name suffixes in WS03DOMAIN01.LOCAL:

Name Suffix	Routing Status

Enable   Disable

To save a file with the details about the status of the name suffixes associated with this trust, click Save As.   Save As...

OK   Cancel

FIGURE 4.49
Add Excluded Name Suffix page.

Configure Authentication Scope for a Trust

Scenario/Problem: Authentication across forest trusts and external trusts might be required for a subset of your users or all users in your domain or forest.

Solution: The scope of authentication can be configured on a forest trust and on an external trust to provide domain-wide/forest-wide authentication or selective authentication.

To complete this task, you must use an AD DS account that has membership in the following AD DS group:

▶ Domain Admins

To configure authentication scope for a trust, perform the following steps:

1. Log on to a domain controller or a member computer that has Windows Server 2008 Remote Server Administration Tools installed.

2. Click Start, click Administrative Tools, and then click Active Directory Domains and Trusts.

3. In the console tree, right-click the domain node for the forest root domain; then click Properties.

4. Click the Trusts tab.

5. Select an outgoing or incoming trust, and click Properties.

6. On the Trust Properties page, click the Authentication tab, shown in Figure 4.50.

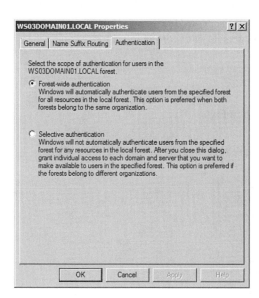

FIGURE 4.50
The Trust Properties Authentication tab.

7. If the trust is a forest trust, select Forest-wide authentication or Selective authentication. If the trust is an external trust, select Domain-wide authentication or Selective authentication.

Validate Trusts

Scenario/Problem: Trust relationships simply provide a means for users to access resources. Additional steps are required to ensure the users have the appropriate permissions on these resources. In some cases, you might need to ensure the trust relationship is still functioning.

Solution: Trust validation allows you to test whether the trust relationship is still functional.

To complete this task, you must use an AD DS account that has membership in the following AD DS group:

▶ Domain Admins

To validate trusts, perform the following steps:

1. Log on to a domain controller or a member computer that has Windows Server 2008 Remote Server Administration Tools installed.

2. Click Start, click Administrative Tools, and then click Active Directory Domains and Trusts.

3. In the console tree, right-click the domain node for the forest root domain; then click Properties.

4. Click the Trusts tab.

5. Select an outgoing or incoming trust and click Properties. The properties page for a two-way forest trust is shown in Figure 4.51.

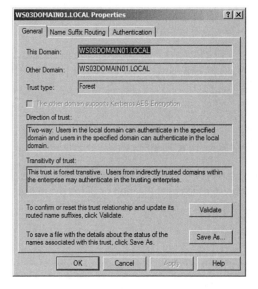

FIGURE 4.51
The Trust Properties General tab.

6. On the Trust Properties page, click Validate.

7. If the trust is a two-way trust, you will be prompted to validate the opposite side of the trust. Select No, do not validate the incoming trust or Yes, validate the incoming trust. If you choose to validate the opposite side of the trust, you must enter the credentials of a user account in the specified domain that has administrative credentials. The prompt for Active Directory Domain Services credentials is shown in Figure 4.52.

FIGURE 4.52
Validating both sides of a trust.

Remove Trusts

Scenario/Problem: Access requirements are not static. At some point, a trust relationship will no longer be required. This is truest when trust relationships are created for short-term tasks, such as migrations.

Solution: You can remove a trust by using the Active Directory Domains and Trusts console.

To complete this task, you must use an AD DS account that has membership in the following AD DS group:

▶ Domain Admins

To remove trusts, perform the following steps:

1. Log on to a domain controller or a member computer that has Windows Server 2008 Remote Server Administration Tools installed.

2. Click Start, click Administrative Tools, and then click Active Directory Domains and Trusts.

3. In the console tree, right-click the domain node for the forest root domain; then click Properties.

4. Click the Trusts tab.

5. Select an outgoing or incoming trust and click Remove.

6. When prompted to remove the trust from the local domain and the other domain, select No, remove the trust from the local domain only or Yes, remove the trust from both the local domain and the other domain, as shown in Figure 4.53. If you select to remove the trust from both domains, you will need to enter the credentials of a user account in the specified domain that has administrative credentials.

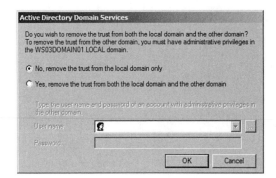

FIGURE 4.53
The Remove Trust Prompt.

Add a User Principal Name to a Forest

Scenario/Problem: Each domain has a default UPN suffix, which uses the DNS name of the domain. In some cases, you might need to provide your users with the use of a different UPN suffix for logon.

Solution: You can use the Active Directory Domains and Trusts console to add a UPN to a forest.

To complete this task, you must use an AD DS account that has membership in the following AD DS group:

▶ Enterprise Admins

To add a user principal name to a forest, perform the following steps:

1. Log on to a domain controller or a member computer that has Windows Server 2008 Remote Server Administration Tools installed.

2. Click Start, click Administrative Tools, and then click Active Directory Domains and Trusts.

3. In the console tree, right-click the Active Directory Domains and Trusts node and then click Properties.

4. On the UPN Suffixes tab, shown in Figure 4.54, type the new UPN suffix you want to add to the forest in the Alternative UPN suffixes field; then click Add.

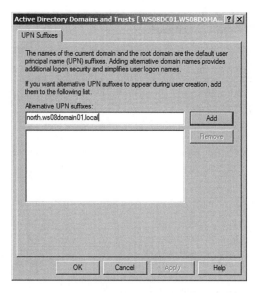

FIGURE 4.54
The UPN Suffixes tab.

Remove a User Principal Name from a Forest

Scenario/Problem: If you have previously added an alternative UPN suffix to your forest, you might need to remove it when it becomes obsolete.

Solution: You can remove a UPN suffix from a forest by using the Active Directory Domains and Trusts console.

To complete this task, you must use an AD DS account that has membership in the following AD DS group:

▶ Enterprise Admins

To remove a user principal name from a forest, perform the following steps:

1. Log on to a domain controller or a member computer that has Windows Server 2008 Remote Server Administration Tools installed.

2. Click Start, click Administrative Tools, and then click Active Directory Domains and Trusts.

3. In the console tree, right-click the Active Directory Domains and Trusts node; then click Properties.

4. On the UPN Suffixes tab, select the UPN suffix you want to remove from the forest in the Alternative UPN suffixes field and click Remove.

Configure Domain Functional Levels

Scenario/Problem: *Domain functional levels* control the advanced features that are available in an Active Directory Domain Services domain. In addition, domain functional levels also control the operating systems that can be installed on domain controllers that are added to the domain.

Solution: You can raise the domain functional level of a domain by using the Active Directory Domains and Trusts console.

To complete this task, you must use an AD DS account that has membership in one of the following AD DS groups:

- ▶ Domain Admins in the forest root domain
- ▶ Enterprise Admins

To configure domain functional levels, perform the following steps:

1. Log on to a domain controller or a member computer that has Windows Server 2008 Remote Server Administration Tools installed.

2. Click Start, click Administrative Tools, and then click Active Directory Domains and Trusts.

3. In the console tree, right-click the domain node for the forest root domain; then click Raise Domain Functional Level, as shown in Figure 4.55.

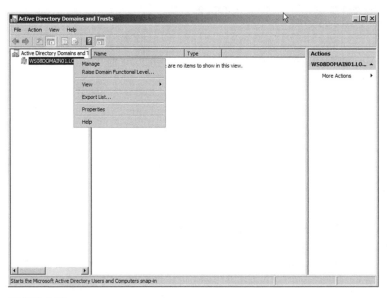

FIGURE 4.55
Selecting Raise Domain Functional Level.

4. On the Raise Domain Functional Level page, select the desired domain functional level from the available list and click Raise, as shown in Figure 4.56.

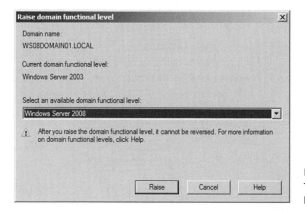

FIGURE 4.56
The Raise Domain Functional
Level page.

5. In the Raise Domain Functional Level warning box, click OK, as shown in Figure 4.57.

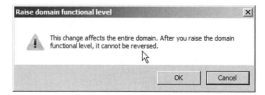

FIGURE 4.57
The Raise Domain Functional Level
warning box.

Configure Forest Functional Levels

Scenario/Problem: *Forest functional levels* control the advanced features that are available in an Active Directory Domain Services forest. In addition, forest functional levels also control the domain functional levels that are permitted in a forest.

Solution: You can raise the forest functional level of a forest by using the Active Directory Domains and Trusts console.

To complete this task, you must use an AD DS account that has membership in one of the following AD DS groups:

▶ Domain Admins in the forest root domain

▶ Enterprise Admins

To configure forest functional levels, perform the following steps:

1. Log on to a domain controller or a member computer that has Windows Server 2008 Remote Server Administration Tools installed.

2. Click Start, click Administrative Tools, and then click Active Directory Domains and Trusts.

3. In the console tree, right-click the Active Directory Domains and Trusts node and then select Raise Forest Functional Level, as shown in Figure 4.58.

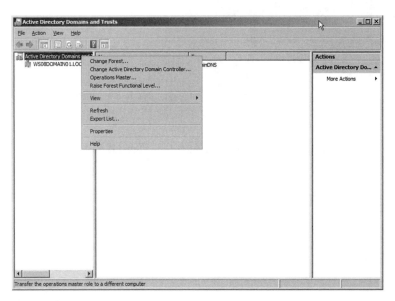

FIGURE 4.58
Selecting Raise Forest Functional Level.

4. On the Raise Forest Functional Level page, shown in Figure 4.59, select the desired forest functional level from the available list and click Raise.

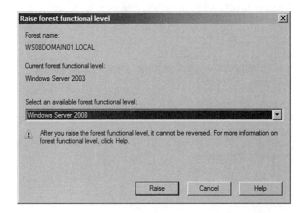

FIGURE 4.59
The Raise Forest Functional Level page.

5. In the Raise Forest Functional Level warning box, shown in Figure 4.60, click OK.

FIGURE 4.60
The Raise Forest Functional Level warning box.

CHAPTER 5

Manage Operations Master Roles and Global Catalog Servers

IN THIS CHAPTER

- ▶ Enable the Global Catalog Role
- ▶ Disable the Global Catalog Role
- ▶ Verify Global Catalog Server Readiness
- ▶ Verify Global Catalog DNS Registrations
- ▶ Determine Global Catalog Servers
- ▶ Identify Operations Master Role Holders
- ▶ Validate Domain Controller Advertising
- ▶ Transfer the Schema Master Role
- ▶ Transfer the Domain Naming Master Role
- ▶ Transfer the RID Master Role
- ▶ Transfer the PDC Emulator Role
- ▶ Transfer the Infrastructure Master Role
- ▶ Seize the Schema Master Role
- ▶ Seize the Domain Naming Master Role
- ▶ Seize the RID Master Role
- ▶ Seize the PDC Emulator Role
- ▶ Seize the Infrastructure Master Role

In every Active Directory Domain Services forest, at least five operations master roles are assigned to one or more domain controllers (DCs). Forest-wide operations master roles, schema master and domain naming master, exist once in the forest. Domain-wide operations master roles, PDC Emulator, RID master, and infrastructure master, exist in each domain in the forest.

Global catalog servers contain the read-only global catalog partition, which contains a subset of the attributes for every object in the forest.

This chapter describes the steps required to manage operations master roles and global catalog servers.

Enable the Global Catalog Role

Scenario/Problem: Each domain controller contains a writable copy of the domain partition for the domain to which the domain controller belongs. In a multiple domain forest, domain controllers are often queried for information pertaining to objects from multiple domains. You might need to configure domain controllers so they also contain a partial list of attributes for objects from all domains in the forest.

Solution: You can enable the global catalog role on a domain controller so that it hosts the global catalog directory partition. The global catalog role can be enabled by using the Windows interface and using the command line.

Enable the Global Catalog Role by Using the Windows Interface

To enable the global catalog role by using the windows interface, perform the following steps:

1. Log on to a domain controller or a member computer that has Windows Server 2008 Remote Server Administration Tools (RSAT) installed.

2. Click Start, click Administrative Tools, and then click Active Directory Sites and Services.

3. In the console tree, as shown in Figure 5.1, select the domain controller where you want to enable the global catalog role.

TIP You can search for a global catalog by right-clicking Sites in the console tree and selecting Find from the menu.

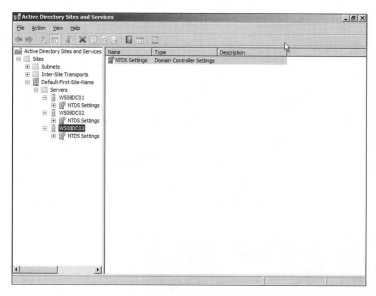

FIGURE 5.1
Active Directory Sites and Services console.

4. In the details pane, right-click NTDS Settings and select Properties.

5. On the NTDS Settings Properties page, shown in Figure 5.2, select the Global Catalog check box and click OK.

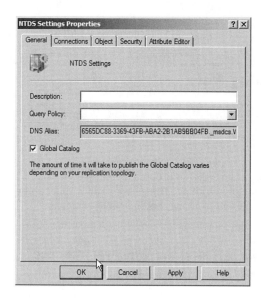

FIGURE 5.2
Enable the global catalog role by using the Windows interface.

Enable the Global Catalog Role by Using the Command Line

To enable the global catalog role by using the command line, perform the following steps:

1. Log on to a domain controller.

2. Click Start, and then click Command Prompt.

3. In the Command Prompt window, type the following command:

   `repadmin /options servername +IS_GC`

   (where *servername* is the domain controller on which you want to enable the global catalog role).

4. Verify that the results show New DSA Options: IS_GC, as shown in Figure 5.3.

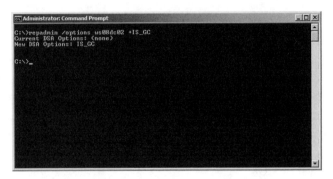

FIGURE 5.3
Enable the global catalog role by using the command line.

Disable the Global Catalog Role

Scenario/Problem: You might need to remove a server from the read-only global catalog partition.

Solution: You can disable the global catalog role on a domain controller so that it no longer hosts the global catalog directory partition. The global catalog role can be disabled by using the Windows interface and by using the command line.

Disable the Global Catalog Role by Using the Windows Interface

To disable the global catalog role by using the windows interface, perform the following steps:

1. Log on to a domain controller or a member computer that has Windows Server 2008 Remote Server Administration Tools installed.

2. Click Start, click Administrative Tools, and then click Active Directory Sites and Services.

3. In the console tree, select the domain controller where you want to disable the global catalog role.

TIP You can search for a global catalog by right-clicking Sites in the console tree and selecting Find from the menu.

---

4. In the details pane, right-click NTDS Settings and select Properties. The NTDS Properties page is shown in Figure 5.4.

5. On the NTDS Settings Properties page, clear the Global Catalog check box and then click OK.

NOTE If this domain controller is the last domain controller in the forest, you will be presented with a confirmation to proceed. You can click Yes on the confirmation to continue with the removal of the global catalog role or No to abort.

TIP In a forest that consists of multiple domains, the global catalog role should reside on one or more domain controllers. Furthermore, each domain should also contain one or more global catalog servers. The global catalog role is important for authentication and for Active Directory-aware applications, such as Microsoft Exchange Server.

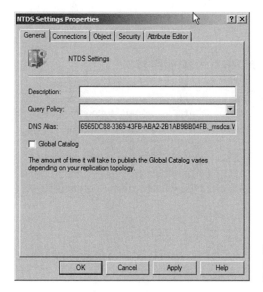

FIGURE 5.4

Disable the global catalog role by using the Windows interface.

Disable the Global Catalog Role by Using the Command Line

To disable the global catalog role by using the command line, perform the following steps:

1. Log on to a domain controller.

2. Click Start, and click Command Prompt.

3. In the Command Prompt window, type the following command:

   `repadmin /options servername -IS_GC`

   (where *servername* is the domain controller on which you want to disable the global catalog role).

4. Verify that the results show New DSA Options: (none), as shown in Figure 5.5.

FIGURE 5.5
Disable the global catalog role by using the command line.

Verify Global Catalog Server Readiness

Scenario/Problem: After you have enabled the global catalog role on a domains controller, you might want to ensure that it is properly functioning as a global catalog server before clients and services start querying the global catalog partition on this server.

Solution: Global catalog server readiness can be verified by using LDP and by using Nltest.

Verify Global Catalog Server Readiness by Using LDP

To verify global catalog server readiness by using LDP, perform the following steps:

1. Log on to a domain controller.

2. Click Start, click Run, type **LDP**, and click OK.

3. On the Connection menu, select Connect.

4. In the Connect box, type the name of the server whose global catalog readiness you want to verify, as shown in Figure 5.6.

FIGURE 5.6
The LDP Connect screen.

5. In the Port box, if 389 is not showing, type **389**.

6. If the Connectionless box is selected, clear it and then click OK.

7. In the details pane, verify that the isGlobalCatalogReady attribute has a value of TRUE, as shown in Figure 5.7.

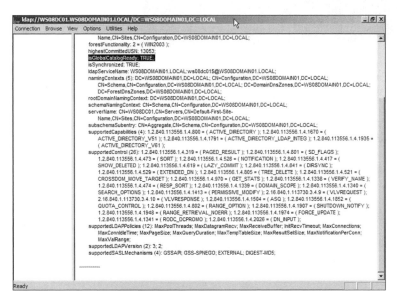

FIGURE 5.7
Verify global catalog server readiness by using LDP.

Verify Global Catalog Server Readiness by Using NLTest

To verify global catalog server readiness by using NLTest, perform the following steps:

1. Log on to a domain controller.

2. Click Start, and click Command Prompt.

3. In the Command Prompt window, type the following command:

   nltest /**server:***servername* /**dsgetdc:***domainname*

   (where *servername* is the domain controller you want to validate global catalog readiness and *domainname* is the name of the domain to which the domain controller belongs).

4. Verify that GC is listed under the Flags section of the results, as shown in Figure 5.8.

FIGURE 5.8
Verify global catalog server readiness by using Nltest.

Verify Global Catalog DNS Registrations

Scenario/Problem: Service query DNS for information on global catalog servers. After you have enabled the global catalog role on a domain controller, you might need to verify that the appropriate DNS registrations exist.

Solution: You can verify global catalog DNS registrations by using the DNS console.

To verify global catalog DNS registrations, perform the following steps:

1. Log on to a domain controller or a member computer that has Windows Server 2008 Remote Server Administration Tools installed.

2. Click Start, click Administrative Tools, and then click DNS.

3. In the console tree, expand the server name, expand Forward Lookup Zones, and then expand the forest root domain, as shown in Figure 5.9.

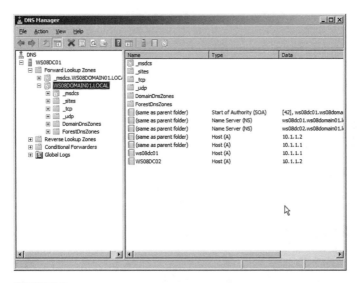

FIGURE 5.9
The forest root DNS zone.

4. In the console tree, click the _tcp container.

5. In the details pane, look in the Name column for _gc and in the Data column for the name of the server, as shown in Figure 5.10.

NOTE One DNS record per global catalog server will exist in DNS. In the case of Figure 5.10, there are two global catalog servers, which each have a DNS record.

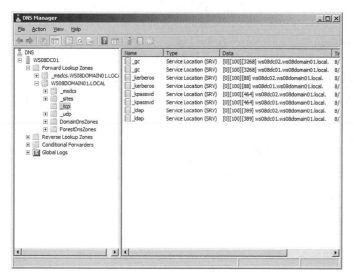

FIGURE 5.10
Global catalog DNS registrations.

Determine Global Catalog Servers

Scenario/Problem: In complex environments, it is not uncommon to have a large number of global catalog servers. You might need to produce a list of all global catalog servers or identify whether a particular domain controller is a global catalog server.

Solution: You can identify all global catalog servers in the forest or identify all global catalog servers in a domain by using the dsquery command-line tool.

Identify All Global Catalog Servers in the Forest

To identify all global catalog servers in the forest, perform the following steps:

1. Log on to a domain controller.

2. Click Start and click Command Prompt.

3. In the Command Prompt window, enter the following command and press Enter.

   ```
   dsquery server -forest -isgc
   ```

NOTE The distinguished name of each global catalog server in the forest is returned, as shown in Figure 5.11.

FIGURE 5.11
Use dsquery to identify all global catalog servers in the forest.

Identify All Global Catalog Servers in a Domain

To identify all global catalog servers in a domain, perform the following steps:

1. Log on to a domain controller.

2. Click Start and click Command Prompt.

3. In the Command Prompt window, enter the following command and press Enter.

    dsquery server -domain *domainname* -isgc

    (where *domainname* is the name of the domain you want to query for global catalog servers).

> **NOTE** The distinguished name of each global catalog server in the forest is returned, as shown in Figure 5.12.

FIGURE 5.12
Use dsquery to identify all global catalog servers in the domain.

Identify Operations Master Role Holders

Scenario/Problem: Certain domain controllers, referred to as *operations master role holders*, have special roles installed. These roles are used for various tasks that require a single server to be authoritative for the given task.

Solution: You can use the dsquery and netdom command-line tools to identify operations master role holders.

Identify Operations Master Role Holders by Using Dsquery

To identify operations master role holders by using Dsquery, perform the following steps:

1. Log on to a domain controller.

2. Click Start, and click Command Prompt.

3. In the Command Prompt window, enter the following command and press Enter:

    `dsquery server -hasfsmo rolename`

    (where *rolename* is the name of the role you want to query for).

Table 5.1 lists the role names used by dsquery.

Table 5.1   **Operations Master Role Names Used by** dsquery

Role Name	Operations Master Role
Schema	Schema Master
Name	Domain Naming Master
Infr	Infrastructure Master
PDC	PDC Emulator
RID	RID Master

NOTE The distinguished name of the operations master role holder is returned, as shown in Figure 5.13.

FIGURE 5.13
Using dsquery to identify operations master role holders.

Identify Operations Master Role Holders by Using Netdom

To identify operations master role holders by using the netdom, perform the following steps:

1. Log on to a domain controller.

2. Click Start, and click Command Prompt.

3. In the Command Prompt window, enter the following command and press Enter:

   netdom query /domain:*domainname*.local fsmo

   (where *domainname* is the name of the domain in which you want to query operations master role holders).

> **NOTE** The names of the operations master role holders are returned, as shown in Figure 5.14.

FIGURE 5.14
Using Netdom to identify operations master role holders.

Validate Domain Controller Advertising

Scenario/Problem: Domain controllers provide a number of services. During troubleshooting, you might need to determine whether a domain controller is providing all the required services.

Solution: You can validate domain controller advertising by using the dcdiag command-line tool.

To validate domain controller advertising, perform the following steps:

1. Log on to a domain controller.

2. Click Start, and click Command Prompt.

3. In the Command Prompt window, enter the following command and press Enter:

   dcdiag /s:*servername* /test:advertising

   (where *servername* is the name of the server you want to test for advertising).

NOTE The results of the Advertising test are returned, as shown in Figure 5.15.

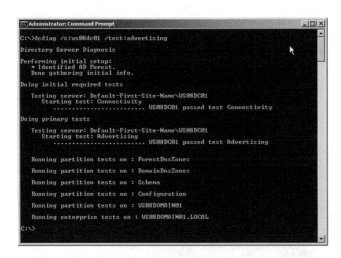

FIGURE 5.15
Using dcdiag to test domain controller advertising.

Transfer the Schema Master Role

Scenario/Problem: Each Active Directory Domain Services forest has a single domain controller that is authoritative for the schema. This domain controller is called the *schema master* and is responsible for performing updates to the directory schema. This role can be enabled on only a single domain controller in the forest root domain. When you first install AD DS, the first domain controller you introduce into the forest holds this role. You might need to transfer this role from one domain controller to another.

Solution: The schema master operations master role can be transferred by using the Windows interface or the command line.

Transfer the Schema Master Role by Using the Windows Interface

To transfer the schema master role by using the Windows interface, perform the following steps:

1. Log on to a domain controller or a member computer that has Windows Server 2008 RSAT installed.

2. Click Start, click Administrative Tools, and then click Active Directory Schema.

TIP The Active Directory Schema Snap-in is not installed by default. You must perform the steps in Chapter 7 to install the snap-in before you can use it.

3. Right-click the Active Directory Schema node in the console tree and select Change Active Directory Domain Controller, as shown in Figure 5.16.

4. On the Change Directory Server page, select the domain controller to which you want to transfer the schema master role; then click OK.

5. A warning displays stating that the snap-in is not connected to the schema master, as shown in Figure 5.17. Click OK.

6. Right-click the Active Directory Schema node in the console tree and select Operations Master.

7. On the Change Schema Master window, ensure the domain controller you selected in Step 4 is listed as the targeted server, as shown in Figure 5.18; then click Change.

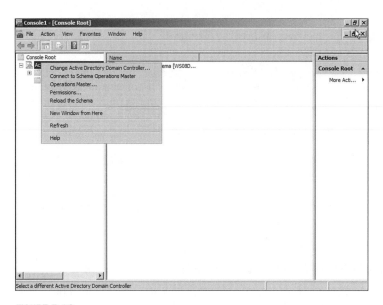

FIGURE 5.16
The Active Directory Schema Snap-In.

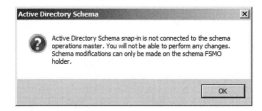

FIGURE 5.17
Active Directory Schema Snap-In
warning.

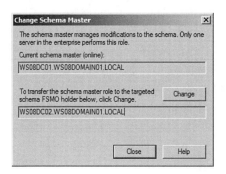

FIGURE 5.18
The Change Schema Master window.

8. In the confirmation box, click Yes.

9. A message that indicates the operation completed successfully displays, as
    shown in Figure 5.19.

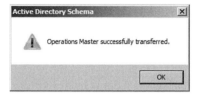

FIGURE 5.19
Active Directory Schema Transfer confirmation
screen.

Transfer the Schema Master Role by Using the Command Line

To transfer the schema master role by using the command line, perform the following
steps:

1. Log on to a domain controller.

2. Click Start, and click Command Prompt.

3. In the Command Prompt window, type **ntdsutil** and press Enter.

4. At the ntdsutil command prompt, type **roles** and press Enter.

5. At the fsmo maintenance command prompt, type **connections** and press Enter.

6. At the fsmo maintenance command prompt, type **connect to server**
   DomainController, where *DomainController* is the domain controller you want
   to transfer the role to; then press Enter.

7. At the server connections command prompt, type **quit** and press Enter.

8. At the fsmo maintenance command prompt, type **transfer schema master**
   and press Enter.

Transfer the Domain Naming Master Role

Scenario/Problem: Each Active Directory Domain Services forest has a single
domain controller that is authoritative for domain naming. This domain controller
is called the *domain naming master* and is responsible for making changes to
the forest-wide domain name space of the directory. This role can be enabled on
only a single domain controller in the forest root domain. When you first install
AD DS, the first domain controller you introduce into the forest holds this role.
You might need to transfer this role from one domain controller to another.

Solution: The domain naming master operations master role can be transferred by
using the Windows interface or the command line.

Transfer the Domain Naming Master Role by Using the Windows Interface

To transfer the domain naming master role by using the Windows interface, perform the following steps:

1. Log on to a domain controller or a member computer that has Windows Server 2008 RSAT installed.

2. Click Start, click Administrative Tools, and click Active Directory Domains and Trusts.

3. Right-click the Active Directory Domains and Trusts node in the console tree; then select Change Active Directory Domain Controller, as shown in Figure 5.20.

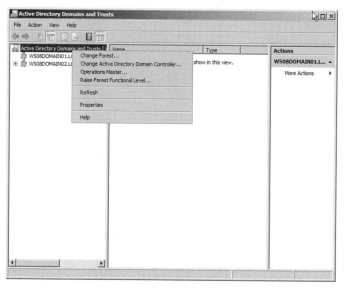

FIGURE 5.20
Active Directory Domains and Trusts console.

4. On the Change Directory Server page, shown in Figure 5.21, select the domain controller to which you want to transfer the domain naming master role; then click OK.

5. Right-click the Active Directory Domains and Trust node in the console tree and select Operations Master.

6. On the Operations Master window, ensure the domain controller you selected in Step 4 is listed as the targeted server, as shown in Figure 5.22, and click Change.

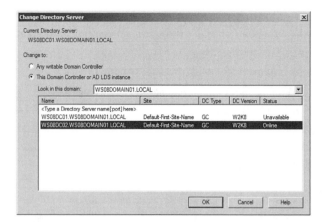

FIGURE 5.21
Change Directory Server page.

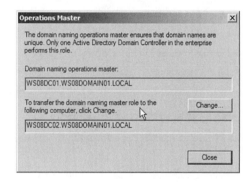

FIGURE 5.22
The Operations Master Window.

7. On the confirmation screen, click Yes.

8. A message displays that indicates the operation completed successfully.

Transfer the Domain Naming Master Role by Using the Command Line

To transfer the domain naming master role by using the command line, perform the following steps:

1. Log on to a domain controller.

2. Click Start, and click Command Prompt.

3. In the Command Prompt window, type **ntdsutil** and press Enter.

4. At the ntdsutil command prompt, type **roles** and press Enter.

5. At the fsmo maintenance command prompt, type **connections** and press Enter.

6. At the fsmo maintenance command prompt, type **connect to server** **DomainController**, where *DomainController* is the domain controller you want to transfer the role to, and press Enter.

7. At the server connections command prompt, type **quit** and press Enter.

8. At the fsmo maintenance command prompt, type **transfer naming master** and press Enter.

Transfer the RID Master Role

Scenario/Problem: Each Active Directory Domain Services domain has a single domain controller that is authoritative for processing RID Pool requests from all DCs within a given domain. This domain controller is called the *RID master*. Each domain in a forest has a domain controller configured as the RID master for that given domain. By default, this role is enabled on the first domain controller you add to a domain.

Solution: The RID master operations master role can be transferred by using the Windows interface or the command line.

Transfer the RID Master Role by Using the Windows Interface

To transfer the RID master role by using the Windows interface, perform the following steps:

1. Log on to a domain controller or a member computer that has Windows Server 2008 RSAT installed.

2. Click Start, click Administrative Tools, and click Active Directory Users and Computers.

3. Right-click the domain node in the console tree and select Change Domain Controller, as shown in Figure 5.23.

4. On the Change Directory Server page, shown in Figure 5.24, select the domain controller to which you want to transfer the RID master role; then click OK.

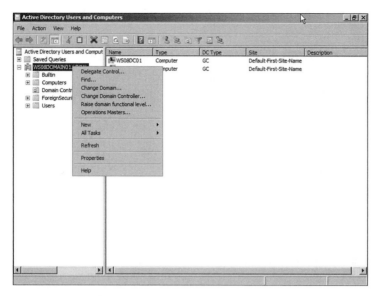

FIGURE 5.23
Active Directory Users and Computers console.

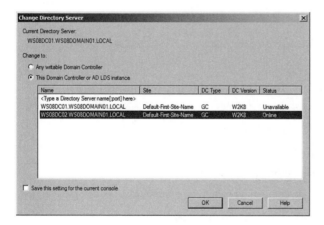

FIGURE 5.24
Change Directory Server page.

5. Right-click the domain node in the console tree and select Operations Masters.

6. On the Operations Masters page, select the RID tab, shown in Figure 5.25.

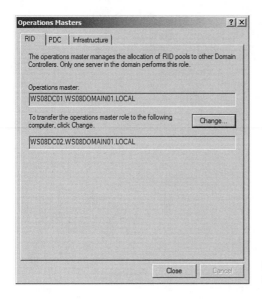

FIGURE 5.25
Operations Masters RID tab.

7. Ensure the domain controller you selected in Step 4 is listed as the targeted server and click Change.

8. On the confirmation page, click Yes.

9. A message displays that indicates the operation completed successfully.

Transfer the RID Master Role by Using the Command Line

1. Log on to a domain controller.

2. Click Start, and click Command Prompt.

3. In the Command Prompt window, type **ntdsutil** and press Enter.

4. At the ntdsutil command prompt, type **roles** and press Enter.

5. At the fsmo maintenance command prompt, type **connections** and press Enter.

6. At the fsmo maintenance command prompt, type **connect to server** *DomainController*, where *DomainController* is the domain controller to which you want to transfer the role, and press Enter.

7. At the server connections command prompt, type **quit** and press Enter.

8. At the fsmo maintenance command prompt, type **transfer RID master** and press Enter.

9. On the Role Transfer Confirmation page, click Yes to confirm the transfer.

Transfer the PDC Emulator Role

Scenario/Problem: Each Active Directory Domain Services domain has a single domain controller that is configured as the PDC emulator. The PDC emulator is ultimately responsible for password changes, validating authentication failures, account lockouts, and synchronizing the time. By default, this role is enabled on the first domain controller you add to a domain.

Solution: The PDC emulator operations master role can be transferred by using the Windows interface or the command line.

Transfer the PDC Emulator Role by Using the Windows Interface

To transfer the PDC master role by using the Windows interface, perform the following steps:

1. Log on to a domain controller or a member computer that has Windows Server 2008 RSAT installed.

2. Click Start, click Administrative Tools, and click Active Directory Users and Computers.

3. Right-click the domain node in the console tree and select Change Domain Controller.

4. On the Change Directory Server page, select the domain controller to which you want to transfer the PDC master role, and click OK.

5. Right-click the domain node in the console tree and select Operations Masters.

6. On the Operations Masters page, select the PDC tab, shown in Figure 5.26.

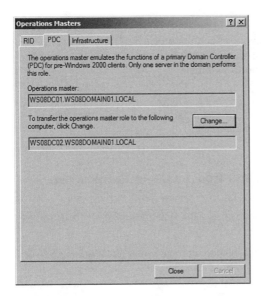

FIGURE 5.26
Operations Masters PDC tab.

7. Ensure the domain controller you selected in Step 4 is listed as the targeted server and click Change.

8. On the confirmation page, click Yes.

9. A message displays that indicates the operation completed successfully.

Transfer the PDC Emulator Role by Using the Command Line

To transfer the PDC master role by using the command line, perform the following steps:

1. Log on to a domain controller.

2. Click Start, and click Command Prompt.

3. In the Command Prompt window, type **ntdsutil** and press Enter.

4. At the ntdsutil command prompt, type **roles** and press Enter.

5. At the fsmo maintenance command prompt, type **connections** and press Enter.

6. At the fsmo maintenance command prompt, type **connect to server** **DomainController**, where *DomainController* is the domain controller to which you want to transfer the role, and press Enter.

7. At the server connections command prompt, type **quit** and press Enter.

8. At the fsmo maintenance command prompt, type **transfer PDC** and press Enter.

9. On the Role Transfer Confirmation page, click Yes to confirm the transfer.

Transfer the Infrastructure Master Role

Scenario/Problem: Each Active Directory Domain Services domain has a single domain controller that is responsible for updating an object's SID and distinguished name in a cross-domain object reference. By default, this role is enabled on the first domain controller you add to a domain.

Solution: The infrastructure master operations master role can be transferred by using the Windows interface or the command line.

Transfer the Infrastructure Master Role by Using the Windows Interface

To transfer the infrastructure master role by using the Windows interface, perform the following steps:

1. Log on to a domain controller or a member computer that has Windows Server 2008 RSAT installed.

2. Click Start, click Administrative Tools, and click Active Directory Users and Computers.

3. Right-click the domain node in the console tree and select Change Domain Controller.

4. On the Change Directory Server page, select the domain controller to which you want to transfer the infrastructure master role, and click OK.

5. Right-click the domain node in the console tree and select Operations Masters.

6. On the Operations Masters page, select the Infrastructure tab, shown in Figure 5.27.

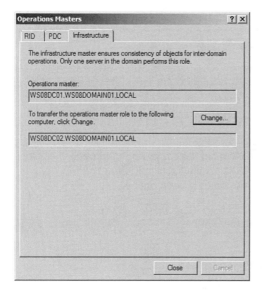

FIGURE 5.27
Operations Masters Infrastructure tab.

7. Ensure the domain controller you selected in Step 4 is listed as the targeted server and click Change.

8. On the confirmation page, click Yes.

9. A message displays that indicates the operation completed successfully.

Transfer the Infrastructure Master Role by Using the Command Line

To transfer the infrastructure master role by using the command line, perform the following steps:

1. Log on to a domain controller.

2. Click Start, and click Command Prompt.

3. In the Command Prompt window, type **ntdsutil** and press Enter.

4. At the ntdsutil command prompt, type **roles** and press Enter.

5. At the fsmo maintenance command prompt, type **connections** and press Enter.

6. At the fsmo maintenance command prompt, type **connect to server** *DomainController*, where *DomainController* is the domain controller to which you want to transfer the role, and press Enter.

7. At the server connections command prompt, type **quit** and press Enter.

8. At the fsmo maintenance command prompt, type **transfer infrastructure master** and press Enter.

Seize the Schema Master Role

Scenario/Problem: If the current schema master role holder becomes unavailable and cannot be recovered, you will need to move that role to another domain controller.

Solution: When the current schema master has failed, you need to seize the role and move it to another domain controller. It is important that, after the role has been seized, the original role holder is not brought back online.

To seize the schema master role, perform the following steps:

1. Log on to a domain controller.

2. Click Start, and click Command Prompt.

3. In the Command Prompt window, type **ntdsutil** and press Enter.

4. At the ntdsutil command prompt, type **roles** and press Enter.

5. At the fsmo maintenance command prompt, type **connections** and press Enter.

6. At the fsmo maintenance command prompt, type **connect to server** *DomainController*, where *DomainController* is the domain controller you want to assign the new operations master role, and press Enter.

7. At the server connections command prompt, type **quit** and press Enter.

8. At the fsmo maintenance command prompt, type **seize schema master** and press Enter.

9. In the Role Seizure Confirmation Dialog screen, click Yes, as shown in Figure 5.28.

10. Ntdsutil first attempts to safe transfer the role before seizing the role. If a safe transfer fails, ntdsutil proceeds with the role seizure, as shown in Figure 5.29.

FIGURE 5.28
The Role Seizure Confirmation Dialog
screen.

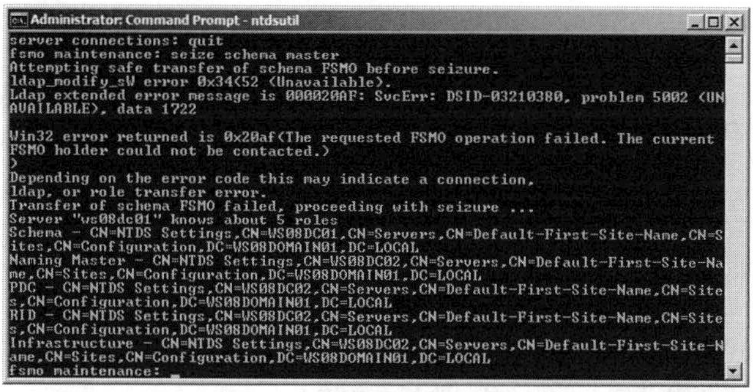

FIGURE 5.29
Seizing the schema master role.

Seize the Domain Naming Master Role

Scenario/Problem: If the current domain naming master role holder becomes
unavailable and cannot be recovered, you need to move that role to another
domain controller.

Solution: When the current domain naming master has failed, you need to seize
the role and move it to another domain controller. It is important that, after the role
has been seized, the original role holder is not brought back online.

To seize the domain naming master role, perform the following steps:

1. Log on to a domain controller.

2. Click Start, and click Command Prompt.

3. In the Command Prompt window, type **ntdsutil** and press Enter.

4. At the ntdsutil command prompt, type **roles** and press Enter.

5. At the fsmo maintenance command prompt, type **connections** and press Enter.

6. At the fsmo maintenance command prompt, type **connect to server** *DomainController*, where *DomainController* is the domain controller you want to assign the new operations master role, and press Enter.

7. At the server connections command prompt, type **quit** and press Enter.

8. At the fsmo maintenance command prompt, type **seize naming master** and press Enter.

9. In the Role Seizure Confirmation Dialog screen, click Yes.

10. Ntdsutil first attempts to safe transfer the role before seizing the role. If a safe transfer fails, ntdsutil proceeds with the role seizure, as shown in Figure 5.30.

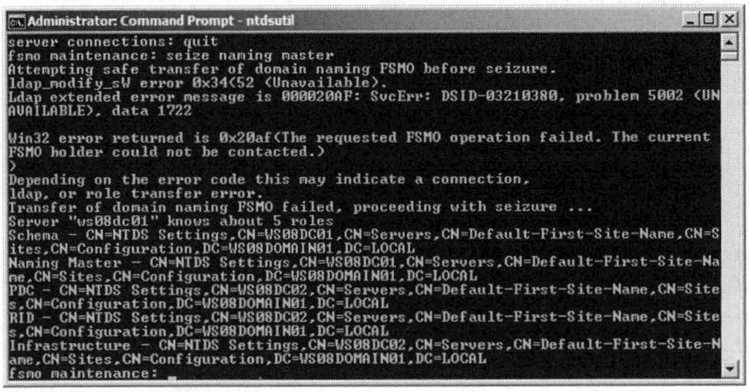

FIGURE 5.30
Seizing the domain naming master role.

Seize the RID Master Role

Scenario/Problem: If the current RID master role holder becomes unavailable and cannot be recovered, you must move that role to another domain controller.

Solution: When the current RID master has failed, you need to seize the role and move it to another domain controller. It is important that, after the role has been seized, the original role holder is not brought back online.

To seize the RID master role, perform the following steps:

1. Log on to a domain controller.

2. Click Start, and click Command Prompt.

3. In the Command Prompt window, type **ntdsutil** and press Enter.

4. At the ntdsutil command prompt, type **roles** and press Enter.

5. At the fsmo maintenance command prompt, type **connections** and press Enter.

6. At the fsmo maintenance command prompt, type **connect to server** **DomainController**, where *DomainController* is the domain controller you want to assign the new operations master role, and press Enter.

7. At the server connections command prompt, type **quit** and press Enter.

8. At the fsmo maintenance command prompt, type **seize RID master** and press Enter.

9. In the Role Seizure Confirmation Dialog screen, click Yes.

10. Ntdsutil first attempts to safe transfer the role before seizing the role. If a safe transfer fails, ntdsutil proceeds with the role seizure, as shown in Figure 5.31.

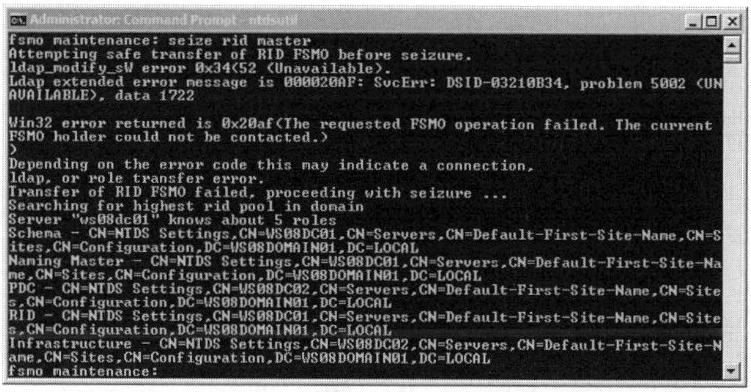

FIGURE 5.31
Seizing the RID master role.

Seize the PDC Emulator Role

Scenario/Problem: If the current PDC emulator role holder becomes unavailable and cannot be recovered, you need to move that role to another domain controller.

Solution: When the current PDC emulator has failed, you need to seize the role and move it to another domain controller. It is important that, after the role has been seized, the original role holder is not brought back online.

To seize the PDC emulator role, perform the following steps:

1. Log on to a domain controller.

2. Click Start, and click Command Prompt.

3. In the Command Prompt window, type **ntdsutil** and press Enter.

4. At the ntdsutil command prompt, type **roles** and press Enter.

5. At the fsmo maintenance command prompt, type **connections** and press Enter.

6. At the fsmo maintenance command prompt, type **connect to server** *DomainController*, where *DomainController* is the domain controller you want to assign the new operations master role, and press Enter.

7. At the server connections command prompt, type **quit** and press Enter.

8. At the fsmo maintenance command prompt, type **seize PDC** and press Enter.

9. In the Role Seizure Confirmation Dialog screen, click Yes.

10. Ntdsutil first attempts to safe transfer the role before seizing the role. If a safe transfer fails, ntdsutil proceeds with the role seizure, as shown in Figure 5.32.

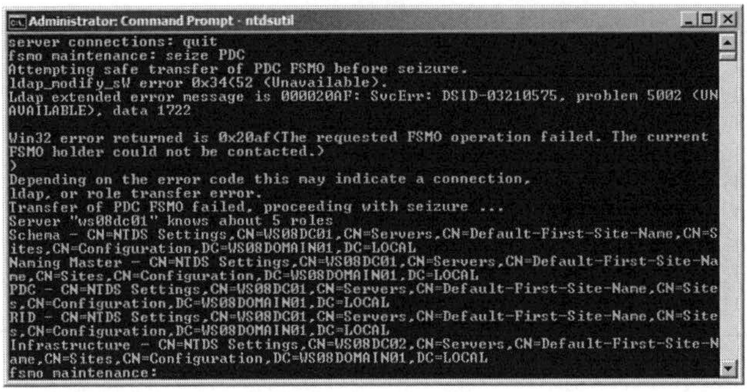

FIGURE 5.32
Seizing the PDC Emulator role.

Seize the Infrastructure Master Role

Scenario/Problem: If the current infrastructure master role holder becomes unavailable and cannot be recovered, you need to move that role to another domain controller.

Solution: When the current infrastructure master has failed, you need to seize the role and move it to another domain controller. It is important that, after the role has been seized, the original role holder is not brought back online.

To seize the infrastructure master role, perform the following steps:

1. Log on to a domain controller.

2. Click Start, and click Command Prompt.

3. In the Command Prompt window, type **ntdsutil** and press Enter.

4. At the ntdsutil command prompt, type **roles** and press Enter.

5. At the fsmo maintenance command prompt, type **connections** and press Enter.

6. At the fsmo maintenance command prompt, type **connect to server** *DomainController*, where *DomainController* is the domain controller you want to assign the new operations master role, and press Enter.

7. At the server connections command prompt, type **quit** and press Enter.

8. At the fsmo maintenance command prompt, type **seize infrastructure master** and press Enter.

9. In the Role Seizure Confirmation Dialog screen, click Yes.

10. Ntdsutil first attempts to safe transfer the role before seizing the role. If a safe transfer fails, ntdsutil proceeds with the role seizure, as shown in Figure 5.33.

FIGURE 5.33
Seizing the infrastructure master role.

CHAPTER 6

Manage Sites and Replication

Active Directory Domain Services (AD DS) sites represent the physical topology of your network. AD DS uses this topology information, which is stored in sites and site links, to build the most efficient replication topology. AD DS sites are used for replication, authentication, and directory-aware applications and services.

Active Directory Domain Services replication is used to maintain replicas of the directory data on multiple domain controllers. AD DS replication ensures directory availability and performance.

This chapter describes the steps required to manage sites and replication.

Create Sites

Scenario/Problem: When AD DS is first installed, a single site exists in the forest. This site is called the Default-First-Site-Name. If your network topology consists of multiple physical locations, you might need to control authentication and replication.

Solution: Create site objects to control authentication and replication. The creation of site objects is required whenever new offices are added to your network.

To create a site, perform the following steps:

1. Log on to a domain controller or a member computer that has Windows Server 2008 Remote Server Administration Tools (RSAT) installed.

2. Click Start, click Administrative Tools, and then click Active Directory Sites and Services.

3. In the console tree, shown in Figure 6.1, right-click the Sites node and click New Site.

4. In the New Object — Site window, shown in Figure 6.2, type a name for the site in the Name field, select a site link from the list, and click OK.

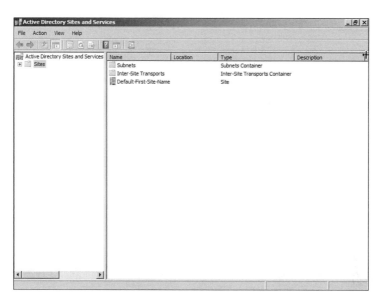

FIGURE 6.1
Active Directory Sites and Services console.

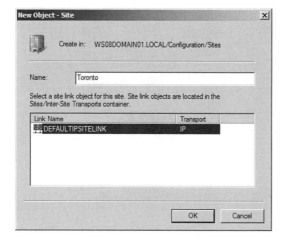

FIGURE 6.2
New Object — Site window.

5. If this is the first site you have created, a notification, shown in Figure 6.3, displays that reminds you that additional configuration steps are required. Click OK.

FIGURE 6.3

The new site additional configuration steps reminder.

6. Notice that, as shown in Figure 6.4, a node for the new site now exists in the console tree in Active Directory Sites and Services.

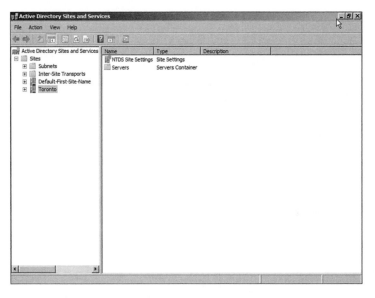

FIGURE 6.4

The new site node in Active Directory Sites and Services.

Remove Sites

Scenario/Problem: Remote offices, which are typically represented by a separate segment on your network, can become obsolete. When your network topology changes, you need to incorporate these changes into your AD DS site design.

Solution: You can remove site objects by using the Active Directory Sites and Services console.

To delete a site, perform the following steps:

1. Log on to a domain controller or a member computer that has Windows Server 2008 RSAT installed.

2. Click Start, click Administrative Tools, and then click Active Directory Sites and Services.

3. In the console tree, right-click the site you want to remove and click Delete, as shown in Figure 6.5.

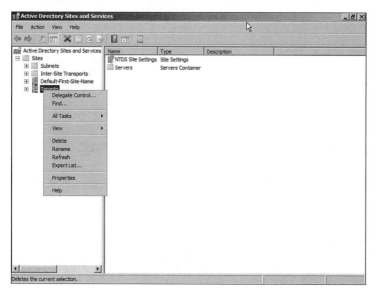

FIGURE 6.5
Deleting a site.

4. In the confirmation dialog box, shown in Figure 6.6, click Yes to delete the site.

FIGURE 6.6
The Delete Site confirmation dialog box.

5. If the site object contains other objects, you are presented with the Confirm Subtree Deletion dialog box, shown in Figure 6.7. Click Yes to delete the site and any subobjects.

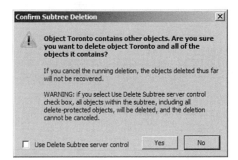

FIGURE 6.7
The Confirm Subtree Deletion dialog box.

NOTE When a site is created in Active Directory, a number of objects are automatically created within the site. These objects are used to store Server objects for domain controllers and NTDS site settings, which define the configuration of the site.

Enable Universal Group Membership Caching

Scenario/Problem: Universal groups can contain members that are users and groups from any domain in the forest. Universal groups enable you to assign permissions on a resource in any domain in the forest. These groups are particularly useful when you have multiple domains in your forest and you need to provide resource access across these domains. When a user logs on to his PC by using his AD DS credentials, the logon process contacts a global catalog server to retrieve a list of the universal groups of which the user is a member. In some cases, you might not have a global catalog server in every AD DS site, which can impede the logon process for the user.

Solution: You can enable universal group membership caching to ensure the user's universal group membership is retrieved without the need to contact a global catalog server.

To enable universal group membership caching, perform the following steps:

1. Log on to a domain controller or a member computer that has Windows Server 2008 RSAT installed.

2. Click Start, click Administrative Tools, and then click Active Directory Sites and Services.

3. In the console tree, expand the Sites node and select the site on which you want to enable Universal Group Membership Caching.

4. In the details pane, right-click NTDS Settings and click Properties.

5. In the NTDS Site Settings Properties page, shown in Figure 6.8, select Enable Universal Group Membership Caching.

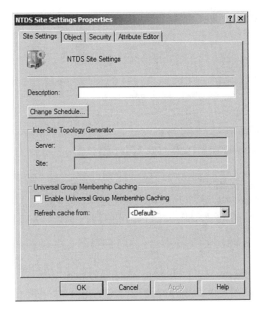

FIGURE 6.8
NTDS Site Settings Properties screen.

6. If you want to define which site the cache is refreshed from, select the site name in the drop-down menu as shown in Figure 6.9, and click OK.

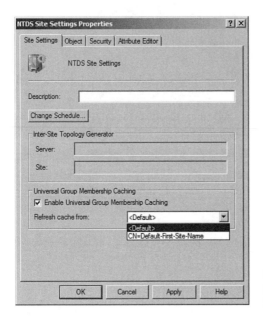

FIGURE 6.9
Selecting Enable Universal Group
Membership Caching.

Disable Universal Group Membership Caching

Scenario/Problem: In some cases, you might have had a previous requirement to enable universal group membership caching. If that requirement no longer exists, you need to ensure the user's membership in the universal group is retrieved from the global catalog at logon.

Solution: You disable universal group membership caching when you want to ensure the user's membership in the universal groups is retrieved from the global catalog at the time of logon.

To disable universal group membership caching, perform the following steps:

1. Log on to a domain controller or a member computer that has Windows Server 2008 RSAT installed.

2. Click Start, click Administrative Tools, and then click Active Directory Sites and Services.

3. In the console tree, expand the Sites node and select the site on which you want to disable universal group membership caching.

4. In the details pane, right-click NTDS Settings and click Properties.

5. Uncheck the Enable Universal Group Membership Caching option, as shown in Figure 6.10; then click OK.

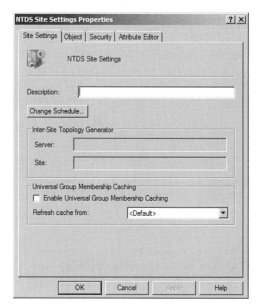

FIGURE 6.10
Disabling universal group membership caching.

Configure Site Properties

Scenario/Problem: In a complex AD DS environment, forests commonly have multiple site objects. You might need to store additional information on these site objects for administration purposes. You might also need to modify the security of these site objects.

Solution: You can modify site properties to store description and location informa-tion on a site object. You can also protect a site object from accidental deletions. Last, you can modify the security on a site object. All this can be done by modifying the site properties using Active Directory Sites and Services.

To configure site properties, perform the following steps:

1. Log on to a domain controller or a member computer that has Windows Server 2008 RSAT installed.

2. Click Start, click Administrative Tools, and then click Active Directory Sites and Services.

3. In the console tree, expand the Sites node, right-click the site for which you want to configure site properties, and click Properties.

4. On the General tab of the site properties page, shown in Figure 6.11, enter a description in the Description field.

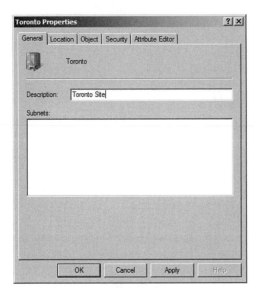

FIGURE 6.11
The General tab of the site's properties page.

5. Click the Location tab.

6. Enter a location in the Location field, as shown in Figure 6.12.

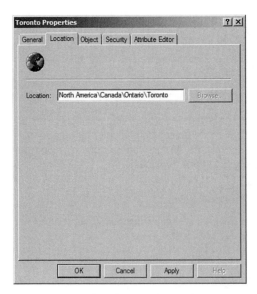

FIGURE 6.12
The Location tab of the site's properties page.

7. Click the Object tab.

8. Select Protect Object from Accidental Deletion, shown in Figure 6.13, if you want to ensure the site is not accidently deleted.

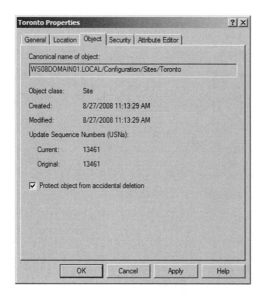

FIGURE 6.13
The Object tab of the site's properties
page.

TIP   This is a new option in Windows Server 2008. By enabling this option, an
Access Control Entry (ACE) is added to the object's Access Control List (ACL) that
denies the Delete permission.

---

9. Click the Security tab, shown in Figure 6.14.

10. Modify the security of the site as required.

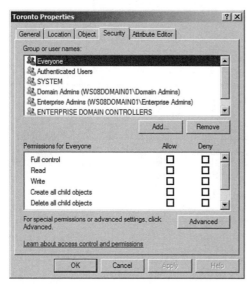

FIGURE 6.14
The Security tab of the site's properties
page.

11. Click the Attribute Editor tab, shown in Figure 6.15.

12. Modify any attributes as required.

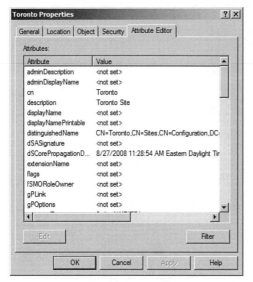

FIGURE 6.15
The Attribute Editor tab of the site's properties page.

> **TIP**   The Attribute Editor is a new feature in Windows Server 2008. The Attribute Editor enables you to view and modify all the attributes for a given object, including any custom attributes you have added to the AD DS schema. In previous versions of Windows, the only attributes that were exposed through the AD DS interfaces were those included with the base schema.

13. Click OK to save your changes.

Create Site Links

> **Scenario/Problem:** When your AD DS forest has more than one site object, you need to configure replication between these sites.

Solution: Connect sites together for replication by creating site links.

To create site links, perform the following steps:

1. Log on to a domain controller or a member computer that has Windows Server 2008 RSAT installed.

2. Click Start, click Administrative Tools, and then click Active Directory Sites and Services.

3. In the console tree, expand the Sites node and then expand the Inter-Site Transports node, as shown in Figure 6.16.

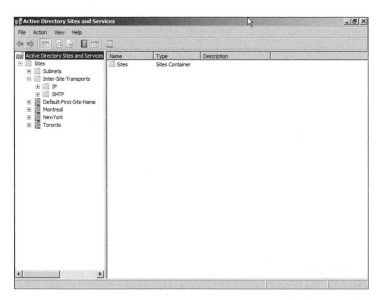

FIGURE 6.16
The Inter-Site Transports node.

4. In the console tree, under the Inter-Site Transports node, right-click the IP or SMTP node; then click New Site Link, as shown in Figure 6.17.

5. In the New Object — Site Link window, shown in Figure 6.18, type a name for the site link in the Name field, select at least two sites you want to add to the site link in the Sites Not in This Site Link section, and click Add.

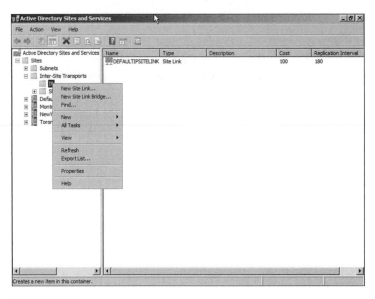

FIGURE 6.17
The New Site Link action.

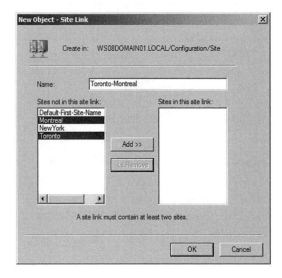

FIGURE 6.18
The Sites Not in this Site Link section.

6. The sites are moved to the Sites in This Site Link section, as shown in Figure 6.19. Click OK.

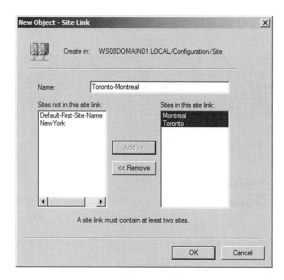

FIGURE 6.19
The Sites in this Site Link section.

7. Notice that, as shown in Figure 6.20, the new site link now exists in the details pane under the transport in which you created the site link.

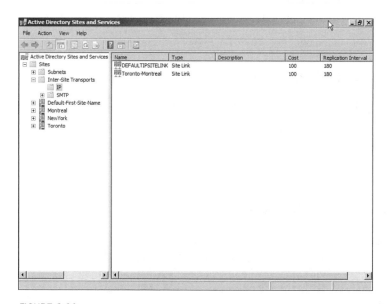

FIGURE 6.20
The new site link in the details pane.

Remove Site Links

Scenario/Problem: As your network topology changes and remote offices close, you need to ensure that any obsolete connections between sites are removed.

Solution: You remove site links to remove a connection between sites.

To remove site links, perform the following steps:

1. Log on to a domain controller or a member computer that has Windows Server 2008 RSAT installed.

2. Click Start, click Administrative Tools, and then click Active Directory Sites and Services.

3. In the console tree, expand the Sites node and then expand the Inter-Site Transports node.

4. In the console tree, under the Inter-Site Transports node, select the transport—IP or SMTP—for which the site link belongs.

5. In the details pane, right-click the site link you want to delete and click Delete.

6. In the confirmation dialog box, shown in Figure 6.21, click Yes.

FIGURE 6.21
Deleting the site link confirmation dialog box.

Configure Site Link Properties

Scenario/Problem: In a complex AD DS environment, forests commonly have multiple site link objects. You might need to store additional information on these site link objects for administration purposes. You might also need to modify the security of these site link objects. Last, you might need to modify the cost, replication frequency, and replication schedule between sites.

Solution: You can modify site link properties to store description and location information on a site object. You can also protect a site link object from accidental deletions. You can modify the security on a site link object. You can configure the site link cost, replication frequency, and replication schedule on a site link. All this can be done by modifying the site link properties using Active Directory Sites and Services.

To configure site link properties, perform the following steps:

1. Log on to a domain controller or a member computer that has Windows Server 2008 RSAT installed.

2. Click Start, click Administrative Tools, and then click Active Directory Sites and Services.

3. In the console tree, expand the Sites node and then expand the Inter-Site Transports node.

4. In the console tree, under the Inter-Site Transports node, select the transport—IP or SMTP—for which the site link belongs.

5. In the details pane, right-click the site link you want to modify and select Properties.

6. On the General tab of the site link properties page, shown in Figure 6.22, enter a description in the Description field, enter a site link cost in the Cost field, and enter a replication interval in the Replicate Every field.

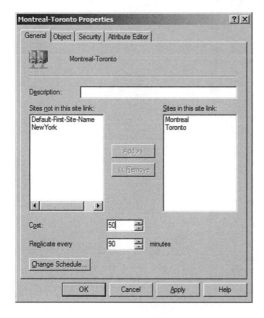

FIGURE 6.22
The General tab of the site link's Properties page.

7. To modify the replication schedule, click Change Schedule.

8. On the Schedule for Site Link page, shown in Figure 6.23, modify the schedule according to your requirements and then click OK.

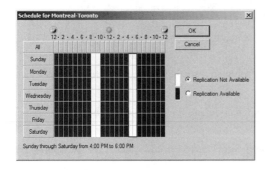

FIGURE 6.23
The site link's Schedule for page.

9. Click the Object tab.

10. Select Protect Object from Accidental Deletion if you want to ensure the site link is not accidently deleted, as shown in Figure 6.24.

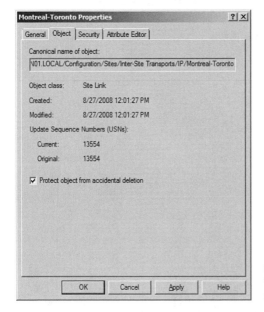

FIGURE 6.24
The Object tab of the site link's Properties page.

11. Click the Security tab, shown in Figure 6.25.

12. Modify the security of the site link as required.

13. Click the Attribute Editor tab, shown in Figure 6.26.

14. Modify any attributes as required.

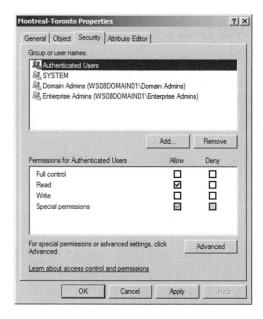

FIGURE 6.25
The Security tab of the site link's
Properties page.

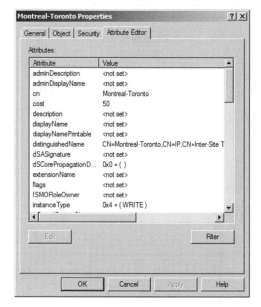

FIGURE 6.26
The Attribute Editor tab of the site link's
Properties page.

15. Click OK to save your changes.

Associate a Site with a Site Link

Scenario/Problem: A number of organizations have a hub and spoke network topology, where remote offices are connected to a central office. If this is the case, you need to ensure that your AD DS site and replication topology match your network topology.

Solution: You can associate a site with a site link to connect sites together.

To asociate a site with a site link, perform the following steps:

1. Log on to a domain controller or a member computer that has Windows Server 2008 RSAT installed.

2. Click Start, click Administrative Tools, and then click Active Directory Sites and Services.

3. In the console tree, expand the Sites node and then expand the Inter-Site Transports node.

4. In the console tree, under the Inter-Site Transports node, select the transport—IP or SMTP—for which the site link belongs.

5. In the details pane, right-click the site link you want to modify and select Properties.

6. In the site link's properties page, shown in Figure 6.27, select the site you want to add to the site link in the Sites Not in This Site Link section; then click Add.

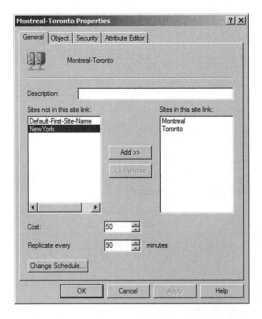

FIGURE 6.27
The Sites Not in This Site Link section.

7. The site is moved to the Sites in This Site Link section, as shown in Figure 6.28. Click OK.

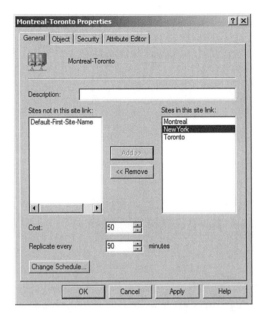

FIGURE 6.28
The Sites in This Site Link section.

Create Site Link Bridges

Scenario/Problem: By default, site links are bridged together. This ensures AD DS replication follows the route with the lowest cost between sites. In some cases, you might want to prevent a specific route to a site from being used for replication.

Solution: You create a site link bridge to prevent a certain route to a site from being used for AD DS replication.

To create site link bridges, perform the following steps:

1. Log on to a domain controller or a member computer that has Windows Server 2008 RSAT installed.

2. Click Start, click Administrative Tools, and then click Active Directory Sites and Services.

3. In the console tree, expand the Sites node and then expand the Inter-Site Transports node.

4. In the console tree, under the Inter-Site Transports node, right-click the IP or SMTP node and click New Site Link Bridge, as shown in Figure 6.29.

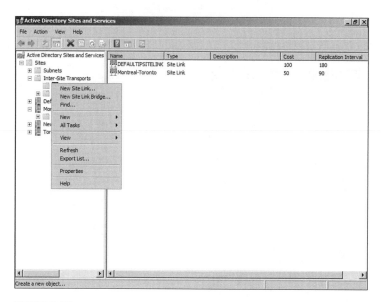

FIGURE 6.29
The New Site Link Bridge action.

5. In the New Object — Site Link Bridge window, shown in Figure 6.30, type a
   name for the site link bridge in the Name field, select at least two site links you
   want to add to the site link bridge in the Site Links Not in This Site Link Bridge
   section, and click Add.

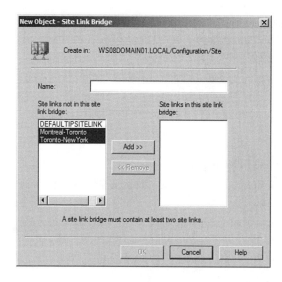

FIGURE 6.30
The Site Links Not in This Site Link
Bridge section.

6. The sites links are moved to the Site Links in This Site Link Bridge section, as shown in Figure 6.31. Click OK.

FIGURE 6.31
The Site Links in This Site Link
Bridge section.

7. Notice that, as shown in Figure 6.32, the new site link bridge now exists in the details pane under the transport in which you created the site link bridge.

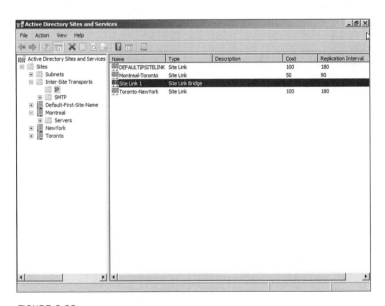

FIGURE 6.32
The new site link bridge in the details pane.

Remove Site Link Bridges

Scenario/Problem: As your network topology changes over time, you need to remove any restrictions you manually created for connections between sites.

Solution: You remove manual site link bridges to remove any restrictions you created for connections between sites.

To remove a site link bridge, perform the following steps:

1. Log on to a domain controller or a member computer that has Windows Server 2008 RSAT installed.

2. Click Start, click Administrative Tools, and then click Active Directory Sites and Services.

3. In the console tree, expand the Sites node and then expand the Inter-Site Transports node.

4. In the console tree, under the Inter-Site Transports node, select the transport—IP or SMTP—for which the site link bridge belongs.

5. In the details pane, right-click the site link bridge you want to delete and click Delete.

6. In the confirmation dialog box, shown in Figure 6.33, click Yes to delete the site link bridge.

FIGURE 6.33
The delete site link bridge confirmation dialog box.

Add a Subnet

Scenario/Problem: AD DS requires a mechanism to know which network segments are in use in a particular office. This is more relevant when the office is represented by a site object in AD DS.

Solution: You add a subnet to AD DS to create an object that represents each network segment.

To add a subnet, perform the following steps:

1. Log on to a domain controller or a member computer that has Windows Server 2008 RSAT installed.

2. Click Start, click Administrative Tools, and then click Active Directory Sites and Services.

3. In the console tree, expand the Sites node, right-click the Subnets node and click New Subnet.

4. In the New Object — Subnet, shown in Figure 6.34, enter a prefix for the subnet in the Prefix field, select the site with which to associate the subnet, and click OK.

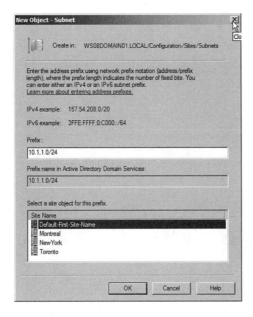

FIGURE 6.34
The New Object — Subnet window.

5. Click the Subnets node in the console tree.

6. Notice that, as shown in Figure 6.35, the new subnet is listed in the details pane, along with the site with which the subnet is associated.

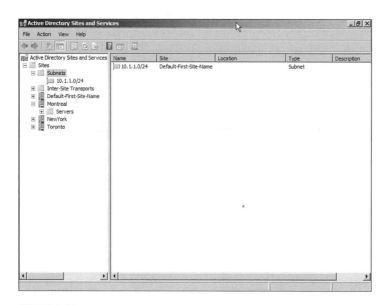

FIGURE 6.35
The new subnet in the details pane.

Remove a Subnet

Scenario/Problem: As your network topology changes, you will inevitability have network segments that are decommissioned. You need to ensure that AD DS is aware of the removal of these network segments.

Solution: You remove a subnet from AD DS when the network segment is no longer in use.

To remove a subnet, perform the following steps:

1. Log on to a domain controller or a member computer that has Windows Server 2008 RSAT installed.

2. Click Start, click Administrative Tools, and then click Active Directory Sites and Services.

3. In the console tree, expand the Sites node and click the Subnets node.

4. Right-click the subnet you want to delete in the details pane, and click Delete.

5. In the confirmation dialog box, shown in Figure 6.36, click Yes to delete the subnet.

FIGURE 6.36
Deleting the subnet confirmation dialog box.

Move Domain Controllers Between Sites

Scenario/Problem: The location of domain controllers within sites is important for authentication, replication, and service location. Users are directed to a domain controller in their site; replication within a site operates differently than replication between sites; and site-aware applications leverage sites to service clients.

Solution: You move domain controllers between sites to control authentication, replication, and service location.

To move domain controllers between sites, perform the following steps:

1. Log on to a domain controller or a member computer that has Windows Server 2008 RSAT installed.

2. Click Start, click Administrative Tools, and then click Active Directory Sites and Services.

3. In the console tree, expand the Sites node.

4. Expand the site node for the site to which the domain controller currently belongs.

> **TIP** If you do not know to which site a domain controller belongs, you can use the Find feature in Active Directory Sites and Services to locate the domain controller. The Find feature is accessed by right clicking on Find on any node below the Active Directory Sites and Services node in the console tree.

5. Expand the Servers node, as shown in Figure 6.37.

6. In the console tree, under the Servers node, right-click the domain controller you want to move and click Move.

7. In the Move Server window, shown in Figure 6.38, select the site to which you want to move the domain controller; then click OK.

FIGURE 6.37
The Servers node in Active Directory Sites and Services.

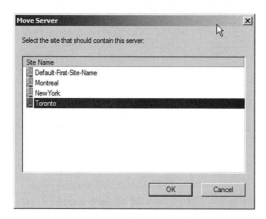

FIGURE 6.38
The Move Server window.

8. Notice that the domain controller is no longer listed under the current site in Active Directory Sites and Services.

9. Expand the site to which the domain controller was moved, and verify the server object exists, as shown in Figure 6.39.

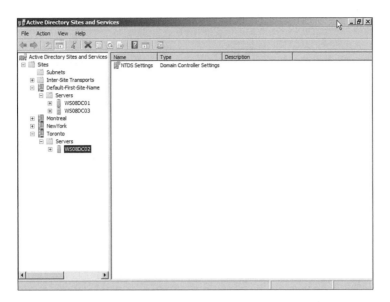

FIGURE 6.39
The domain controller moved between sites.

Enable a Domain Controller as a Preferred Bridgehead Server

Scenario/Problem: Each site object can contain multiple domain controllers. When replication occurs between two sites, all the domain controllers in one site replicating with all the domain controllers in another site is inefficient. A *bridgehead server* is a server that is responsible for requesting changes from its source replication partner in another site. The bridgehead server then replicates these changes with the domain controllers within its site.

Bridgehead servers are automatically selected in each site. However, you might need to prevent a server from becoming a bridgehead if that server, for example, is unreliable or incapable of handling the additional load.

Solution: You enable a domain controller as a preferred bridgehead server to ensure that domain controller participates in intersite replication with other sites.

WARNING Microsoft does not recommend that you configure preferred bridgehead servers manually. This has to do with the fact that by manually configuring preferred bridgehead servers, you limit the ability of the Active Directory Knowledge Consistency Checker (KCC) to automatically configure a fault-tolerant inter-site replication topology.

To enable a domain controller as a preferred bridgehead server, perform the following steps:

1. Log on to a domain controller or a member computer that has Windows Server 2008 RSAT installed.

2. Click Start, click Administrative Tools, and then click Active Directory Sites and Services.

3. In the console tree, expand the Sites node.

4. Expand the site node for the site to which the domain controller belongs.

WARNING If you do not know to which site a domain controller belongs, you can use the Find feature in Active Directory Sites and Services to locate the domain controller. The Find feature is accessed by right clicking on Find on any node below the Active Directory Sites and Services node in the console tree.

---

5. Expand the Servers node.

6. In the console tree, under the Servers node, right-click the domain controller you want to move and click Properties, as shown in Figure 6.40.

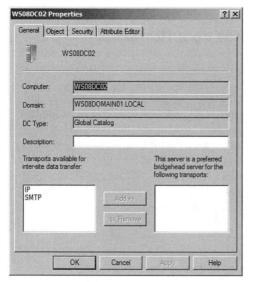

FIGURE 6.40
The domain controller's Properties window.

7. On the domain controller's Properties page, under Transports Available for Inter-site Data Transfer, select the inter-site transport or transports for which the computer will be a preferred bridgehead server; then click Add, as shown in Figure 6.41.

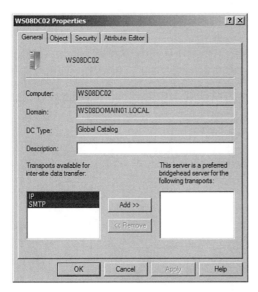

FIGURE 6.41
The transports available for inter-site data transfer.

8. The transports are moved to the This Server Is a Preferred Bridgehead Server for the Following Transports section, as shown in Figure 6.42. Click OK.

FIGURE 6.42
This Server Is a Preferred Bridgehead Server for the Following Transports section.

9. Click the Servers node under the site. Notice that the transports are listed under the Bridgehead column.

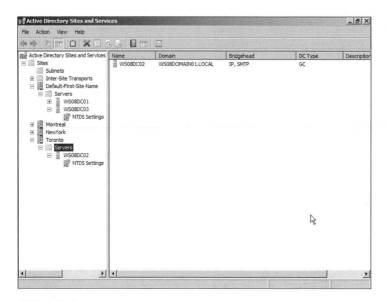

FIGURE 6.43
The transports listed under Bridgehead column.

Disable a Domain Controller as a Preferred Bridgehead Server

Scenario/Problem: You need to remove a previous manual designation as a preferred bridgehead server when the requirement no longer exists.

Solution: You disable a domain controller as a preferred bridgehead server.

To disable a domain controller as a preferred bridgehead server, perform the following steps:

1. Log on to a domain controller or a member computer that has Windows Server 2008 RSAT installed.

2. Click Start, click Administrative Tools, and then click Active Directory Sites and Services.

3. In the console tree, expand the Sites node.

4. Expand the site node for the site to which the domain controller belongs.

TIP If you do not know to which site a domain controller belongs, you can use the Find feature in Active Directory Sites and Services to locate the domain controller. The Find feature is accessed by right clicking on Find on any node below the Active Directory Sites and Services node in the console tree.

5. Expand the Servers node.

6. In the console tree, under the Servers node, right-click the domain controller you want to modify and click Properties.

7. On the domain controller properties page, under This Server Is a Preferred Bridgehead Server for the Following Transports, select the inter-site transport or transports for which you want to remove the preferred bridgehead role from this computer as shown in Figure 6.44,; then click Remove.

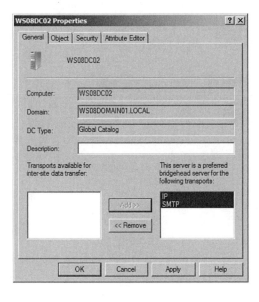

FIGURE 6.44
The This Server Is a Preferred Bridgehead Server for the Following Transports section.

8. The transports are moved to the Transports Available for Inter-site Data Transfer section, as shown in Figure 6.45. Click OK.

9. Click the Servers node under the site. Notice the transports are not listed under the Bridgehead column.

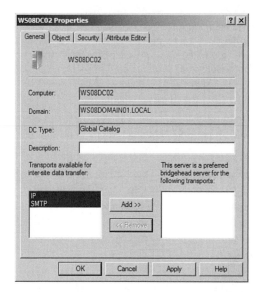

FIGURE 6.45

The Transports Available for Inter-Site Data Transfer section.

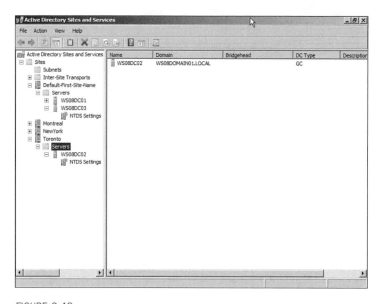

FIGURE 6.46

The transports not listed under the Bridgehead column.

Create Manual Connection Objects

Scenario/Problem: AD DS creates replication connections between domain controllers based on the site and services design. You might need to ensure that a particular domain controller replicates only with another domain controller.

Solution: You create manual connection objects when you want more granular control over replication between specific domain controllers.

To create manual connection objects, perform the following steps:

1. Log on to a domain controller or a member computer that has Windows Server 2008 RSAT installed.

2. Click Start, click Administrative Tools, and then click Active Directory Sites and Services.

3. In the console tree, expand the Sites node.

4. Expand the site node for the site to which the domain controller belongs.

TIP If you do not know to which site a domain controller belongs, you can use the Find feature in Active Directory Sites and Services to locate the domain controller. The Find feature is accessed by right clicking on Find on any node below the Active Directory Sites and Services node in the console tree.

5. Expand the Servers node.

6. In the console tree, select the server you want to create the manual connection object on; then select NTDS Settings.

7. The current connection objects—those generated manually and those generated automatically—are listed in the details pane, as shown in Figure 6.47.

8. In the console tree, right-click NTDS Settings, click New, and then click Connection. as shown in Figure 6.48.

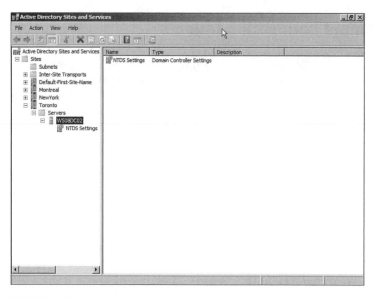

FIGURE 6.47
The connection objects shown in the details pane.

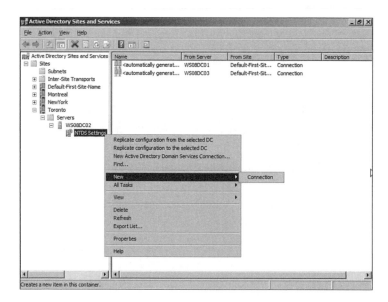

FIGURE 6.48
The New Connection action.

9. In the Find Active Directory Domain Controllers window, shown in Figure 6.49, select the domain controller with which you want to create the manual connection and click OK.

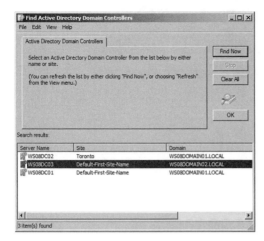

FIGURE 6.49
The Find Active Directory Domain
Controllers window.

10. In the New Object — Connection window, shown in Figure 6.50, enter a name
for the connection in the Name field and then click OK.

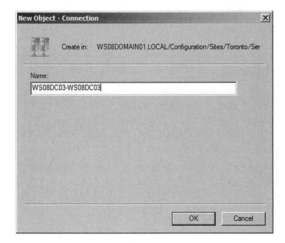

FIGURE 6.50
The New Object — Connection
window.

11. Notice that, as shown in Figure 6.51, the new connection object now appears in
the details pane of the NTDS Settings for the domain controller.

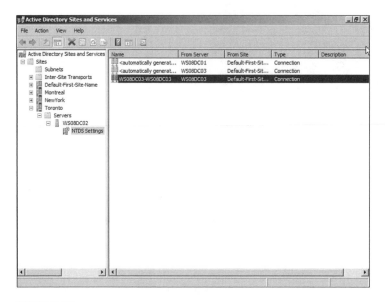

FIGURE 6.51
The new connection object in the details pane.

Remove Connection Objects

Scenario/Problem: As your network topology changes, you might no longer have a requirement to force two domain controllers to be replication partners.

Solution: You remove connection objects from domain controllers to enable AD DS to build automatic connection objects.

To remove connection objects, perform the following steps:

1. Log on to a domain controller or a member computer that has Windows Server 2008 RSAT installed.

2. Click Start, click Administrative Tools, and then click Active Directory Sites and Services.

3. In the console tree, expand the Sites node.

4. Expand the site node for the site to which the domain controller belongs.

> **TIP** If you do not know to which site a domain controller belongs, you can use the Find feature in Active Directory Sites and Services to locate the domain controller. The Find feature is accessed by right clicking on Find on any node below the Active Directory Sites and Services node in the console tree.

5. Expand the Servers node.

6. In the console tree, select the server from which you want to remove a connection object; then select NTDS Settings.

7. The current connection objects—those generated manually and those generated automatically—are listed in the details pane.

8. In the details pane, right-click the connection object you want to remove and select Delete.

9. On the confirmation box for deleting the connection object, shown in Figure 6.52, click Yes.

FIGURE 6.52
Confirming to delete the connection object.

10. Notice that the connection object is no longer listed in the details pane.

Disable KCC for a Site

Scenario/Problem: The knowledge consistency checker is a process that runs on every domain controller and generates the AD DS replication topology for the forest. By default, KCC creates separate replication topologies for intrasite replication and intersite replication. You might want to prevent KCC from creating replication topologies for replication within a site (intrasite), replication between sites (intersite), or both.

Solution: You disable automatic intrasite topology generation, automatic intersite topology generation, or both for a site.

To disable KCC for a site, perform the following steps:

1. Log on to a domain controller or a member computer that has Windows Server 2008 RSAT installed.

2. Click Start, click Administrative Tools, and then click Active Directory Sites and Services.

3. In the console tree, expand the Sites node.

4. In the console tree, select the site on which you want to disable KCC.

5. In the details pane, right-click NTDS Site Settings and click Properties, as shown in Figure 6.53.

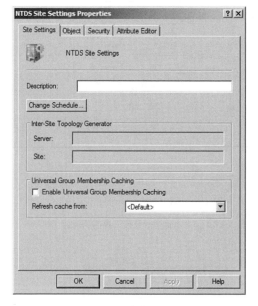

FIGURE 6.53
The NTDS Site Settings Properties window.

6. In the NTDS Site Settings Properties window, click the Attribute Editor tab.

7. On the Attribute Editor tab, select the options attribute and click Edit.

8. In the Integer Attribute Editor window, shown in Figure 6.54, type one of the following:

   ▶ **1** to disable automatic intrasite topology generation

   ▶ **16** to disable automatic intersite topology generation

   ▶ **17** to disable both intrasite and intersite topology generation

9. Click OK.

10. The options attribute, shown in Figure 6.55, is updated based on the value you provided in Step 8. Table 6.1 shows the decimal values, the meaning, and the corresponding value that display in Attribute Editor.

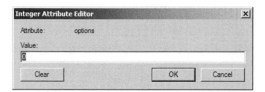

FIGURE 6.54
The Integer Attribute Editor window.

TABLE 6.1   **Disabling KCC by Using the Attribute Editor in Windows Server 2008**

Decimal Value	Meaning	Value in Attribute Editor
<not set>	Automatic intrasite topology generation enabled	<not set>
1	Automatic intrasite topology generation disabled	0x1=(IS_AUTO_ TOPOLOGY_DISABLED)
16	Automatic intersite topology generation disabled	0x10=(IS_INTER_ SITE_AUTO_ TOPOLOGY_ DISABLED)
17	Intrasite and intersite topology generation	0x11=(IS_AUTO_ TOPOLOGY_DISABLED ¦ IS_INTER_SITE_ AUTO_TOPOLOGY_DISABLED)

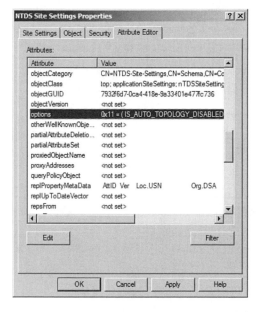

FIGURE 6.55
The updated options attribute.

Enable KCC for a Site

Scenario/Problem: You might have previously had a requirement to prevent KCC from generating the intrasite and/or intersite replication topology for a site. If this requirement no longer exists, you need to ensure that KCC generates these topologies.

Solution: You enable automatic intrasite topology generation, automatic intersite topology generation, or both for a site.

TIP KCC is enabled by default. The steps in this section are required only if KCC was previously disabled and you want to reenable it.

To enable KCC for a site, perform the following steps:

1. Log on to a domain controller or a member computer that has Windows Server 2008 RSAT installed.

2. Click Start, click Administrative Tools, and then click Active Directory Sites and Services.

3. In the console tree, expand the Sites node.

4. In the console tree, select the site on which you want to disable KCC.

5. In the details pane, right-click NTDS Site Settings and click Properties.

6. In the NTDS Site Settings Properties window, click the Attribute Editor tab.

7. On the Attribute Editor tab, select the options attribute and click Edit.

8. In the Integer Attribute Editor window, click Clear.

9. Click OK.

10. The options attribute is changed to <not set>.

Disable Inbound Replication

Scenario/Problem: You want to temporarily prevent a domain controller from receiving updates from other domain controllers.

Solution: You disable inbound replication on the domain controller.

To disable inbound replication, perform the following steps:

1. Log on to a domain controller.

2. Click Start, and click Command Prompt.

3. In the Command Prompt window, type the following command:

   repadmin /options *servername* +DISABLE_INBOUND_REPL

   (where *servername* is the domain controller on which you want to perform the change).

4. Verify that DISABLE_INBOUND_REPL is listed in the results under New DSA Options, as shown in Figure 6.56:

FIGURE 6.56
Disabling inbound replication.

Enable Inbound Replication

Scenario/Problem: You previously disabled a domain controller from receiving updates from other domain controllers. You now might want the domain controller to receive updates.

Solution: You enable inbound replication on the domain controller.

To enable inbound replication, perform the following steps:

1. Log on to a domain controller.

2. Click Start, and click Command Prompt.

3. In the Command Prompt window, type the following command:

`repadmin /options servername -DISABLE_INBOUND_REPL`

(where *servername* is the domain controller on which you want to perform the change).

4. Verify that `DISABLE_INBOUND_REPL` is listed in the results under Current DSA Options: and not New DSA Options, as shown in Figure 6.57:

FIGURE 6.57
Enabling inbound replication.

Disable Outbound Replication

Scenario/Problem: You might want to temporarily prevent a domain controller from sending updates to other domain controllers.

Solution: You disable outbound replication on the domain controller.

To disable outbound replication, perform the following steps:

1. Log on to a domain controller.
2. Click Start, and click Command Prompt.
3. In the Command Prompt window, type the following command:

`repadmin /options servername +DISABLE_OUTBOUND_REPL`

(where *servername* is the domain controller on which you want to perform the change).

4. Verify that `DISABLE_OUTBOUND_REPL` is listed in the results under New DSA Options, as shown in Figure 6.58:

FIGURE 6.58
Disabling outbound replication.

Enable Outbound Replication

Scenario/Problem: You previously disabled a domain controller from sending updates to other domain controllers. You now might want the domain controller to send updates.

Solution: You enable outbound replication on the domain controller.

To enable outbound replication, perform the following steps:

1. Log on to a domain controller.
2. Click Start, and click Command Prompt.
3. In the Command Prompt window, type the following command:

   `repadmin /options servername -DISABLE_OUTBOUND_REPL`

   (where *servername* is the domain controller on which you want to perform the change).

4. Verify that DISABLE_OUTBOUND_REPL is listed in the results under Current DSA Options: and not New DSA Options, as shown in Figure 6.59:

FIGURE 6.59
Enabling outbound replication.

Disable the Bridge All Site Links Option

Scenario/Problem: By default, all site links are transitive in AD DS. You might have a network that is not fully routed, or you might need to control the replication flow of changes made in AD DS.

Solution: You disable the bridge all site links option for the given transport.

To disable the bridge all site links option, perform the following steps:

1. Log on to a domain controller or a member computer that has Windows Server 2008 RSAT installed.

2. Click Start, click Administrative Tools, and then click Active Directory Sites and Services.

3. In the console tree, expand the Sites node and then expand the Inter-Site Transports node.

4. In the console tree, under the Inter-Site Transports node, right-click either the IP node if you want to disable this setting for the IP transport or the SMTP node if you want to disable this setting for the SMTP transport. Then click Properties.

5. On the transport properties page, shown in Figure 6.60, uncheck the Bridge All Site Links option and click OK.

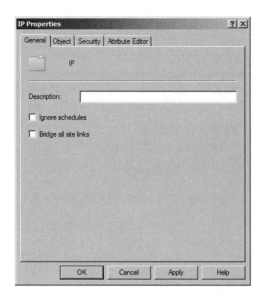

FIGURE 6.60
Disabling the Bridge All Site Links
option.

Enable the Bridge All Site Links Option

Scenario/Problem: You previously might have had a network that was not fully routed or previously wanted to control the replication flow of changes made in AD DS. This requirement no longer exists.

Solution: You enable the bridge all site links option for the given transport.

TIP   The bridge all site links option is enabled by default. The steps in this section are required only if the bridge all site links option was previously disabled and you want to re-enable it.

To enable the bridge all site links option, perform the following steps:

1. Log on to a domain controller or a member computer that has Windows Server 2008 RSAT installed.

2. Click Start, click Administrative Tools, and then click Active Directory Sites and Services.

3. In the console tree, expand the Sites node and then expand the Inter-Site Transports node.

4. In the console tree, under the Inter-Site Transports node, right-click either the IP node if you want to enable this setting for the IP transport or SMTP node if you want to enable this setting for the SMTP transport. Then click Properties.

5. On the transport properties page, shown in Figure 6.61, check the Bridge All Site Links option and click OK.

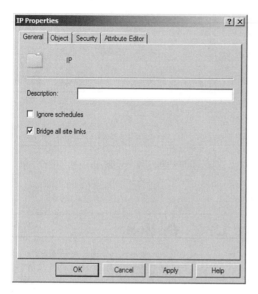

FIGURE 6.61
Disabling the Bridge All Site Links option.

Verify Replication Is Functioning

Scenario/Problem: You might have made a change to your AD DS site design and now want to ensure that replication is occurring as expected.

Solution: Verify replication is functioning.

To verify replication is functioning, perform the following steps:

1. Log on to a domain controller.

2. Click Start, and click Command Prompt.

3. In the Command Prompt window, type the following command and press Enter:

   `dcdiag /test:replications`

4. The results are presented in the Command Prompt window.

Trigger Replication

Scenario/Problem: You might have made a change to AD DS and now cannot wait for the replication interval for the change to be replicated.

Solution: You trigger replication.

To trigger replication, perform the following steps:

1. Log on to a domain controller.
2. Click Start, and click Command Prompt.
3. In the Command Prompt window, type the following command and press Enter:

   `repadmin /replicate DEST-DC SOURCE-DC NAMINGCONTEXT`

   (where *DEST-DC* is the name of the destination domain controller, *SOURCE-DC* is the name of the source domain controller, and *NAMINGCONTEXT* is the naming context you want to replicate).

   Continuing with the previous example, if you have a destination DC with a name of WS08DC01 and a source DC with a naming of WS08DC02 and you want to replicate the DC=DOMAIN,DC=LOCAL naming context, you would type the following command:

   `repadmin /replicate WS08DC02 WS08DC01 DC=DOMAIN,DC=LOCAL`

4. The results are presented in the Command Prompt window.

CHAPTER 7

Manage the Active Directory Domain Services Schema

IN THIS CHAPTER

- ▶ Install the Active Directory Schema Snap-In
- ▶ Apply Active Directory Schema Administrative Permissions
- ▶ View Schema Class and Attribute Definitions
- ▶ Create Attributes
- ▶ Deactivate Attributes
- ▶ Activate Attributes
- ▶ Index Attributes
- ▶ Remove Attributes from the Index
- ▶ Add Attributes to Ambiguous Name Resolution Filter
- ▶ Remove Attributes from Ambiguous Name Resolution Filter
- ▶ Add Attributes to Global Catalog Replication
- ▶ Remove Attributes from Global Catalog Replication
- ▶ Configure Attributes to Be Copied When Duplicating Users
- ▶ Configure Attributes Not to Be Copied When Duplicating Users
- ▶ Configuring Attributes to Be Indexed for Containerized Searches
- ▶ Configuring Attributes Not to Be Indexed for Containerized Searches
- ▶ Configure Attribute Range
- ▶ Create Classes
- ▶ Deactivate Classes
- ▶ Activate Classes
- ▶ Configure Classes to Be Visible in Advanced View
- ▶ Configure Classes Not to Be Visible in Advanced View
- ▶ Configure Class Relationships
- ▶ Configure Class Attributes

The Active Directory Domain Services (AD DS) schema contains formal definitions of every object class that can be created in an AD DS forest. The schema also contains formal definitions of every attribute that can exist in an AD DS object.

This chapter describes the steps required to manage the schema.

Install the Active Directory Schema Snap-In

Scenario/Problem: You need to manage the AD DS schema, which can include extending the schema, modifying existing attributes and classes.

Solution: You need to install the Active Directory Schema snap-in.

To install the Active Directory Schema snap-in, perform the following steps:

1. Log on to a domain controller or a member computer that has Windows Server 2008 Remote Server Administration Tools (RSAT) installed.

2. Click Start, and click Command Prompt.

3. In the Command Prompt window, type the following command and press Enter:

   `regsvr32 schmmgmt.dll`

4. You will receive a notification that `schmmgmt.dll` was registered successfully, as shown in Figure 7.1. Click OK and close the Command Prompt window.

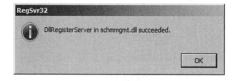

FIGURE 7.1
`schmmgmt.dll` was registered successfully.

5. Click Start, click Run, type **mmc** /**a**, and click OK.

6. On the File menu, click Add/Remove Snap-In.

7. In the Add or Remove Snap-ins window, shown in Figure 7.2, select Active Directory Schema under Available Snap-ins, click Add, and then click OK. The Active Directory Schema snap-in is added to the MMC console, as shown in Figure 7.3.

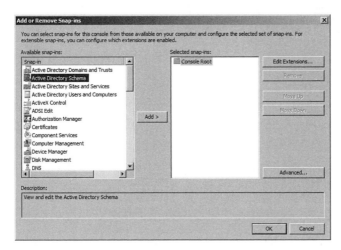

FIGURE 7.2
Adding the Active Directory Schema snap-in to the MMC console.

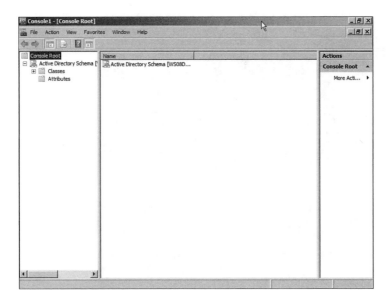

FIGURE 7.3
The Active Directory Schema snap-in.

8. On the File menu, click Save As.

9. In the Save As window, shown in Figure 7.4, type **systemroot%\System32\ schmmgmt.msc** in the File name field, and click Save.

FIGURE 7.4
Saving the Active Directory
Schema snap-in.

10. Close the console.

11. Right-click Start, and click Open All Users, shown in Figure 7.5.

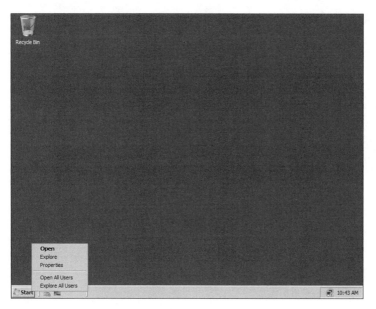

FIGURE 7.5
Selecting Open All Users.

12. Double-click Programs and double-click Administrative Tools.

13. On the File menu, click New; then click Shortcut.

14. In the Create Shortcut Wizard, shown in Figure 7.6, in the Type the Location of the Item box, type **schmmgmt.msc**; then click Next.

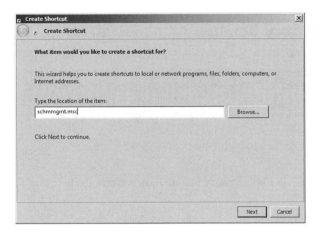

FIGURE 7.6
The Create Shortcut Wizard.

15. On the Select a Title for the Program page, in the Type a name for this shortcut, type **Active Directory Schema**; then click Finish.

16. To verify that the Active Directory Schema shortcut was created successfully, click Start, click Administrative Tools, and verify that Active Directory Schema is listed, as shown in Figure 7.7.

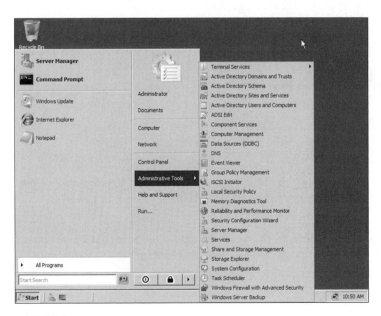

FIGURE 7.7
The Active Directory Schema Snap-in.

Apply Active Directory Schema Administrative Permissions

Scenario/Problem: You need to modify the default permissions on an attribute or a class in the schema.

Solution: Apply permissions to schema attributes or classes.

To apply Active Directory schema administrative permissions, perform the following steps:

1. Log on to a domain controller or a member computer that has Windows Server 2008 RSAT installed.

2. Click Start, click Administrative Tools, and click ADSI Edit.

3. In the console tree, right-click the ADSI Edit node and click Connect to.

4. On the Connection Settings window, under Select a well known Naming Context, select Schema, as shown in Figure 7.8; then click OK.

FIGURE 7.8
Connecting to the schema naming context in ADSI Edit.

5. In the console tree, click the Schema node, expand the Schema node, and then click the node that begins with CN=Schema,CN=Configuration, as shown in Figure 7.9.

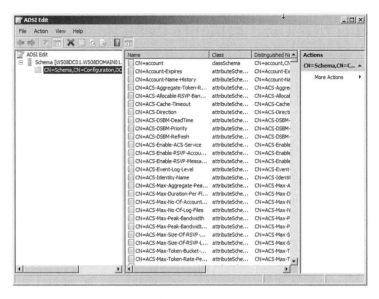

FIGURE 7.9
Viewing the schema naming context in ADSI Edit.

6. In the details pane, right-click the attribute or class to which you want to apply permissions, and click Properties.

7. On the attribute or class properties page, click the Security tab, shown in Figure 7.10.

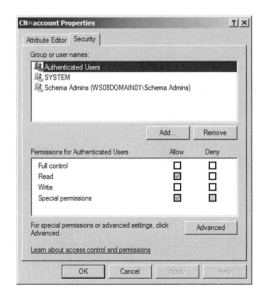

FIGURE 7.10
The Attribute and Class Security tab.

8. Modify the permissions according to your requirements and then click OK.

View Schema Class and Attribute Definitions

Scenario/Problem: You need to determine the configuration of a particular attribute or class.

Solution: Use the Active Directory Schema snap-in to view schema class and attribute definitions.

To view schema class and attribute definitions, perform the following steps:

1. Log on to a domain controller or a member computer that has Windows Server 2008 RSAT installed.

2. Click Start, click Administrative Tools, and click Active Directory Schema.

3. In the console tree, expand Active Directory Schema.

4. To view schema class definitions, click the Classes node in the console tree, as shown in Figure 7.11.

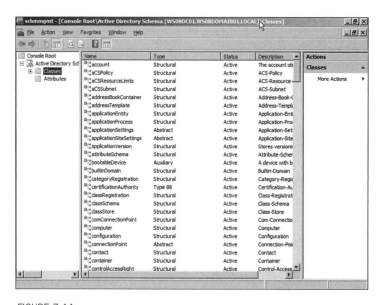

FIGURE 7.11
Classes in the Active Directory Schema snap-in.

5. To view schema attribute definitions, click the Attributes node in the console tree, as shown in Figure 7.12.

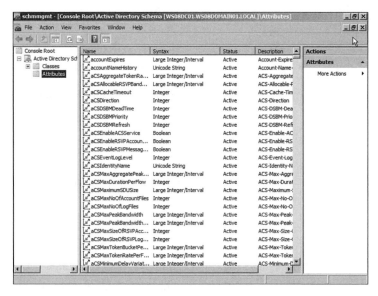

FIGURE 7.12
Attributes in the Active Directory Schema snap-in.

Create Attributes

Scenario/Problem: Your company requires a number of custom attributes in which to store employee information.

Solution: Use the Active Directory Schema snap-in to create attributes in the schema.

To create an attribute, perform the following steps:

1. Log on to a domain controller or a member computer that has Windows Server 2008 RSAT installed.

2. Click Start, click Administrative Tools, and click Active Directory Schema.

3. In the console tree, expand Active Directory Schema and then click Attributes.

4. On the Action menu, click Create Attribute.

5. On the Schema Object Creation warning, shown in Figure 7.13, click Continue.

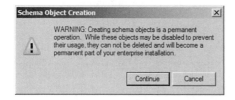

FIGURE 7.13
The Schema Object Creation warning box.

6. On the Create New Attribute window, shown in Figure 7.14, do the following:

    ▶ Type a common name in the Common Name field.

    ▶ Type an LDAP display name in the LDAP Display Name field.

    ▶ Type the OID in the Unique X500 Object ID field.

    ▶ Type a description in the Description field, if required.

    ▶ Select the attribute syntax in the Syntax field.

    ▶ Type a minimum acceptable value in the Minimum field, if required.

    ▶ Type a maximum acceptable value in the Maximum field, if required.

    ▶ Select Multi-Valued if the attributed is a multivalued attribute.

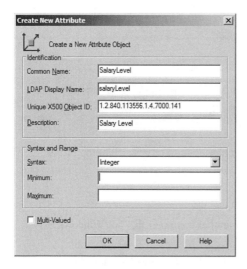

FIGURE 7.14
The Create New Attribute window.

7. Click OK to create the new attribute.

Deactivate Attributes

Scenario/Problem: You previously created a custom attribute that is no longer used.

Solution: Deactivate the attribute using the Active Directory Schema snap-in.

To deactivate an attribute, perform the following steps:

1. Log on to a domain controller or a member computer that has Windows Server 2008 RSAT installed.

2. Click Start, click Administrative Tools, and click Active Directory Schema.

3. In the console tree, expand Active Directory Schema and then click Attributes.

4. In the details pane, right-click the attribute you want to deactivate and click Properties.

5. On the attribute's properties page, shown in Figure 7.15, deselect the check box next to Attribute is active.

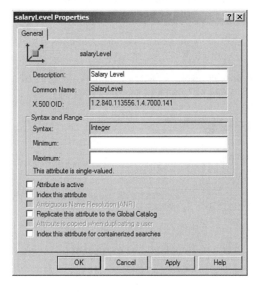

FIGURE 7.15
Deactivating an attribute.

6. On the warning box for making the schema object defunct, shown in Figure 7.16, click Yes.

7. Click OK to save the changes.

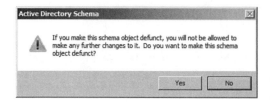

FIGURE 7.16
The warning box for making the
schema object defunct.

Activate Attributes

Scenario/Problem: You previously deactivated an attribute in the schema.

Solution: Activate the attribute by using the Active Directory Schema snap-in.

To activate an attribute, perform the following steps:

1. Log on to a domain controller or a member computer that has Windows Server
   2008 RSAT installed.

2. Click Start, click Administrative Tools, and click Active Directory Schema.

3. In the console tree, expand Active Directory Schema and then click Attributes.

4. In the details pane, right-click the attribute you want to activate and click
   Properties.

5. A notification that the attribute is defunct displays, and no changes are allowed
   on the object until it is made active again, as shown in Figure 7.17. Click OK.

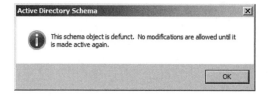

FIGURE 7.17
The message that the schema object
is defunct.

6. On the attribute properties page, select the check box next to Attribute is active,
   as shown in Figure 7.18.

7. Click OK to save the changes.

FIGURE 7.18
Activating an attribute.

Index Attributes

Scenario/Problem: You have an application that queries users who have a specific value in an attribute. You need to optimize the queries.

Solution: Index the attribute by using the Active Directory Schema snap-in.

To index an attribute, perform the following steps:

1. Log on to a domain controller or a member computer that has Windows Server 2008 RSAT installed.

2. Click Start, click Administrative Tools, and click Active Directory Schema.

3. In the console tree, expand Active Directory Schema and then click Attributes.

4. In the details pane, right-click the attribute you want to index and click Properties.

5. On the attribute properties page, select the check box next to Index this attribute, as shown in Figure 7.19.

6. Click OK to save the changes.

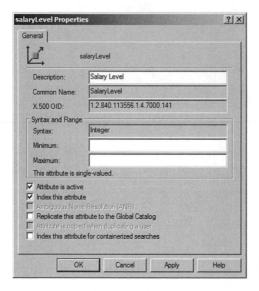

FIGURE 7.19
Indexing an attribute.

Remove Attributes from the Index

Scenario/Problem: You previously indexed an attribute so that queries responded more quickly; however, this is no longer required.

Solution: Remove the attribute from the index by using the Active Directory Schema snap-in.

To remove an attribute from the index, perform the following steps:

1. Log on to a domain controller or a member computer that has Windows Server 2008 RSAT installed.

2. Click Start, click Administrative Tools, and click Active Directory Schema.

3. In the console tree, expand Active Directory Schema and then click Attributes.

4. In the details pane, right-click the attribute you want to remove from the index and click Properties.

5. On the attribute properties page, deselect the check box next to Index this attribute, as shown in Figure 7.20.

6. Click OK to save the changes.

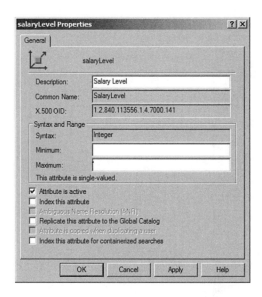

FIGURE 7.20
Removing an attribute from the index.

Add Attributes to Ambiguous Name Resolution Filter

Scenario/Problem: You need to provide clients the capability to search multiple naming-related attributes on objects via a single clause in a search filter. You want a custom naming-related attribute to be searched as well.

Solution: Add the attribute to the ambiguous name resolution (ANR) filter by using the Active Directory Schema snap-in.

To add attributes to the Ambiguous Name Resolution filter, perform the following steps:

1. Log on to a domain controller or a member computer that has Windows Server 2008 RSAT installed.

2. Click Start, click Administrative Tools, and click Active Directory Schema.

3. In the console tree, expand Active Directory Schema and then click Attributes.

4. In the details pane, right-click the attribute you want to add to the ANR filter and click Properties.

NOTE Attributes that use the string syntax, and have been configured to be indexed, can only be added to the ANR filter. You cannot add attributes that use another syntax type, such as integrator or Boolean. Furthermore, the option to add an attribute that uses the string syntax to the ANR filter is limited to indexed attributes.

5. On the attribute properties page, select the check box next to Ambiguous Name Resolution (ANR), as shown in Figure 7.21.

FIGURE 7.21
Adding attributes to the ANR filter.

6. Click OK to save the changes.

Remove Attributes from Ambiguous Name Resolution Filter

Scenario/Problem: You previously added an attribute to the ANR filter, but you do not need it to be searched.

Solution: Remove the attribute from the ANR filter by using the Active Directory Schema snap-in.

To remove attributes from the Ambiguous Name Resolution filter, perform the following steps:

1. Log on to a domain controller or a member computer that has Windows Server 2008 RSAT installed.

2. Click Start, click Administrative Tools, and click Active Directory Schema.

3. In the console tree, expand Active Directory Schema and then click Attributes.

4. In the details pane, right-click the attribute you want to remove from the ANR filter and click Properties.

5. On the attribute properties page, deselect the check box next to Ambiguous Name Resolution (ANR), as shown in Figure 7.22.

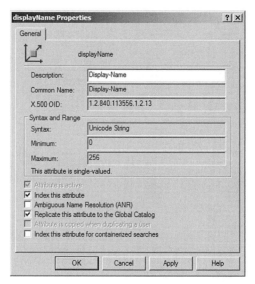

FIGURE 7.22
Removing attributes from the ANR filter.

6. Click OK to save the changes.

Add Attributes to Global Catalog Replication

Scenario/Problem: You created a custom attribute in your schema and want users from all domains in the forest to be able to see the values in that attribute.

Solution: Add the attribute to global catalog replication by using the Active Directory Schema snap-in.

To add an attribute to global catalog replication, perform the following steps:

1. Log on to a domain controller or a member computer that has Windows Server 2008 RSAT installed.

2. Click Start, click Administrative Tools, and click Active Directory Schema.

3. In the console tree, expand Active Directory Schema and then click Attributes.

4. In the details pane, right-click the attribute you want to add to global catalog replication and click Properties.

5. On the attribute properties page, select the check box next to Replicate this attribute to the Global Catalog, as shown in Figure 7.23.

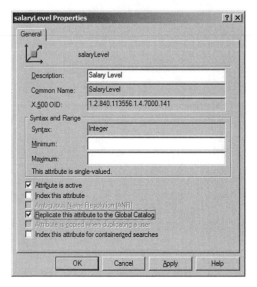

FIGURE 7.23
Adding attributes to global catalog replication.

6. Click OK to save the changes.

Remove Attributes from Global Catalog Replication

Scenario/Problem: You previously added an attribute to global catalog replication but no longer require this attribute to be replicated to the global catalog.

Solution: Remove the attribute from global catalog replication by using the Active Directory Schema snap-in.

To remove an attribute from global catalog replication, perform the following steps:

1. Log on to a domain controller or a member computer that has Windows Server 2008 RSAT installed.

2. Click Start, click Administrative Tools, and click Active Directory Schema.

3. In the console tree, expand Active Directory Schema and then click Attributes.

4. In the details pane, right-click the attribute you want to remove from global catalog replication and click Properties.

5. On the attribute properties page, deselect the check box next to Replicate this attribute to the Global Catalog, as shown in Figure 7.24.

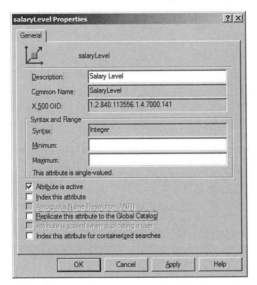

FIGURE 7.24
Removing attributes from global catalog replication.

6. Click OK to save the changes.

Configure Attributes to Be Copied When Duplicating Users

Scenario/Problem: You have a custom attribute you added to your schema and want this attribute to be copied when users are duplicated.

Solution: Configure the attribute to be copied when duplicating users.

To configure an attribute to be copied when duplicating users, perform the following steps:

1. Log on to a domain controller or a member computer that has Windows Server 2008 RSAT installed.

2. Click Start, click Administrative Tools, and click Active Directory Schema.

3. In the console tree, expand Active Directory Schema and then click Attributes.

4. In the details pane, right-click the attribute you want to be copied when duplicating users and click Properties.

5. On the attribute properties page, select the check box next to Attribute is copied when duplicating a user, as shown in Figure 7.25.

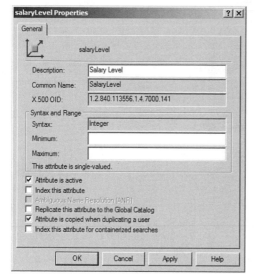

FIGURE 7.25

Configuring an attribute to be copied when duplicating a user.

6. Click OK to save the changes.

Configure Attributes Not to Be Copied When Duplicating Users

Scenario/Problem: You do not want an attribute to be copied when users are duplicated.

Solution: Configure the attribute not to be copied when duplicating users.

To configure an attribute not to be copied when duplicating users, perform the following steps:

1. Log on to a domain controller or a member computer that has Windows Server 2008 RSAT installed.

2. Click Start, click Administrative Tools, and click Active Directory Schema.

3. In the console tree, expand Active Directory Schema and then click Attributes.

4. In the details pane, right-click the attribute you do not want to be copied when duplicating users and click Properties.

5. On the attribute properties page, deselect the check box next to Attribute is copied when duplicating a user, as shown in Figure 7.26.

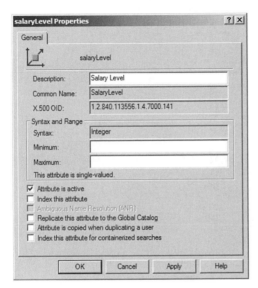

FIGURE 7.26
Configuring an attribute not to be copied when duplicating a user.

6. Click OK to save the changes.

Configuring Attributes to Be Indexed for Containerized Searches

Scenario/Problem: You need to define a search for an attribute located in a specific organizational unit.

Solution: Configure the attribute to be indexed for containerized searches.

To configure an attribute to be indexed for containerized searches, perform the following steps:

1. Log on to a domain controller or a member computer that has Windows Server 2008 RSAT installed.

2. Click Start, click Administrative Tools, and click Active Directory Schema.

3. In the console tree, expand Active Directory Schema and then click Attributes.

4. In the details pane, right-click the attribute you want to be indexed for categorized containerized searches and click Properties.

5. On the attribute properties page, select the check box next to Index this attribute for containerized searches, as shown in Figure 7.27.

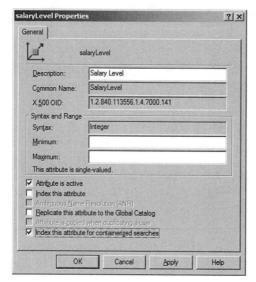

FIGURE 7.27
Configuring an attribute to be indexed for containerized searches.

6. Click OK to save the changes.

Configuring Attributes Not to Be Indexed for Containerized Searches

Scenario/Problem: You do not want an attribute to be defined for a search located in a specific organizational unit.

Solution: Configure the attribute not to be indexed for containerized searches.

To configure an attribute not to be indexed for containerized searches, perform the following steps:

1. Log on to a domain controller or a member computer that has Windows Server 2008 RSAT installed.

2. Click Start, click Administrative Tools, and click Active Directory Schema.

3. In the console tree, expand Active Directory Schema and then click Attributes.

4. In the details pane, right-click the attribute you do not want to be indexed for categorized containerized searches and click Properties.

5. On the attribute properties page, deselect the check box next to Index this attribute for containerized searches, as shown in Figure 7.28.

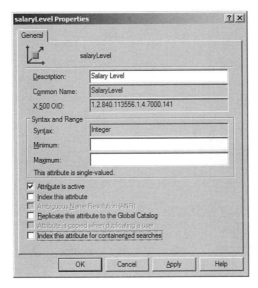

FIGURE 7.28
Configuring an attribute not to be indexed for containerized searches.

6. Click OK to save the changes.

Configure Attribute Range

Scenario/Problem: You need to define the upper and lower values an attribute can have.

Solution: Configure the attribute range by using the Active Directory Schema snap-in.

To configure the attribute range, perform the following steps:

1. Log on to a domain controller or a member computer that has Windows Server 2008 RSAT installed.

2. Click Start, click Administrative Tools, and click Active Directory Schema.

3. In the console tree, expand Active Directory Schema and then click Attributes.

4. In the details pane, right-click the attribute for which you want to configure the range and click Properties.

5. On the attribute properties page, enter a minimum value in the Minimum field and enter a maximum value in the Maximum field, as shown in Figure 7.29.

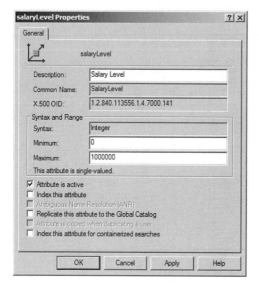

FIGURE 7.29
Configuring an attribute's range.

6. Click OK to save the changes.

Attribute Range Acceptable Values

The minimum acceptable value is determined by the attribute's syntax. Integer, Large Integer, and Enumeration syntaxes accept negative numbers. For these syntaxes, the smallest value that can be entered is -2,147,483,648. For all other syntaxes, the smallest value that can be entered is 0 (zero).

The maximum acceptable value is determined by the attribute's syntax. If minimum and maximum values are defined, the maximum value must be greater than or equal to the minimum value.

Valid characters for minimum and maximum are 0–9.

Create Classes

Scenario/Problem: You need to group a number of attributes together.

Solution: Create a class by using the Active Directory Schema snap-in.

To create a class, perform the following steps:

1. Log on to a domain controller or a member computer that has Windows Server 2008 RSAT installed.

2. Click Start, click Administrative Tools, and click Active Directory Schema.

3. In the console tree, expand Active Directory Schema and then click Classes.

4. On the Action menu, click Create Class.

5. On the Schema Object Creation warning box, shown in Figure 7.30, click Continue.

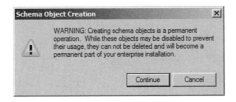

FIGURE 7.30
The warning box for schema object creation.

6. On the Create New Schema Class window, shown in Figure 7.31, do the following:

   ▶ Type a common name in the Common Name field.

   ▶ Type an LDAP display name in the LDAP Display Name field.

   ▶ Type the OID in the Unique X500 Object ID field.

   ▶ Type a description in the Description field, if required.

   ▶ Type a parent class in the Parent Class field, if required.

   ▶ Select a class type of Structural, Abstract, or Auxiliary in the Class Type field.

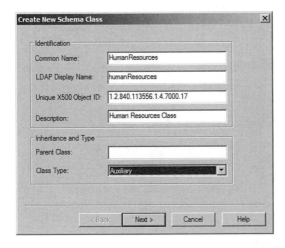

FIGURE 7.31
The Create New Schema Class window.

7. Click Next.

8. To add mandatory attributes to the class, click Add beside the mandatory field, shown in Figure 7.32, and select the attributes you want to add as mandatory.

9. To add optional attributes to the class, click Add beside the optional field, shown in Figure 7.32, and select the attributes you want to add as mandatory.

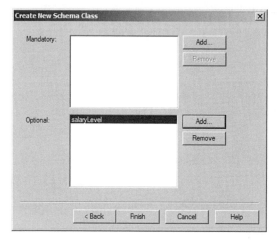

FIGURE 7.32
The window for adding attributes.

10. Click Finish.

Deactivate Classes

Scenario/Problem: You previously created a class you no longer require.

Solution: Deactivate the class by using the Active Directory Schema snap-in.

To deactivate a class, perform the following steps:

1. Log on to a domain controller or a member computer that has Windows Server 2008 RSAT installed.

2. Click Start, click Administrative Tools, and click Active Directory Schema.

3. In the console tree, expand Active Directory Schema and then click Classes.

4. In the details pane, right-click the class you want to deactivate and click Properties.

5. On the class properties page, deselect the check box next to Class is active, as shown in Figure 7.33.

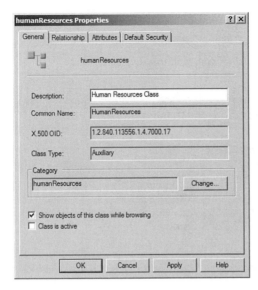

FIGURE 7.33
Deactivating a class.

6. On the warning box for making a schema object defunct, shown in Figure 7.34, click Yes.

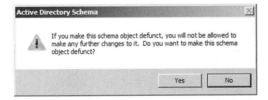

FIGURE 7.34
The warning box for making a schema object defunct.

7. Click OK to save the changes.

Activate Classes

Scenario/Problem: You previously deactivated a class, and now you require it.

Solution: Activate the class by using the Active Directory Schema snap-in.

To activate a class, perform the following steps:

1. Log on to a domain controller or a member computer that has Windows Server 2008 RSAT installed.

2. Click Start, click Administrative Tools, and click Active Directory Schema.

3. In the console tree, expand Active Directory Schema and then click Classes.

4. In the details pane, right-click the class you want to activate and click Properties.

5. A notification that the class is defunct displays, and no changes are allowed on the object until it is made active again, as shown in Figure 7.35. Click OK.

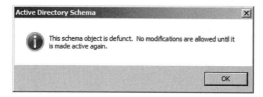

FIGURE 7.35
The message that the schema object is defunct.

6. On the class properties page, select the check box next to Class is active, as shown in Figure 7.36.

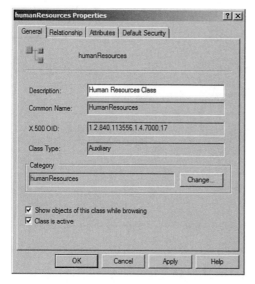

FIGURE 7.36
Activating a class.

7. Click OK to save the changes.

Configure Classes to Be Visible in Advanced View

Scenario/Problem: You want a class to be visible only in advanced view.

Solution: Configure the class to be visible in advanced view by using the Active Directory Schema snap-in.

To configure a class to be visible in advanced view, perform the following steps:

1. Log on to a domain controller or a member computer that has Windows Server 2008 RSAT installed.

2. Click Start, click Administrative Tools, and click Active Directory Schema.

3. In the console tree, expand Active Directory Schema and then click Classes.

4. In the details pane, right-click the class you want to make visible in advanced view and click Properties.

5. On the class properties page, select the check box next to Show objects of this class while browsing, as shown in Figure 7.37.

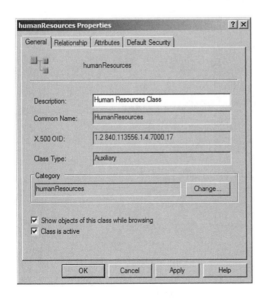

FIGURE 7.37
Configuring a class to be visible in advanced view.

6. Click OK to save the changes.

Configure Classes Not to Be Visible in Advanced View

Scenario/Problem: You do not want an attribute to be visible in advanced view.

Solution: Configure the class to not be visible in advanced view by using the Active Directory Schema snap-in.

To configure a class not to be visible in advanced view, perform the following steps:

1. Log on to a domain controller or a member computer that has Windows Server 2008 RSAT installed.

2. Click Start, click Administrative Tools, and click Active Directory Schema.

3. In the console tree, expand Active Directory Schema and then click Classes.

4. In the details pane, right-click the class you want to make invisible in advanced view and click Properties.

5. On the class properties page, deselect the check box next to Show objects of this class while browsing, as shown in Figure 7.38.

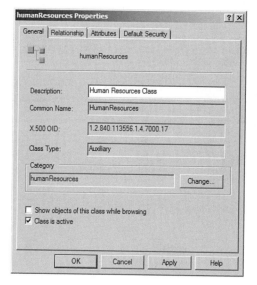

FIGURE 7.38
Configuring a class not to be visible in advanced view.

6. Click OK to save the changes.

Configure Class Relationships

Scenario/Problem: You want to configure the subclasses of a parent class.

Solution: Configure class relationships by using the Active Directory Schema snap-in.

To configure class relationships, perform the following steps:

1. Log on to a domain controller or a member computer that has Windows Server 2008 RSAT installed.

2. Click Start, click Administrative Tools, and click Active Directory Schema.

3. In the console tree, expand Active Directory Schema and then click Classes.

4. In the details pane, right-click the class on which you want to configure the relationship and click Properties.

5. On the class properties page, click the Relationship tab, as shown in Figure 7.39.

6. To add auxiliary classes, click Add Class and select the class you want to add as an auxiliary class.

7. To remove auxiliary classes, click the auxiliary class you want to remove and then click Remove.

8. To add superior classes, click Add Superior.

9. To remove superior classes, click the superior class you want to remove and then click Remove.

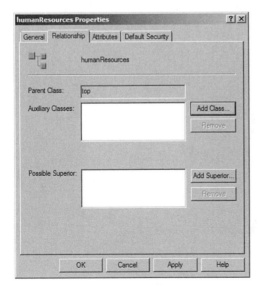

FIGURE 7.39
The Relationship tab.

10. Click OK to save the changes.

Configure Class Attributes

Scenario/Problem: You do not want to define the mandatory and optional attributes within a class.

Solution: Configure class attributes by using the Active Directory Schema snap-in.

To configure class attributes, perform the following steps:

1. Log on to a domain controller or a member computer that has Windows Server 2008 RSAT installed.

2. Click Start, click Administrative Tools, and click Active Directory Schema.

3. In the console tree, expand Active Directory Schema and then click Classes.

4. In the details pane, right-click the class on which you want to configure class attributes and click Properties.

5. On the class properties page, click the Attributes tab, as shown in Figure 7.40.

6. To add optional attributes to the class, click Add and select the attributes you want to add as optional.

7. To remove optional attributes to the class, click the optional attribute you want to remove and then click Remove.

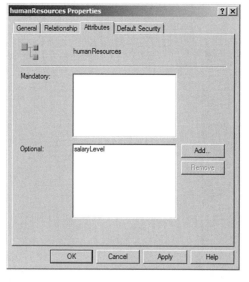

FIGURE 7.40
The Attributes tab.

8. Click OK to save the changes.

CHAPTER 8

Manage Active Directory Domain Services Data

IN THIS CHAPTER

- ▶ Create User Object
- ▶ Delete User Object
- ▶ Rename User Object
- ▶ Copy User Object
- ▶ Move User Object
- ▶ Add User to Group
- ▶ Disable a User Object
- ▶ Enable a User Object
- ▶ Reset a User Account Password
- ▶ Modify a User Object's General Properties
- ▶ Modify a User Object's Address Properties
- ▶ Modify a User Object's Account Properties
- ▶ Modify a User's Logon Hours
- ▶ Modify the Computers a User Can Log On To
- ▶ Modify a User Object's Profile Properties
- ▶ Modify a User's Object Telephone Properties
- ▶ Modify a User's Object Organization Properties
- ▶ Modify a User's Manager
- ▶ View a User Object's Direct Reports
- ▶ Modify a User's Group Membership
- ▶ Modify a User Object's Dial-in Properties
- ▶ Modify a User Object's Environment Properties
- ▶ Modify a User Object's Sessions Properties

- ▶ Modify a User Object's Remote Control Properties
- ▶ Modify a User Object's Terminal Services Properties
- ▶ Modify a User Object's COM+ Properties
- ▶ Modify a User Object's Published Certificates Properties
- ▶ View the Password Replication Policies Applied to a User Object
- ▶ Modify a User Object's Protection from Deletion Properties
- ▶ Modify a User Object's Custom Attributes
- ▶ Create a Group Object
- ▶ Delete a Group Object
- ▶ Rename a Group Object
- ▶ Move a Group Object
- ▶ Add a Group to a Group
- ▶ Modify a Group Object's General Properties
- ▶ Modify a Group Object's Scope
- ▶ Modify a Group Object's Type
- ▶ Modify a Group Object's Members
- ▶ Modify a Group Object Managed By Properties
- ▶ Modify a Group Object Protection from Deletion
- ▶ Modify a Group Object's Custom Attributes
- ▶ Create a Computer Object
- ▶ Delete a Computer Object

- ▶ Move a Computer Object
- ▶ Add a Computer to a Group
- ▶ Disable a Computer Object
- ▶ Enable a Computer Object
- ▶ Modify a Computer Object's General Properties
- ▶ View a Computer Object's Operating System Properties
- ▶ Modify a Computer Object's Delegation Properties
- ▶ View the Password Replication Policies Applied to a Computer Object
- ▶ Modify a Computer Object's Location Properties
- ▶ Modify a Computer Object's Managed By Properties
- ▶ Modify a Computer Object's Protection from Deletion
- ▶ Modify a Computer Object's Custom Attributes
- ▶ Create an Organizational Unit
- ▶ Delete an Organizational Unit
- ▶ Rename an Organizational Unit
- ▶ Move an Organizational Unit
- ▶ Modify an Organizational Unit's General Properties
- ▶ Modify an Organizational Unit's Managed By Properties
- ▶ Modify an Organizational Unit's COM+ Properties
- ▶ Modify an Organizational Unit's Protection from Deletion
- ▶ Modify an Organizational Unit's Custom Attributes

Each Active Directory Domain Services (AD DS) domain contains data in the form of objects and accounts. Domain data mainly consists of users, groups, computers, and organizational units (OUs).

This chapter describes the steps required to manage the data within the AD DS directory.

Create User Object

Scenario/Problem: Your employees need to log on to their desktops by using AD DS authentication.

Solution: Create an AD DS user account by using the Windows interface or by using the command line.

Create User Object by Using the Windows Interface

To create user objects by using the Windows interface, perform the following steps:

1. Log on to a domain controller or a member computer that has Windows Server 2008 Remote Server Administration Tools (RSAT) installed.

2. Click Start, click Administrative Tools, and then click Active Directory Users and Computers.

3. In the console tree, right-click the OU or container where want to store the user object, click New, and click User.

4. As shown in Figure 8.1, type the user's first name in the First name field, type the user's initials in the Initials field if required, type the user's last name in the Last name field, type the user's logon name in the User logon name field, and click Next.

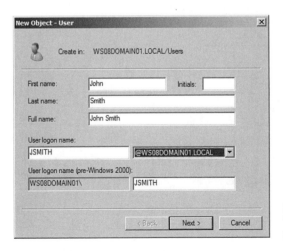

FIGURE 8.1
The New Object - User account information page.

> **TIP** The Full name and User logon name (pre-Windows 2000) fields are automatically populated by the wizard. You can modify these fields if required.

5. Type a password into the Password and Confirm password fields; then click Next, as shown in Figure 8.2.

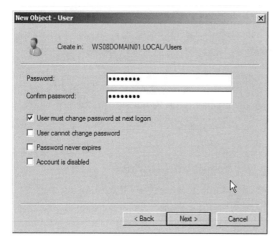

FIGURE 8.2
The New Object - User account password page.

> **TIP** Password options can be set on this page as well.

6. Confirm the user object options, as shown in Figure 8.3, and click Finish.

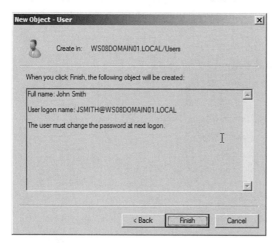

FIGURE 8.3
The New Object - User confirmation page.

Create User Object by Using the Command Line

To create user objects by using the command line, perform the following steps:

1. Log on to a domain controller.

2. Click Start, and click Command Prompt.

3. In the Command Prompt window, type the following command and press Enter:

   ```
   Dsadd user "CN=John Doe,CN=Users,DC=WS08DOMAIN01,DC=local" -samid
   JDOE -UPN JDOE@WS08DOMAIN01.LOCAL -disabled NO -pwd Today01!
   ```

   Table 8.1 lists each parameter used in the previous command.

TABLE 8.1   **Parameters to Create User Objects by Using the Command Line**

Parameter	Meaning
`"CN=John Doe,CN=Users,` `DC=WS08DOMAIN01,DC=local"`	Distinguished name
`-samid`	Pre-Windows 2000 logon name
`-UPN`	User principle name
`-disabled`	Status of user account after creation
`-pwd`	Password

3. Verify that the results of the dsadd command entered above returns dsadd succeeded, as shown in Figure 8.4.

FIGURE 8.4
Creating the user object using the command line.

> **TIP**   For a full list of dsadd user parameters, go to http://technet.microsoft.com/en-us/library/cc731279.aspx.

Delete User Object

Scenario/Problem: An employee has left your company, and you need to remove the employee's identify from your AD DS environment.

Solution: Delete an AD DS user account by using the Windows interface or the command line.

Delete User Object by Using the Windows Interface

To delete user objects by using the Windows interface, perform the following steps:

1. Log on to a domain controller or a member computer that has Windows Server 2008 RSAT installed.

2. Click Start, click Administrative Tools, and then click Active Directory Users and Computers.

3. In the details pane, right-click the user object you want to delete and click Delete.

4. Click Yes on the confirmation page, shown in Figure 8.5.

FIGURE 8.5
Confirming the user object deletion.

Delete User Object by Using the Command Line

To delete user objects by using the command line, perform the following steps:

1. Log on to a domain controller.

2. Click Start, and click Command Prompt.

3. In the Command Prompt window, type the following command and press Enter:

   `Dsrm "CN=John Doe,CN=Users,DC=WS08DOMAIN01,DC=local"`

   (where `"CN=John Doe,CN=Users,DC=WS08DOMAIN01,DC=local"` is the distinguished name of the user object you want to delete).

4. Type **Y** to confirm the deletion and press Enter.

> **TIP** For a full list of dsrm parameters, go to http://technet.microsoft.com/en-us/library/cc731865.aspx.

5. Verify that the results of the dsrm command entered above returns dsrm succeeded, as shown in Figure 8.6.

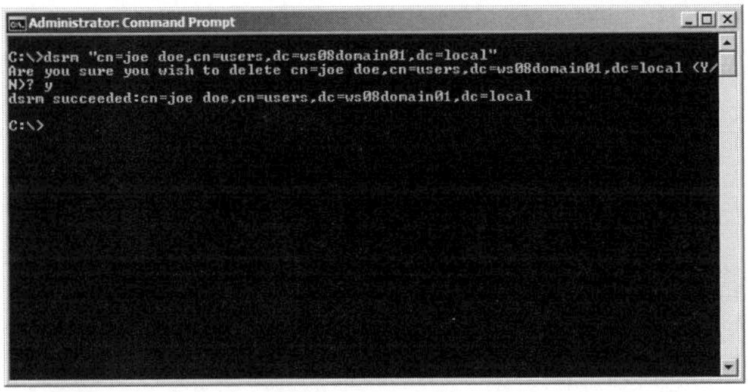

FIGURE 8.6
Deleting the user object using the command line.

Rename User Object

Scenario/Problem: An employee was married recently and her last name has changed.

Solution: Rename an AD DS user account by using the Windows interface or the command line.

Rename User Object by Using the Windows Interface

To rename a user object by using the Windows interface, perform the following steps:

1. Log on to a domain controller or a member computer that has Windows Server 2008 RSAT installed.

2. Click Start, click Administrative Tools, and then click Active Directory Users and Computers.

3. In the details pane, right-click the user object you want to rename and click Rename.

4. Type the new full name of the user and press Enter.

5. On the Rename User window, shown in Figure 8.7, modify the applicable name fields; then click OK.

FIGURE 8.7
The Rename User page.

Rename User Object by Using the Command Line

To rename a user object by using the command line, perform the following steps:

1. Log on to a domain controller.

2. Click Start, and click Command Prompt.

> **NOTE** Renaming a user account by using the command line is a two phase process. The first step uses the dsmod command to modify the applicable name attributes for the object. The second step uses the dsmove command to modify the distinguished name of the object.

3. In the Command Prompt window, type the following command and press Enter:

   Dsmod user "CN=John Smith,CN=Users,DC=WS08DOMAIN01,DC=local" -fn
   Jonathan -display "Jonathan Smith"

   (where "*CN=John Smith,CN=Users,DC=WS08DOMAIN01,DC=local*" is the distinguished name of the user, *-fn Jonathan* is the new first name of the user, and *-display "Jonathan Smith"* is the new display name of the user).

> **TIP** For a full list of dsmod user parameters, go to http://technet.microsoft.com/en-us/library/cc732954.aspx.

4. Verify that the results of the dsmod command entered above returns dsmod succeeded, as shown in Figure 8.8.

FIGURE 8.8
Modifying the user's name using the command line.

5. In the Command Prompt window, type the following command and press Enter:

Dsmove "CN=John Smith,CN=Users,DC=WS08DOMAIN01,DC=local" -newname
"Jonathan Smith"

(where "CN=John Smith,CN=Users,DC=WS08DOMAIN01,DC=local" is the
distinguished name of the user, -fn Jonathan is the new first name of the user,
and -display "Jonathan Smith" is the new display name of the user).

6. Verify that the results of the dsmove command entered above returns dsmove
succeeded, as shown in Figure 8.9.

TIP For a full list of dsmove parameters, go to http://technet.microsoft.com/
en-us/library/cc731094.aspx.

FIGURE 8.9
Renaming the user using the command line.

Copy User Object

Scenario/Problem: A new employee has been hired and requires the same access as his counterpart.

Solution: Copy an AD DS user account.

To copy a user object, perform the following steps:

1. Log on to a domain controller or a member computer that has Windows Server 2008 RSAT installed.

2. Click Start, click Administrative Tools, and then click Active Directory Users and Computers.

3. In the details pane, right-click the user object you want to copy and click Copy.

4. On the Copy Object – User page, shown in Figure 8.10, type the user's first name in the First name field, type the user's initials in the Initials field if required, type the user's last name in the Last name field, type the user's logon name in the User logon name field, and click Next.

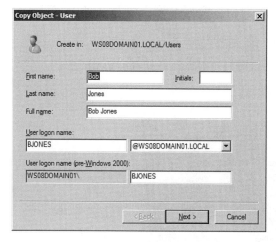

FIGURE 8.10

The Copy Object - User account information page.

TIP The Full name and User logon name (pre-Windows 2000) fields are automatically populated by the wizard. You can modify these fields if required.

5. Type a password into the Password and Confirm password fields as shown in Figure 8.11, and click Next.

FIGURE 8.11
The Copy Object - User account
password page.

TIP Password options can be set on this page as well.

6. Confirm the user object options, as shown in Figure 8.12, and click Finish.

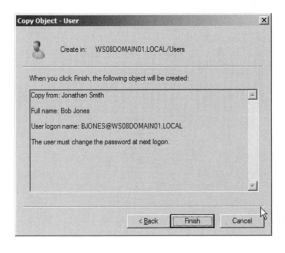

FIGURE 8.12
Copy Object – User confirmation
page.

Move User Object

> **Scenario/Problem:** Your company's AD DS logical design uses OUs to group employees by region. An employee has moved offices.

Solution: Move an AD DS user account by using the Windows interface or by using the command line.

Move User Object by Using the Windows Interface

To move a user object by using the Windows interface, perform the following steps:

1. Log on to a domain controller or a member computer that has Windows Server 2008 RSAT installed.

2. Click Start, click Administrative Tools, and then click Active Directory Users and Computers.

3. In the details pane, right-click the user object you want to move and click Move.

4. On the Move window, shown in Figure 8.13, select the OU or container to which you want to move the user object; then click OK.

FIGURE 8.13
The Move object window.

Move User Object by Using the Command Line

To move a user object by using the command line, perform the following steps:

1. Log on to a domain controller.

2. Click Start, and click Command Prompt.

3. In the Command Prompt window, type the following command and press Enter:

```
Dsmove  "CN=Jonathan Smith,CN=Users,DC=WS08DOMAIN01,DC=local"
-newparent "OU=New York,DC=WS08DOMANI01,DC=local"
```

(where "*CN=Jonathan Smith,CN=Users,DC=WS08DOMAIN01,DC=local*" is the distinguished name of the user and "*OU=New York,DC=WS08DOMANI01,DC=local*" is the location to which you want to move the user).

4. Verify that the results of the dsmove command entered above returns dsmove succeeded, as shown in Figure 8.14.

TIP For a full list of dsmove parameters, go to http://technet.microsoft.com/en-us/library/cc731094.aspx.

FIGURE 8.14
Moving a user using the command line.

Add User to Group

Scenario/Problem: Your company has an application that uses AD DS groups to grant access to the application. You need to provide an employee with access to the application.

Solution: Add an AD DS user account to a group by using the Windows interface or by using the command line.

Add User to Group by Using the Windows Interface

To add a user to a group by using the Windows interface, perform the following steps:

1. Log on to a domain controller or a member computer that has Windows Server 2008 RSAT installed.

2. Click Start, click Administrative Tools, and then click Active Directory Users and Computers.

3. In the details pane, right-click the user object you want to add to the group and click Add to a group.

4. In the Select Groups window, shown in Figure 8.15, enter the name of the group to which you want to add the user, click Check Names, and click OK.

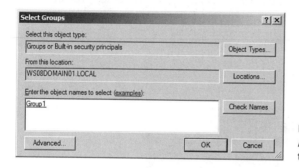

FIGURE 8.15
Adding a user to a group using the Windows interface.

Add User to Group by Using the Command Line

To add a user to a group by using the command line, perform the following steps:

1. Log on to a domain controller.
2. Click Start, and click Command Prompt.
3. In the Command Prompt window, type the following command and press Enter:

```
Dsmod group "CN=Group1,OU=New York,DC=WS08DOMAIN01,DC=local"
-addmbr "CN=Jonathan Smith,CN=Users,DC=WS08DOMAIN01,DC=local"
```

(where "CN=Group1,OU=New York,DC=WS08DOMAIN01,DC=local" is the distinguished name of the group and "CN=Jonathan Smith,CN=Users,DC=WS08DOMAIN01,DC=local" is the distinguished name of the user that you want to add to the group).

4. Verify that the results of the dsmod group command entered above returns dsmod succeeded, as shown in Figure 8.16.

TIP For a full list of dsmod group parameters, go to http://technet.microsoft.com/en-us/library/cc732423.aspx.

FIGURE 8.16
Adding a user to a group using the command line.

Disable a User Object

Scenario/Problem: An employee has left for maternity leave, and you need to ensure her account cannot be used until she returns.

Solution: Disable an AD DS user account by using the Windows interface or by using the command line.

Disable User Object by Using the Windows Interface

To disable a user object by using the Windows interface, perform the following steps:

1. Log on to a domain controller or a member computer that has Windows Server 2008 RSAT installed.

2. Click Start, click Administrative Tools, and then click Active Directory Users and Computers.

3. In the details pane, right-click the user object you want to disable and click Disable Account.

4. Verify the status message that indicates the account was disabled, as shown in Figure 8.17.

FIGURE 8.17
Disabling a user object using the Windows interface.

Disable a User Object by Using the Command Line

To disable a user object by using the command line, perform the following steps:

1. Log on to a domain controller.

2. Click Start, and click Command Prompt.

3. In the Command Prompt window, type the following command and press Enter:

   **Dsmod user "CN=Jonathan Smith,OU=New York,DC=WS08DOMAIN01,DC=local"
   -disabled yes**

   (where "*CN=Jonathan Smith,OU=New York,DC=WS08DOMAIN01,DC=local*" is
   the distinguished name of the user that you want to disable).

4. Verify that the results of the dsmod user command entered above returns dsmod
   succeeded, as shown in Figure 8.18.

TIP For a full list of dsmod user parameters, go to http://technet.microsoft.com/
en-us/library/cc732954.aspx.

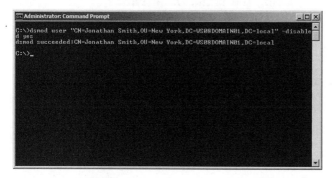

FIGURE 8.18
Disabling a user object using the command line.

Enable a User Object

> **Scenario/Problem:** An employee who was away on maternity leave has returned to work.

Solution: Enable an AD DS user account by using the Windows interface or by using the command line.

Enable User Object by Using the Windows Interface

To enable a user object by using the Windows interface, perform the following steps:

1. Log on to a domain controller or a member computer that has Windows Server 2008 RSAT installed.

2. Click Start, click Administrative Tools, and then click Active Directory Users and Computers.

3. In the details pane, right-click the user object you want to enable and click Enable Account.

4. Verify the status message that indicates the account was enabled, as shown in Figure 8.19.

FIGURE 8.19
Enabling a user object using the Windows interface.

Enable User Object by Using the Command Line

To enable a user object by using the command line, perform the following steps:

1. Log on to a domain controller.

2. Click Start, and click Command Prompt.

3. In the Command Prompt window, type the following command and press Enter:

   Dsmod user "CN=Jonathan Smith,OU=New York,DC=WS08DOMAIN01,DC=local"
   -disabled no

   (where "*CN=Jonathan Smith,OU=New York,DC=WS08DOMAIN01,DC=local*" is the distinguished name of the user you want to enable).

4. Verify that the of results the dsmod user command entered above returns dsmod succeeded, as shown in Figure 8.20.

> **TIP** For a full list of dsmod user parameters, go to http://technet.microsoft.com/
> en-us/library/cc732954.aspx.

FIGURE 8.20
Enabling a user object using the command line.

Reset a User Account Password

> **Scenario/Problem:** An employee recently changed his password, but he cannot
> remember what his new password is.

Solution: Reset an AD DS user account password by using the Windows interface
or by using the command line.

Reset a User Account Password by Using the Windows Interface

To reset a user account password by using the Windows interface, perform the following steps:

1. Log on to a domain controller or a member computer that has Windows Server
   2008 RSAT installed.

2. Click Start, click Administrative Tools, and then click Active Directory Users
   and Computers.

3. In the details pane, right-click the user account on which you want to reset the
   password; then click Reset Password.

4. In the Reset Password window, shown in Figure 8.21, type a password in the
   Password and Confirm password fields, specify whether the user must change
   his password at next logon, specify whether the user account should be
   unlocked, and click OK.

FIGURE 8.21

Resetting a user account password using the Windows interface.

Reset a User Account Password by Using the Command Line

To reset a user account password by using the command line, perform the following steps:

1. Log on to a domain controller.

2. Click Start, and click Command Prompt.

3. In the Command Prompt window, type the following command and press Enter:

   Dsmod user "CN=Jonathan Smith,OU=New York,DC=WS08DOMAIN01,DC=local" -pwd Hello01! -mustchpwd no

   (where "*CN=Jonathan Smith,OU=New York,DC=WS08DOMAIN01,DC=local*" is the distinguished name of the user for which you want to reset the password, *-pwd* is the new password, and *-mustchpwd* specifies whether the user must change his password at next logon).

4. Verify that the results of the dsmod user command entered above returns dsmod succeeded, as shown in Figure 8.22.

TIP For a full list of dsmod user parameters, go to http://technet.microsoft.com/en-us/library/cc732954.aspx.

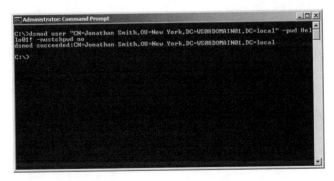

FIGURE 8.22

Resetting a user account password using the command line.

Modify a User Object's General Properties

Scenario/Problem: Your company uses the description field on AD DS user objects to identify to which business unit a user belongs.

Solution: Modify a user object's general properties.

To modify a user object's general properties, perform the following steps:

1. Log on to a domain controller or a member computer that has Windows Server 2008 RSAT installed.

2. Click Start, click Administrative Tools, and then click Active Directory Users and Computers.

3. In the details pane, right-click the user account you want to modify, and click Properties.

4. Click the General tab, shown in Figure 8.23.

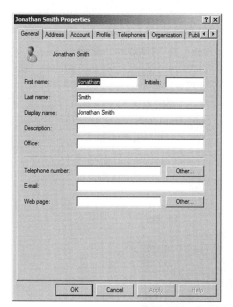

FIGURE 8.23
Modifying a user object's general properties.

5. Modify the applicable properties, and then click OK.

Modify a User Object's Address Properties

Scenario/Problem: Your company stores address information on user objects in AD DS. An employee has recently changed offices.

Solution: Modify a user object's address properties.

To modify a user object's address properties, perform the following steps:

1. Log on to a domain controller or a member computer that has Windows Server 2008 RSAT installed.

2. Click Start, click Administrative Tools, and then click Active Directory Users and Computers.

3. In the details pane, right-click the user account you want to modify, and click Properties.

4. Click the Address tab, shown in Figure 8.24.

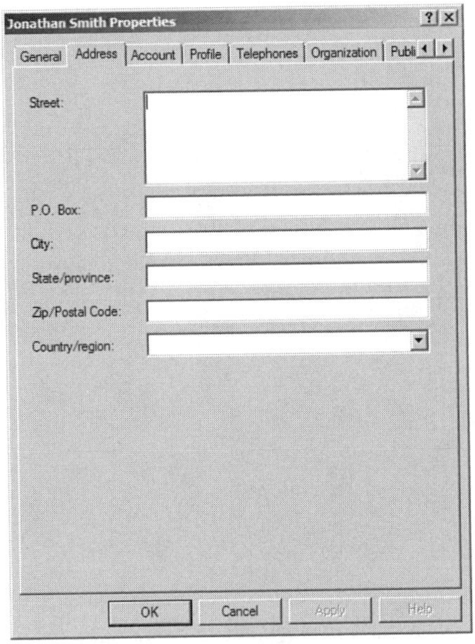

FIGURE 8.24
Modifying a user object's general properties.

5. Modify the applicable properties, and then click OK.

Modify a User Object's Account Properties

Scenario/Problem: You need to force a user to change her password the next time she logs on.

Solution: Modify a user object's account properties.

To modify a user object's account properties, perform the following steps:

1. Log on to a domain controller or a member computer that has Windows Server 2008 RSAT installed.

2. Click Start, click Administrative Tools, and then click Active Directory Users and Computers.

3. In the details pane, right-click the user account you want to modify, and click Properties.

4. Click the Account tab, shown in Figure 8.25.

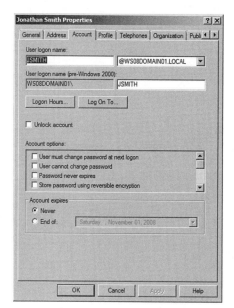

FIGURE 8.25
Modifying a user object's account properties.

5. Modify the applicable properties, and then click OK.

Modify a User's Logon Hours

Scenario/Problem: You need to prevent a user from logging on outside of business hours.

Solution: Modify user logon hours.

To modify a user object's logon hours, perform the following steps:

1. Log on to a domain controller or a member computer that has Windows Server 2008 RSAT installed.

2. Click Start, click Administrative Tools, and then click Active Directory Users and Computers.

3. In the details pane, right-click the user account you want to modify, and click Properties.

4. Click the Account tab.

5. Click Logon Hours. The Logon Hours properties window will open, as shown in Figure 8.26.

6. To deny a user from logging on during a particular day and/or time, select the days and/or time, click the Logon Denied radio button, and then click OK.

7. To allow a user to log on during a particular day and/or time, select the days and/or time, click the Logon Permitted radio button, and then click OK.

8. Click OK to save the account changes.

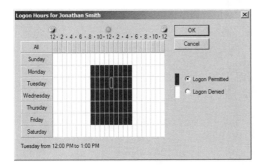

FIGURE 8.26
Modifying a user's logon hours.

Modify the Computers a User Can Log On To

Scenario/Problem: You need to limit a particular user to log on to a single computer.

Solution: Modify the computers a user can log on to.

To modify the computers that a user can log on to, perform the following steps:

1. Log on to a domain controller or a member computer that has Windows Server 2008 RSAT installed.

2. Click Start, click Administrative Tools, and then click Active Directory Users and Computers.

3. In the details pane, right-click the user account you want to modify, and click Properties.

4. Click the Account tab.

5. Click Log On To. The Logon Workstations window will open, as shown in Figure 8.27.

6. To allow the user to log on to all computers, select All Computers and click OK.

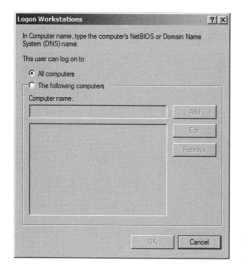

FIGURE 8.27
Allowing a user to log on to all computers.

TIP By default, users are allowed to log on to all computers.

7. To restrict the user to log on to specific computers, select The following computers, type the computer name in the Computer name field, click Add, and then click OK.

8. Click OK to save the account changes.

Modify a User Object's Profile Properties

Scenario/Problem: You created a logon script that should be run each time a user logs on.

Solution: Modify a user object's profile properties.

To modify a user object's profile properties, perform the following steps:

1. Log on to a domain controller or a member computer that has Windows Server 2008 RSAT installed.

2. Click Start, click Administrative Tools, and then click Active Directory Users and Computers.

3. In the deails pane, right-click the user account you want to modify and click Properties.

4. Click the Profile tab, shown in Figure 8.28.

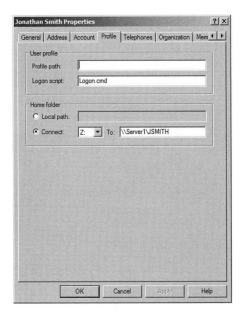

FIGURE 8.28
Modifying a user's object profile properties.

5. Modify the applicable properties, and then click OK.

Modify a User's Object Telephone Properties

Scenario/Problem: The phone number for an employee was recently changed.

Solution: Modify a user object's telephone properties.

To modify a user object's telephone properties, perform the following steps:

1. Log on to a domain controller or a member computer that has Windows Server 2008 RSAT installed.

2. Click Start, click Administrative Tools, and then click Active Directory Users and Computers.

3. In the details pane, right-click the user account you want to modify and click Properties.

4. Click the Telephones tab, shown in Figure 8.29.

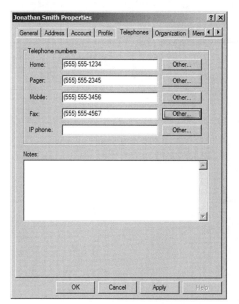

FIGURE 8.29
Modifyinjg a user's object telephone properties.

5. Modify the applicable properties, and then click OK.

Modify a User's Object Organization Properties

Scenario/Problem: Your company stores job title information for each employee in AD DS. An employee recently changed jobs and has a new title.

Solution: Modify a user object's organization properties.

To modify a user object's organization properties, perform the following steps:

1. Log on to a domain controller or a member computer that has Windows Server 2008 RSAT installed.

2. Click Start, click Administrative Tools, and then click Active Directory Users and Computers.

3. In the console tree, right-click the user account you want to modify; then click Properties.

4. Click the Organization tab, shown in Figure 8.30.

FIGURE 8.30
Modifying a user's object organization properties.

5. Modify the applicable properties, and then click OK.

Modify a User's Manager

Scenario/Problem: Your company stores manager information for each employee using AD DS. An employee recently moved to another team and has a new manager.

Solution: Modify a user's manager.

To modify a user object's manager, perform the following steps:

1. Log on to a domain controller or a member computer that has Windows Server 2008 RSAT installed.

2. Click Start, click Administrative Tools, and then click Active Directory Users and Computers.

3. In the details pane, right-click the user account you want to modify and click Properties.

4. Click the Organization tab.

5. Click the Change button under the Manager section.

6. On the Select User or Contact window, shown in Figure 8.31, type the name of the user's manager, click Check Names, and click OK.

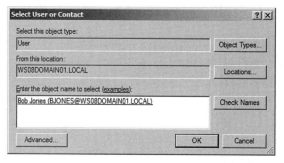

FIGURE 8.31
Modifying a user's manager.

7. Click OK to save the changes.

View a User Object's Direct Reports

Scenario/Problem: Your company stores manager information for each employee using AD DS. You need to determine all the individuals who report to a particular manager.

Solution: View a user object's direct reports.

To view a user object's direct reports, perform the following steps:

1. Log on to a domain controller or a member computer that has Windows Server 2008 RSAT installed.

2. Click Start, click Administrative Tools, and then click Active Directory Users and Computers.

3. In the details pane, right-click the user account you want to view and click Properties.

4. Click the Organization tab.

5. The user's direct reports are listed under the Direct Reports section, as shown in Figure 8.32.

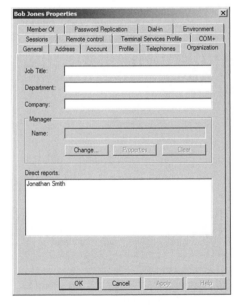

FIGURE 8.32
Viewing a user's direct reports.

6. Click OK to save the changes.

Modify a User's Group Membership

Scenario/Problem: Your company's applications use AD DS groups for authorization. You need to allow a particular user the ability to use an application.

Solution: Modify a user object's group membership.

To modify a user object's group membership, perform the following steps:

1. Log on to a domain controller or a member computer that has Windows Server 2008 RSAT installed.

2. Click Start, click Administrative Tools, and then click Active Directory Users and Computers.

3. In the details pane, right-click the user account you want to modify; then click Properties.

4. Click the Member Of tab, shown in Figure 8.33.

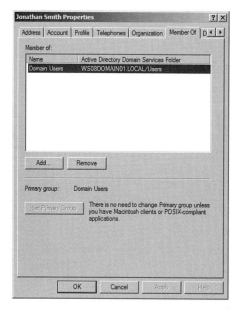

FIGURE 8.33
Modifying a user's group membership.

5. To add the user to a group, click the Add button, type the name of the group in the Select Groups window, as shown in Figure 8.34, and then click OK.

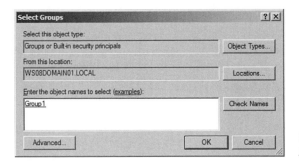

FIGURE 8.34
Adding a user to a group.

6. To remove a user from a group, select the group in the Member Of section and then click Remove.

7. On the Remove user from group confirmation screen, shown in Figure 8.35, click Yes.

FIGURE 8.35
Removing a user from a group.

8. Click OK to save the changes.

Modify a User Object's Dial-in Properties

Scenario/Problem: Your company uses Network Access Protection to provide remote access. You need to prevent a particular employee from using your company's remote access solution.

Solution: Modify a user object's dial-in properties.

To modify a user object's dial-in properties, perform the following steps:

1. Log on to a domain controller or a member computer that has Windows Server 2008 RSAT installed.

2. Click Start, click Administrative Tools, and then click Active Directory Users and Computers.

3. In the details pane, right-click the user account you want to modify and click Properties.

4. Click the Dial-in tab, shown in Figure 8.36.

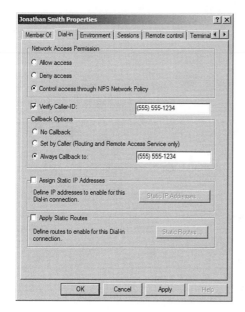

FIGURE 8.36
Modifying a user object's dial-in properties.

5. Modify the applicable properties, and then click OK.

Modify a User Object's Environment Properties

Scenario/Problem: Your company uses Terminal Services to provide remote desktop logon to servers. You need to ensure client drives are connected when users log on using Terminal Services.

Solution: Modify a user object's environment properties.

To modify a user object's environment properties, perform the following steps:

1. Log on to a domain controller or a member computer that has Windows Server 2008 RSAT installed.

2. Click Start, click Administrative Tools, and then click Active Directory Users and Computers.

3. In the details pane, right-click the user account you want to modify. Then click Properties.

4. Click the Environment tab, shown in Figure 8.37.

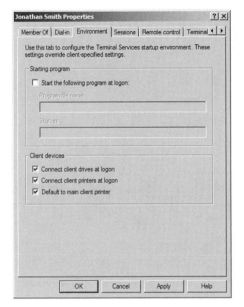

FIGURE 8.37

Modifying a user object's environment properties.

5. Modify the applicable properties, and then click OK.

Modify a User Object's Sessions Properties

Scenario/Problem: Your company uses Terminal Services to provide remote desktop logon to servers. You need to ensure that sessions that are disconnected are automatically ended after 30 minutes.

Solution: Modify a user object's session properties.

To modify a user object's sessions properties, perform the following steps:

1. Log on to a domain controller or a member computer that has Windows Server 2008 RSAT installed.

2. Click Start, click Administrative Tools, and then click Active Directory Users and Computers.

3. In the details pane, right-click the user account you want to modify and click Properties.

4. Click the Sessions tab, shown in Figure 8.38.

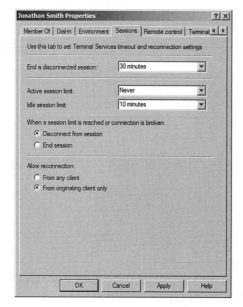

FIGURE 8.38
Modifying a user object's sessions properties.

5. Modify the applicable properties, and then click OK.

Modify a User Object's Remote Control Properties

Scenario/Problem: Your company uses Terminal Services to provide the help desk with the capability to log on to desktops using remote desktop. You need to ensure that the help desk is able to interact with the user's session.

Solution: Modify a user object's remote control properties.

To modify a user object's remote control properties, perform the following steps:

1. Log on to a domain controller or a member computer that has Windows Server 2008 RSAT installed.

2. Click Start, click Administrative Tools, and then click Active Directory Users and Computers.

3. In the details pane, right-click the user account you want to modify and click Properties.

4. Click the Remote Control tab, shown in Figure 8.39.

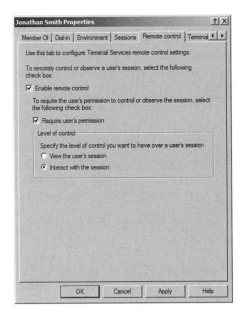

FIGURE 8.39
Modifying a user object's remote control
properties.

5. Modify the applicable properties; then click OK.

Modify a User Object's Terminal Services Properties

Scenario/Problem: Your company uses Terminal Services. You need to configure the Terminal Services profile for your employees.

Solution: Modify a user object's Terminal Services properties.

To modify a user object's Terminal Services properties, perform the following steps:

1. Log on to a domain controller or a member computer that has Windows Server 2008 RSAT installed.

2. Click Start, click Administrative Tools, and then click Active Directory Users and Computers.

3. In the details pane, right-click the user account you want to modify and click Properties.

4. Click the Terminal Services Profile tab, shown in Figure 8.40.

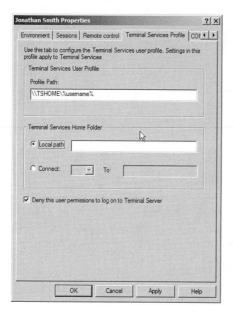

FIGURE 8.40
Modifying a user object's Terminal Services properties.

5. Modify the applicable properties, and then click OK.

Modify a User Object's COM+ Properties

Scenario/Problem: Your company has a COM+ partition set in AD DS. You need to associate users with a COM+ partition set.

Solution: Modify a user object's COM+ properties.

To modify a user object's COM+ properties, perform the following steps:

1. Log on to a domain controller or a member computer that has Windows Server 2008 RSAT installed.

2. Click Start, click Administrative Tools, and then click Active Directory Users and Computers.

3. In the details pane, right-click the user account you want to modify; then click Properties.

4. Click the COM+ tab, shown in Figure 8.41.

5. Modify the applicable properties, and then click OK.

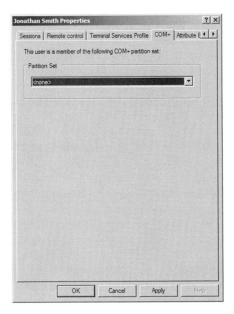

FIGURE 8.41
Modifying a user object's COM+ properties.

Modify a User Object's Published Certificates Properties

Scenario/Problem: Your company uses Active Directory Certificate Services to provide Encrypting File System (EFS) certificates to its employees. You need to view the certificates that are mapped to a particular user account.

Solution: Modify a user object's published certificates properties.

To modify a user object's published certificates properties, perform the following steps:

1. Log on to a domain controller or a member computer that has Windows Server 2008 RSAT installed.

2. Click Start, click Administrative Tools, and then click Active Directory Users and Computers.

3. Ensure that Advanced Features is selected in the View menu.

4. In the details pane, right-click the user account you want to modify and click Properties.

5. Click the Published Certificates tab, shown in Figure 8.42.

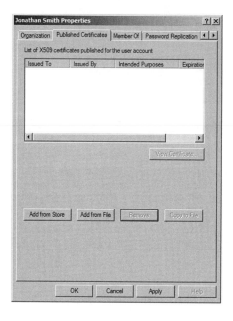

FIGURE 8.42
Modifying a user object's published certificates properties.

6. To add a certificate from the certificate store, click Add from Store, select the certificate to add in the Select Certificate window, shown in Figue 8.43, and then click OK.

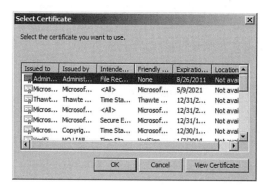

FIGURE 8.43
Adding a certificate from the store.

7. To add a certificate from a certificate file, click Add from File, select the certificate to add in the Add Certificate from a File window, shown in Figure 8.44, and then click OK.

8. To remove a certificate from a user object, select the certificate, and then click Remove. Click Yes in the Remove certificate confirmation window, shown in Figure 8.45.

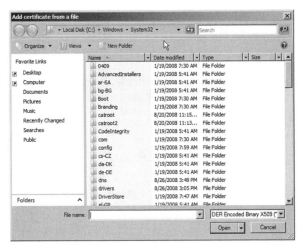

FIGURE 8.44
Adding a certificate from a file.

FIGURE 8.45
The Remove certificate confirmation.

9. To export a certificate, select the certificate and click Copy to file. On the Save certificate to a file window, shown in Figure 8.46, enter a name for the certificate file in the File name field, select whether to save the certificate as a DER Encoded Binary X509 or PKCS #7 file, and click Save.

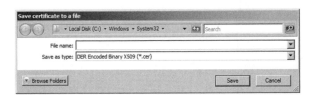

FIGURE 8.46
Exporting a certificate.

10. Click OK to save the changes.

View the Password Replication Policies Applied to a User Object

Scenario/Problem: Your company has a number of read-only domain controllers (RODCs). Each RODC caches passwords for certain employees. You need to determine which RODCs have cached a password for a particular employee.

Solution: View a user object's password replication properties.

To view the password replication properties applied to a user object, perform the following steps:

1. Log on to a domain controller or a member computer that has Windows Server 2008 RSAT installed.

2. Click Start, click Administrative Tools, and then click Active Directory Users and Computers.

3. Ensure that Advanced Features is selected in the View menu.

4. In the details pane, right-click the user account you want to view and click Properties.

5. Click the Password Replication tab.

6. The password replication policies that are applied to the user account are listed, as shown in Figure 8.47.

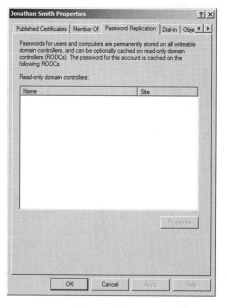

FIGURE 8.47

Viewing a user's password replication policies.

6. To view the properties of a password replication policy, select the password replication policy and click Properties.

7. Click OK to save the changes.

Modify a User Object's Protection from Deletion Properties

Scenario/Problem: You need to prevent user accounts from being accidently deleted from AD DS.

Solution: Modify a user object's accidental deletion properties.

To modify a user object's protection from deletion properties, perform the following steps:

1. Log on to a domain controller or a member computer that has Windows Server 2008 RSAT installed.

2. Click Start, click Administrative Tools, and then click Active Directory Users and Computers.

3. Ensure that Advanced Features is selected in the View menu.

4. In the details pane, right-click the user account you want to modify; then click Properties.

5. Click the Object tab, shown in Figure 8.48.

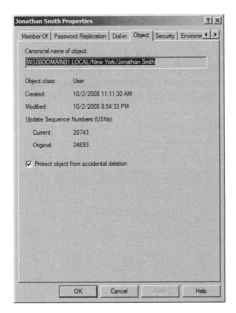

FIGURE 8.48

Modifying a user object's protection from deletion properties.

6. To protect a user object from accidental deletion, select Protect object from accidental deletion.

7. To unprotect a user object from accidental deletion, deselect Protect object from accidental deletion.

8. Click OK to save the changes.

Modify a User Object's Custom Attributes

Scenario/Problem: Your company has a number of custom attributes in its AD DS forest. You need to edit these attributes for a particular user account.

Solution: Modify a user object's custom attributes.

To modify a user object's custom attributes, perform the following steps:

1. Log on to a domain controller or a member computer that has Windows Server 2008 RSAT installed.

2. Click Start, click Administrative Tools, and then click Active Directory Users and Computers.

3. Ensure that Advanced Features is selected in the View menu.

4. In the details pane, right-click the user account you want to modify and click Properties.

5. Click the Attribute Editor tab, shown in Figure 8.49.

FIGURE 8.49
Modifying a user object's custom attributes.

6. Modify the applicable attributes, and then click OK.

Create a Group Object

Scenario/Problem: Your company has a number of applications that use AD DS groups for authorization. You need to create a new AD DS group that can be used by an application.

Solution: Create a group by using the Windows interface or the command line.

Create Group Object by Using the Windows Interface

To create a group object by using the Windows interface, perform the following steps:

1. Log on to a domain controller or a member computer that has Windows Server 2008 RSAT installed.

2. Click Start, click Administrative Tools, and then click Active Directory Users and Computers.

3. In the console tree, right-click the OU or container where you want to store the group object, click New, and click Group.

4. Type the name of the group in the Group name field, select the group scope, select the group type, as shown in Figure 8.50, and click OK.

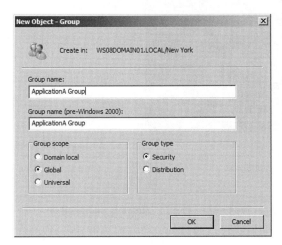

FIGURE 8.50

Creating a new group object by using the Windows interface.

TIP The Group name (pre-Windows 2000) field is automatically populated by the wizard. You can modify these fields if required.

Create Group Object by Using the Command Line

To create a group object by using the command line, perform the following steps:

1. Log on to a domain controller.

2. Click Start, and click Command Prompt.

3. In the Command Prompt window, type the following command and press Enter:

   ```
   dsadd group "CN=GroupA,CN=Users,DC=WS08DOMAIN01,DC=local" -secgrp
   Yes -scope g -samid GroupA
   ```

   Table 8.3 lists each parameter used in the previous command.

TABLE 8.3   **Parameters to Create Group Objects by Using the Command Line**

Parameter	Meaning
`"CN=GroupA,CN=Users,` `DC=WS08DOMAIN01,DC=local"`	Distinguished name
`-secgrp Yes`	Group will be a security group
`-scope g`	Group will be a global
`-samid GroupA`	The SAMID of the group (pre-Windows 2000 name)

4. Verify that the results of the dsadd command entered above returns dsadd succeeded, as shown in Figure 8.51.

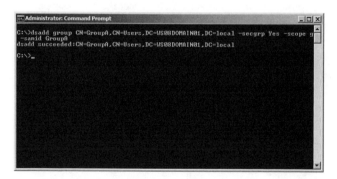

FIGURE 8.51
Creating a group object using the command line.

> **TIP**   For a full list of dsadd group parameters, go to http://technet.microsoft.com/
> en-us/library/cc754037.aspx.

Delete a Group Object

Scenario/Problem: Your company has a number of AD DS groups that are used for authorization. One of the AD DS groups is no longer required.

Solution: Delete the group by using the Windows interface or the command line.

Delete a Group Object by Using the Windows Interface

To delete a group object by using the Windows interface, perform the following steps:

1. Log on to a domain controller or a member computer that has Windows Server 2008 RSAT installed.

2. Click Start, click Administrative Tools, and then click Active Directory Users and Computers.

3. In the details pane, right-click the group object you want to delete and click Delete.

4. Click Yes on the confirmation page, shown in Figure 8.52.

FIGURE 8.52
Deleting a group object using the Windows interface.

Delete a Group Object by Using the Command Line

To delete a group object by using the command line, perform the following steps:

1. Log on to a domain controller.

2. Click Start, and click Command Prompt.

3. In the Command Prompt window, type the following command and press Enter:

   `Dsrm "CN=ApplicationA Group,CN=Users,DC=WS08DOMAIN01,DC=LOCAL"`

   (where `"CN=ApplicationA Group,CN=Users,DC=WS08DOMAIN01,DC=LOCAL"` is the distinguished name of the group you want to delete).

4. Type **Y** to confirm the deletion and press Enter.

TIP For a full list of dsrm parameters, go to http://technet.microsoft.com/en-us/library/cc731865.aspx.

5. Verify that the results of the dsrm command entered above returns dsrm succeeded, as shown in Figure 8.53.

FIGURE 8.53
Deleting a group object using the command line.

Rename a Group Object

Scenario/Problem: Your company has a group that was named incorrectly.

Solution: Rename the group by using the Windows interface or the command line.

Rename a Group Object by Using the Windows Interface

To rename a group object by using the Windows interface, perform the following steps:

1. Log on to a domain controller or a member computer that has Windows Server 2008 RSAT installed.

2. Click Start, click Administrative Tools, and then click Active Directory Users and Computers.

3. In the details pane, right-click the group object you want to rename and click Rename.

4. Type the new group name and press Enter.

5. On the Rename Group page, shown in Figure 8.54, modify the applicable name fields, and click OK.

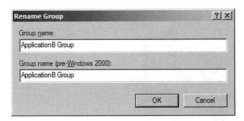

FIGURE 8.54
The Rename Group Wizard.

Rename a Group Object by Using the Command Line

To rename a group object by using the command line, perform the following steps:

1. Log on to a domain controller.

2. Click Start, and click Command Prompt.

NOTE Renaming a group object by using the command line is a two phase process. The first step uses the dsmod command to modify the applicable name attributes for the object. The second step uses the dsmove command to modify the distinguished name of the object.

3. In the Command Prompt window, type the following command and press Enter:

   `Dsmod group "CN=ApplicationA Group,CN=Users,DC=WS08DOMAIN01,DC=LOCAL" -samid "ApplicationB Group"`

   (where *"CN=ApplicationA Group,CN=Users,DC=WS08DOMAIN01,DC=LOCAL"* is the distinguished name of the group you want to rename and *"ApplicationB Group"* is the new name).

TIP For a full list of dsmod group parameters, go to http://technet.microsoft.com/en-us/library/cc732423.aspx.

4. Verify that the results of the dsmod command entered above returns dsmod succeeded, as shown in Figure 8.55.

5. In the command Prompt window, type the following command and press Enter:

   `Dsmove "CN=ApplicationA Group,CN=Users,DC=WS08DOMAIN01,DC=LOCAL" -newname "ApplicationB Group"`

   (where "CN=ApplicationA Group,CN=Users,DC=WS08DOMAIN01,DC=LOCAL" is the distinguished name of the group and "ApplicationB Group" is the new group name).

FIGURE 8.55
Modifying a group name using the command line.

6. Verify that the results of the dsmove command entered above returns dsmove
    succeeded, as shown in Figure 8.56.

> **TIP** For a full list of dsmove parameters, go to http://technet.microsoft.com/
> en-us/library/cc731094.aspx.

FIGURE 8.56
Renaming a group using the command line.

Move a Group Object

> **Scenario/Problem:** Your company's AD DS logical design uses OUs to group AD
> DS groups for administrative purposes. The management of a particular group is
> being moved to a different team.

Solution: Move an AD DS group account by using the Windows interface or the
command line.

Move a Group Object by Using the Windows Interface

To move a group object by using the Windows interface, perform the following steps:

1. Log on to a domain controller or a member computer that has Windows Server 2008 RSAT installed.

2. Click Start, click Administrative Tools, and then click Active Directory Users and Computers.

3. In the details pane, right-click the group object you want to move and click Move.

4. In the Move window, shown in Figure 8.57, select the OU or container to which you want to move the group object; then click OK.

FIGURE 8.57
The Move window.

Move a Group Object by Using the Command Line

To move a group object by using the command line, perform the following steps:

1. Log on to a domain controller.

2. Click Start, and click Command Prompt.

3. In the Command Prompt window, type the following command and press Enter:

```
Dsmove "CN=ApplicationA Group,CN=Users,DC=WS08DOMAIN01,DC=local"
-newparent "OU=New York,DC=WS08DOMAIN01,DC=LOCAL"
```

(where "CN=ApplicationA Group,CN=Users,DC=WS08DOMAIN01,DC=local" is the distinguished name of the group and "OU=New York,DC=WS08DOMANI01,DC=local" is the location to where you want to move the group).

4. Verify that the results of the dsmove command entered above returns dsmove succeeded, as shown in Figure 8.58.

> **TIP** For a full list of dsmove parameters, go to http://technet.microsoft.com/
> en-us/library/cc731094.aspx.

FIGURE 8.58
Moving a group using the command line.

Add a Group to a Group

> **Scenario/Problem:** Your company has a number of universal groups that are
> used to assign access to resources. You need to add a global group to one of
> these universal groups.

Solution: Add a group to a group by using the Windows Interface or the command
line.

Add a Group to a Group by Using the Windows Interface

To add a group to a group by using the Windows interface, perform the following
steps:

1. Log on to a domain controller or a member computer that has Windows Server
   2008 RSAT installed.

2. Click Start, click Administrative Tools, and then click Active Directory Users
   and Computers.

3. In the details pane, right-click the group object you want to add to a group and
   click Properties.

4. Click the Member Of tab.

5. Click Add.

6. On the Select Groups window, shown in Figure 8.59, browse to or type the name
   of the group to which you want to add the group; then click OK.

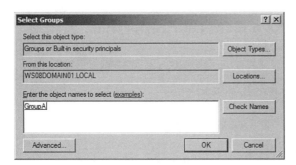

FIGURE 8.59
The Select Groups window.

Add a Group to a Group by Using the Command Line

To add a group to a group by using the command line, perform the following steps:

1. Log on to a domain controller.

2. Click Start, and click Command Prompt.

3. In the Command Prompt window, type the following command and press Enter:

   Dsmod group "CN=GroupA,CN=Users,DC=WS08DOMAIN01,DC=LOCAL" -addmbr "CN=ApplicationA Group,CN=Users,DC=WS08DOMAIN01,DC=LOCAL"

   (where "*CN=ApplicationA Group,CN=Users,DC=WS08DOMAIN01,DC=local*" is the distinguished name of the group and "*OU=New York,DC=WS08DOMANI01,DC=local*" is the location to which you want to move the group).

4. Verify that the results of the dsmod command entered above returns dsmod succeeded, as shown in Figure 8.60.

TIP For a full list of dsmod group parameters, go to http://technet.microsoft.com/en-us/library/cc732423.aspx.

FIGURE 8.60
Adding a group to a group using the command line.

Modify a Group Object's General Properties

Scenario/Problem: Your company uses the description field on AD DS group objects to identify to which business unit a group belongs.

Solution: Modify a group object's general properties.

To modify a group object's general properties, perform the following steps:

1. Log on to a domain controller or a member computer that has Windows Server 2008 RSAT installed.

2. Click Start, click Administrative Tools, and then click Active Directory Users and Computers.

3. In the details pane, right-click the group account you want to modify and click Properties.

4. Click the General tab, shown in Figure 8.61.

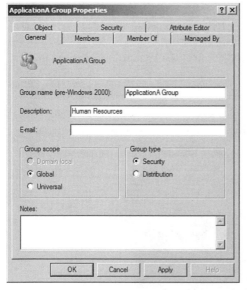

FIGURE 8.61
Modifying a group object's general properties.

5. Modify the applicable properties, and then click OK.

Modify a Group Object's Scope

Scenario/Problem: Your company uses AD DS groups for authorization. You need to ensure a group can contain users from all domains in your forest as members.

Solution: Modify a group object's scope.

To modify a group object's scope, perform the following steps:

1. Log on to a domain controller or a member computer that has Windows Server 2008 RSAT installed.

2. Click Start, click Administrative Tools, and then click Active Directory Users and Computers.

3. In the details pane, right-click the group account you want to modify and click Properties.

4. Click the General tab, shown in Figure 8.62.

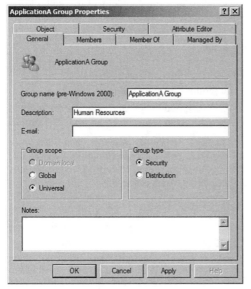

FIGURE 8.62
Modifying a group.

5. Select a group scope of Domain Local, Global, or Universal, as shown in Figure 8.63; then click OK.

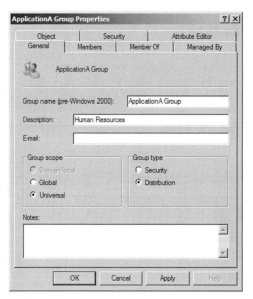

FIGURE 8.63
Modifying a group object's scope.

TIP The existing group scope dictates the scope that you can convert the group to. For example, if the existing group has a scope of Global, it can only be converted to a Universal group, which is why the Domain Local group scope option is not available in Figure 8.62. The following lists the group scope conversion paths:

The group scope for a group that has an existing group scope of Universal can be modified to Domain Local or Global. A Universal group can only be converted to a Global group if there are no other Universal groups as members.

The group scope for a group that has an existing group scope of Global can be modified to Universal. A Global group can only be converted to a Universal group if there are no other Global groups as members.

The group scope for a group that has an existing group scope of Domain Local can be modified to Universal. A Domain Local group can only be converted to a Universal group if there are no other Domain Local groups as members.

Modify a Group Object's Type

Scenario/Problem: Your company uses AD DS groups for authorization and email distribution lists. You need to ensure that a group can contain users to be used for email distribution and to apply security permissions.

Solution: Modify a group object's type.

To modify a group object's type, perform the following steps:

1. Log on to a domain controller or a member computer that has Windows Server 2008 RSAT installed.

2. Click Start, click Administrative Tools, and then click Active Directory Users and Computers.

3. In the details pane, right-click the group account you want to modify and click Properties.

4. Click the General tab.

5. Select a group type of Security or Distribution, as shown in Figure 8.63; then click OK.

Modify a Group Object's Members

Scenario/Problem: Your company uses AD DS groups for email distribution lists. You need to ensure that a particular user receives emails that are sent to the group.

Solution: Modify a group object's members.

To modify a group object's members, perform the following steps:

1. Log on to a domain controller or a member computer that has Windows Server 2008 RSAT installed.

2. Click Start, click Administrative Tools, and then click Active Directory Users and Computers.

3. In the details pane, right-click the group account you want to modify and click Properties.

4. Click the Members tab, shown in Figure 8.64.

5. To add a member to the group, click Add In the Select Users, Contacts, Computers, or Groups window, shown in Figure 8.65, type the name of the object you want to add and click OK.

6. To remove a member from a group, select the object in the Members tab click Remove, shown in Figure 8.66.

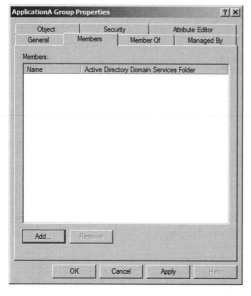

FIGURE 8.64
The group object Members tab.

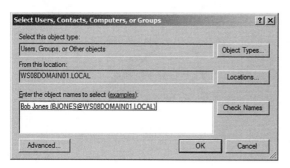

FIGURE 8.65
The Select Users, Contacts,
Computers, or Groups window.

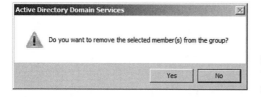

FIGURE 8.66
The Remove Member from Group confirmation.

7. Click Yes on the confirmation screen, shown in Figure 8.66, to remove the group
   member.

Modify a Group Object Managed By Properties

Scenario/Problem: Your company uses AD DS groups for email distribution. You need to assign owners to a group and grant them the ability to manage group membership by using Microsoft Office Outlook.

Solution: Modify a group object's Managed By properties.

To modify a group object's Managed By properties, perform the following steps:

1. Log on to a domain controller or a member computer that has Windows Server 2008 RSAT installed.

2. Click Start, click Administrative Tools, and then click Active Directory Users and Computers.

3. In the details pane, right-click the group account you want to modify and click Properties.

4. Click the Managed By tab, shown in Figure 8.7

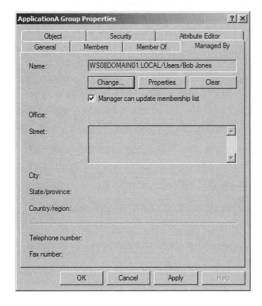

FIGURE 8.67
Modifying a group object's Managed By properties.

5. Click Change.

6. On the Select User, Contact, or Group window, type the name of the object you want to assign as the manager, and click OK.

7. To allow the manager to manage group membership, click the option Manager can update membership list, shown in Figure 8.68, and click OK.

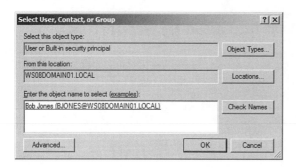

FIGURE 8.68
The Manager Can Update
Membership List check box.

Modify a Group Object Protection from Deletion

Scenario/Problem: You need to prevent group accounts from being accidently deleted from AD DS.

Solution: Modify a group object's accidental deletion properties.

To modify a group object's protection from deletion properties, perform the following steps:

1. Log on to a domain controller or a member computer that has Windows Server 2008 RSAT installed.

2. Click Start, click Administrative Tools, and then click Active Directory Users and Computers.

3. Ensure that Advanced Features is selected in the View menu.

4. In the details pane, right-click the group account you want to modify and click Properties.

5. Click the Object tab, shown in Figure 8.69.

6. To protect a group object from accidental deletion, select Protect object from accidental deletion.

7. To unprotect a group object from accidental deletion, deselect Protect object from accidental deletion.

8. Click OK to save the changes.

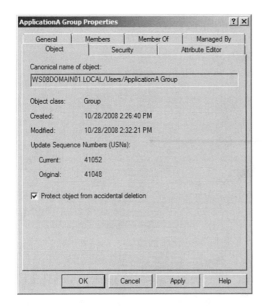

FIGURE 8.69
Modifying a group object's protection
from deletion properties.

Modify a Group Object's Custom Attributes

Scenario/Problem: Your company has a number of custom attributes in its AD
DS forest. You need to edit these attributes for a particular group account.

Solution: Modify a group object's custom attributes.

To modify a group object's custom attributes, perform the following steps:

1. Log on to a domain controller or a member computer that has Windows Server
   2008 RSAT installed.

2. Click Start, click Administrative Tools, and then click Active Directory Users
   and Computers.

3. Ensure that Advanced Features is selected in the View menu.

4. In the details pane, right-click the group account you want to modify and click
   Properties.

5. Click the Attribute Editor tab, shown in Figure 8.70.

6. Modify the applicable attributes, and then click OK.

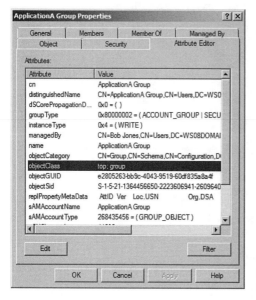

FIGURE 8.70
Modifying a group object's custom attributes.

Create a Computer Object

Scenario/Problem: Your company pre-creates computer objects in AD DS to allow nonadministrator users to join the computers to the domain.

Solution: Create a computer object by using the Windows interface or the command line.

Create a Computer Object by Using the Windows Interface

To create a computer object by using the Windows interface, perform the following steps:

1. Log on to a domain controller or a member computer that has Windows Server 2008 RSAT installed.

2. Click Start, click Administrative Tools, and then click Active Directory Users and Computers.

3. In the console tree, right-click the OU or container where you want to store the computer object, click New, and click Computer.

4. Type the name of the computer in the Computer name field, as shown in Figure 8.71.

FIGURE 8.71
Creating a new computer object using the Windows interface.

TIP The Computer name (pre-Windows 2000) field is automatically populated by the wizard. You can modify this field if required.

5. If you want to permit someone other than the Domain Admins group to join the computer to AD DS, click the Change button.

6. In the Select User or Group window, shown in Figure 8.72, type the name of the user or group you want to permit to join this computer to the domain, and click OK.

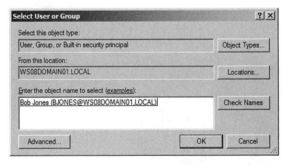

FIGURE 8.72
Select User or Group window.

7. If the computer account is pre-Windows 2000, select the Assign this computer account as a pre-Windows 2000 computer option, as shown in Figure 8.73; then click OK.

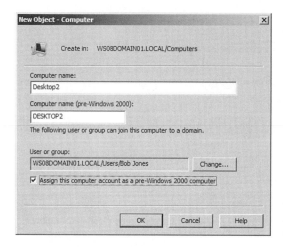

FIGURE 8.73
The Assign This Computer Account as a Pre-Windows 2000 Computer option.

Create a Computer Object by Using the Command Line

To create a computer object by using the command line, perform the following steps:

1. Log on to a domain controller.

2. Click Start, and click Command Prompt.

3. In the Command Prompt window, type the following command and press Enter:

   dsadd computer "CN=Client01,CN=Computers,DC=WS08DOMAIN01,DC=local"

   (where *"CN=Client01,CN=Computers,DC=WS08DOMAIN01,DC=local"* is the distinguished name of the new computer object).

4. Verify that the results of the dsadd command entered above returns dsadd succeeded, as shown in Figure 8.74.

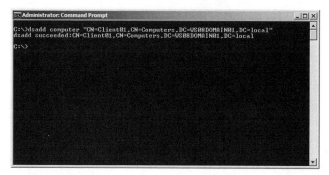

FIGURE 8.74
Creating a computer object using the command line.

> **TIP** For a full list of dsadd computer parameters, go to
> http://technet.microsoft.com/en-us/library/cc754539.aspx.

Delete a Computer Object

> **Scenario/Problem:** A computer experienced a hardware failure and will not be repaired.

Solution: Delete the computer object by using the Windows interface or the command line.

Delete a Computer Object by Using the Windows Interface

To delete a computer object by using the Windows interface, perform the following steps:

1. Log on to a domain controller or a member computer that has Windows Server 2008 RSAT installed.

2. Click Start, click Administrative Tools, and then click Active Directory Users and Computers.

3. In the details pane, right-click the computer object you want to delete and click Delete.

4. On the confirmation screen to delete the computer object, shown in Figure 8.75, click Yes.

FIGURE 8.75
The confirmation to delete a computer account.

Delete a Computer Object by Using the Command Line

To delete a computer object by using the command line, perform the following steps:

1. Log on to a domain controller.

2. Click Start, and click Command Prompt.

3. In the Command Prompt window, type the following command and press Enter:

   `Dsrm "CN=Client01,CN=Computers,DC=WS08DOMAIN01,DC=LOCAL"`

   (where "`CN=Client01,CN=Computers,DC=WS08DOMAIN01,DC=local`" is the distinguished name of the computer object you want to delete).

4. Enter **Y** to confirm the deletion and press Enter.

5. Verify that the results of the `dsrm` command entered above returns `dsrm` succeeded, as shown in Figure 8.76.

FIGURE 8.76
Deleting a computer object using the command line.

> **TIP**   For a full list of `dsrm` computer parameters, go to
> http://technet.microsoft.com/en-us/library/cc731865.aspx.

Move a Computer Object

> **Scenario/Problem:** Your company's AD DS logical design uses OUs to group AD DS computers for group policy purposes. A computer object needs to be moved to an OU that has a different GPO.

Solution: Move an AD DS computer account by using the Windows interface or the command line.

Move a Computer Object by Using the Windows Interface

To move a computer object by using the Windows interface, perform the following steps:

1. Log on to a domain controller or a member computer that has Windows Server 2008 RSAT installed.

2. Click Start, click Administrative Tools, and then click Active Directory Users and Computers.

3. In the details pane, right-click the computer object you want to move and click Move.

4. On the Move window, shown in Figure 8.77, select the OU or container to which you want to move the computer object; then click OK.

FIGURE 8.77
The Move window.

Move a Computer Object by Using the Command Line

To move a computer object by using the command line, perform the following steps:

1. Log on to a domain controller.

2. Click Start, and click Command Prompt.

3. In the Command Prompt window, type the following command and press Enter:

```
Dsmove "CN=Desktop1,CN=Computers,DC=WS08DOMAIN01,DC=LOCAL"
-newparent "OU=New York,DC=WS08DOMAIN01,DC=LOCAL"
```

(where "*CN=Desktop1,CN=Computers,DC=WS08DOMAIN01,DC=LOCAL*" is the distinguished name of the computer and "*OU=New York,DC=WS08DOMANI01,DC=local*" is the location to which you want to move the computer).

4. Verify that the results of the dsmove command entered above returns dsmove succeeded, as shown in Figure 8.78.

> **TIP** For a full list of dsmove parameters, go to http://technet.microsoft.com/en-us/library/cc731094.aspx.

FIGURE 8.78
Moving a computer using the command line.

Add a Computer to a Group

Scenario/Problem: Your company uses AD DS groups to filter the application of GPOs on computers.

Solution: Add a computer account to a group using the Windows interface or the command line.

Add a Computer to a Group by Using the Windows Interface

To add a computer object to a group by using the Windows interface, perform the following steps:

1. Log on to a domain controller or a member computer that has Windows Server 2008 RSAT installed.

2. Click Start, click Administrative Tools, and then click Active Directory Users and Computers.

3. In the details pane, right-click the computer object you want to add to the group and click Add to a group.

4. In the Select Groups window, shown in Figure 8.79, enter the name of the group to which you want to add the user, click Check Names, and click OK.

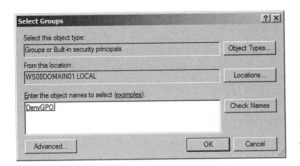

FIGURE 8.79
Adding a computer to a group
using the Windows interface.

Add a Computer to a Group by Using the Command Line

To add a computer object to a group by using the command line, perform the following steps:

1. Log on to a domain controller.

2. Click Start, and click Command Prompt.

3. In the Command Prompt window, type the following command and press Enter:

   Dsmod group "CN=DenyGPO,CN=Users,DC=WS08DOMAIN01,DC=LOCAL" -addmbr
   "CN=Desktop1,CN=Computers,DC=WS08DOMAIN01,DC=LOCAL"

   (WHERE *"CN=DenyGPO,CN=Users,DC=WS08DOMAIN01,DC=LOCAL"* is the distinguished name of the group and
   "CN=Desktop1,CN=Computers,DC=WS08DOMAIN01,DC=LOCAL" is the distinguished name of the computer you want to add to the group).

4. Verify that the results of the dsmod group command entered above returns dsmod succeeded, as shown in Figure 8.80.

TIP For a full list of dsmod group parameters, go to
http://technet.microsoft.com/en-us/library/cc732423.aspx.

FIGURE 8.80
Adding a computer to a group using the command line.

Disable a Computer Object

Scenario/Problem: You need to prevent users on a particular computer from logging on to AD DS.

Solution: Disable a computer account by using the Windows interface or the command line.

Disable a Computer Object by Using the Windows Interface

To disable a computer object by using the Windows interface, perform the following steps:

1. Log on to a domain controller or a member computer that has Windows Server 2008 RSAT installed.

2. Click Start, click Administrative Tools, and then click Active Directory Users and Computers.

3. In the details pane, right-click the computer object you want to disable and click Disable Account.

4. On the confirmation screen to disable the computer account, shown in Figure 8.81, click Yes.

FIGURE 8.81
Disabling a computer object using the Windows interface.

Disable a Computer Object by Using the Command Line

To disable a computer object by using the command line, perform the following steps:

1. Log on to a domain controller.

2. Click Start, and click Command Prompt.

3. In the Command Prompt window, type the following command and press Enter:

   `Dsmod computer "CN=Desktop1,CN=Computers,DC=WS08DOMAIN01,DC=LOCAL" -disabled yes`

   (where `"CN=Desktop1,CN=Computers,DC=WS08DOMAIN01,DC=LOCAL"` is the distinguished name of the computer that you want to disable).

4. Verify that the results of the dsmod computer command entered above returns dsmod succeeded, as shown in Figure 8.82.

TIP For a full list of dsmod computer parameters, go to
http://technet.microsoft.com/en-us/library/cc753733.aspx.

FIGURE 8.82
Disabling a computer object using the command line.

Enable a Computer Object

Scenario/Problem: You previously disabled a computer account and you need to allow users on that particular computer to log on to AD DS.

Solution: Enable a computer account by using the Windows interface or the command line.

Enable a Computer Object by Using the Windows Interface

To enable a computer object by using the Windows interface, perform the following steps:

1. Log on to a domain controller or a member computer that has Windows Server 2008 RSAT installed.

2. Click Start, click Administrative Tools, and then click Active Directory Users and Computers.

3. In the details pane, right-click the computer object you want to disable and click Enable Account.

4. Verify the computer account was enabled, as shown in Figure 8.83, and click OK.

FIGURE 8.83
Enabling a computer object using the Windows interface.

Enable a Computer Object by Using the Command Line

To enable a computer object by using the command line, perform the following steps:

1. Log on to a domain controller.

2. Click Start, and click Command Prompt.

3. In the Command Prompt window, type the following command and press Enter:

   `Dsmod computer "CN=Desktop1,CN=Computers,DC=WS08DOMAIN01,DC=LOCAL"`
   `-disabled no`

   (where `"CN=Desktop1,CN=Computers,DC=WS08DOMAIN01,DC=LOCAL"` is the distinguished name of the computer you want to disable).

4. Verify that the results of the dsmod computer command entered above returns dsmod succeeded, as shown in Figure 8.84.

> **TIP** For a full list of dsmod computer parameters, go to
> http://technet.microsoft.com/en-us/library/cc753733.aspx.

FIGURE 8.84
Enabling a computer object using the command line.

Modify a Computer Object's General Properties

Scenario/Problem: Your company uses the description field on AD DS computer objects to identify to which business unit a computer belongs.

Solution: Modify a computer object's general properties.

To modify a computer object's general properties, perform the following steps:

1. Log on to a domain controller or a member computer that has Windows Server 2008 RSAT installed.

2. Click Start, click Administrative Tools, and then click Active Directory Users and Computers.

3. In the details pane, right-click the computer account you want to modify and click Properties.

4. Click the General tab, shown in Figure 8.85.

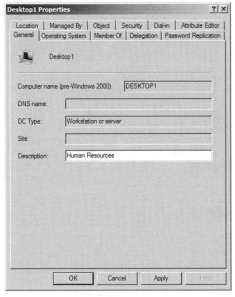

FIGURE 8.85
Modifying a computer object's general properties.

5. Modify the applicable properties, and then click OK.

View a Computer Object's Operating System Properties

Scenario/Problem: You need to determine the operating system and service pack that is installed on a particular computer.

Solution: View a computer object's operating system properties.

To view a computer object's operating system properties, perform the following steps:

1. Log on to a domain controller or a member computer that has Windows Server 2008 RSAT installed.

2. Click Start, click Administrative Tools, and then click Active Directory Users and Computers.

3. In the details pane, right-click the computer account you want to modify and click Properties.

4. Click the Operating System tab, shown in Figure 8.86.

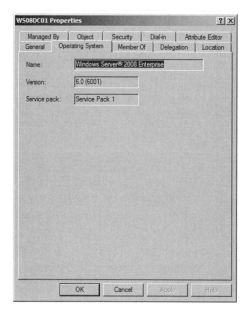

FIGURE 8.86
Viewing a computer object's operating system properties.

5. View the operating system properties and click OK.

Modify a Computer Object's Delegation Properties

Scenario/Problem: Your company has an application that uses Kerberos delegation.

Solution: Modify a computer object's delegation properties.

To modify a computer object's delegation properties, perform the following steps:

1. Log on to a domain controller or a member computer that has Windows Server 2008 RSAT installed.

2. Click Start, click Administrative Tools, and then click Active Directory Users and Computers.

3. In the details pane, right-click the computer account you want to modify and click Properties.

4. Click the Delegation tab, shown in Figure 8.87.

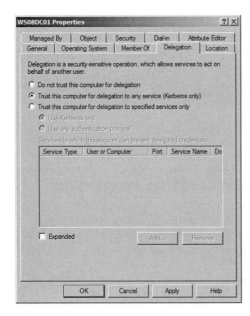

FIGURE 8.87
Modifying a computer object's delegation properties.

5. Modify the applicable properties, and then click OK.

View the Password Replication Policies Applied to a Computer Object

Scenario/Problem: Your company has a number of RODCs. Each RODC caches passwords. You need to determine which RODCs have cached a password for a particular computer.

Solution: View a computers object's password replication properties.

To view the password replication policies applied to a computer object, perform the following steps:

1. Log on to a domain controller or a member computer that has Windows Server 2008 RSAT installed.

2. Click Start, click Administrative Tools, and then click Active Directory Users and Computers.

3. In the details pane, right-click the computer account you want to view; then click Properties.

4. Click the Password Replication tab.

5. The password replication policies that are applied to the computer account are listed.

6. To view the properties of a password replication policy, select the password replication policy and click Properties.

7. Click OK to save the changes.

Modify a Computer Object's Location Properties

Scenario/Problem: Your company stores the physical locations of computer objects in AD DS. You need to configure the location for a particular computer.

Solution: Modify a computer object's location properties.

To modify a computer object's location properties, perform the following steps:

1. Log on to a domain controller or a member computer that has Windows Server 2008 RSAT installed.

2. Click Start, click Administrative Tools, and then click Active Directory Users and Computers.

3. In the details pane, right-click the computer account you want to view and click Properties.

4. Click the Location tab, shown in Figure 8.88.

5. Enter the location into the Location field; then click OK.

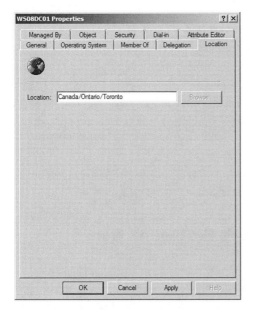

FIGURE 8.88
Modifying a computer object's location properties.

Modify a Computer Object's Managed By Properties

Scenario/Problem: Your company needs to record which IT administrator is responsible for the support of a particular computer.

Solution: Modify a computer object's Managed By properties.

To modify a computer object's Managed By properties, perform the following steps:

1. Log on to a domain controller or a member computer that has Windows Server 2008 RSAT installed.

2. Click Start, click Administrative Tools, and then click Active Directory Users and Computers.

3. In the details pane, right-click the computer account you want to modify and click Properties.

4. Click the Managed By tab.

5. Click Change.

6. On the Select User, Contact, or Group window, shown in Figure 8.89, type the name of the object you want to assign as the manager and click OK.

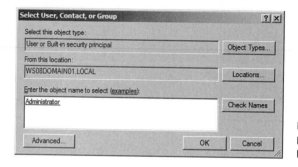

FIGURE 8.89
Modifying a computer object's Managed By properties.

7. Click OK.

Modify a Computer Object's Protection from Deletion

Scenario/Problem: You need to prevent computer accounts from being accidently deleted from AD DS.

Solution: Modify a computer object's accidental deletion properties.

To modify a computer object's protection from deletion properties, perform the following steps:

1. Log on to a domain controller or a member computer that has Windows Server 2008 RSAT installed.

2. Click Start, click Administrative Tools, and then click Active Directory Users and Computers.

3. Ensure that Advanced Features is selected in the View menu.

4. In the details pane, right-click the computer account you want to modify and click Properties.

5. Click the Object tab, shown in Figure 8.90.

6. To protect a computer object from accidental deletion, select Protect object from accidental deletion.

7. To unprotect a computer object from accidental deletion, deselect Protect object from accidental deletion.

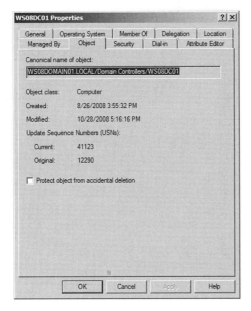

FIGURE 8.90
Modifying a computer object's protection from deletion properties.

8. Click OK to save the changes.

Modify a Computer Object's Custom Attributes

Scenario/Problem: Your company has a number of custom attributes in its AD DS forest. You need to edit these attributes for a particular computer account.

Solution: Modify a computer object's custom attributes.

To modify a computer object's custom attributes, perform the following steps:

1. Log on to a domain controller or a member computer that has Windows Server 2008 RSAT installed.

2. Click Start, click Administrative Tools, and then click Active Directory Users and Computers.

3. Ensure that Advanced Features is selected in the View menu.

4. In the details pane, right-click the computer account you want to modify and click Properties.

5. Click the Attribute Editor tab, shown in Figure 8.91.

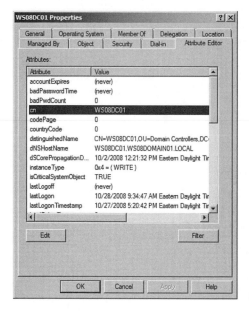

FIGURE 8.91
Modifying a computer object's custom attributes.

6. Modify the applicable attributes, and then click OK.

Create an Organizational Unit

Scenario/Problem: Your company uses OUs to group objects based on their physical locations. Your company is opening a new office in Boston.

Solution: Create an OU by using the Windows interface or the command line.

Create an Organizational Unit by Using the Windows Interface

To create an OU by using the Windows interface, perform the following steps:

1. Log on to a domain controller or a member computer that has Windows Server 2008 RSAT installed.

2. Click Start, click Administrative Tools, and then click Active Directory Users and Computers.

3. In the console tree, right-click the domain or OU where want to store the OU, click New, and click OU.

4. Type the name of the OU in the Name field, as shown in Figure 8.92.

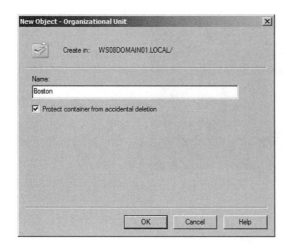

FIGURE 8.92
Creating a new OU using the
Windows interface.

5. If you do not want to protect the OU against accidental deletions, uncheck the Protect container from accidental deletions option and click OK.

Create an Organizational Unit by Using the Command Line

To create an OU by using the command line, perform the following steps:

1. Log on to a domain controller.

2. Click Start, and click Command Prompt.

3. In the Command Prompt window, type the following command and press Enter:

   Dsadd OU "OU=Boston,DC=WS08DOMAIN01,DC=local"

   (where "*OU=Boston,DC=WS08DOMAIN01,DC=local*" is the distinguished name of the new OU).

4. Verify that the results of the dsadd command entered above returns dsadd succeeded, as shown in Figure 8.93.

> **TIP** For a full list of dsadd OU parameters, go to http://technet.microsoft.com/en-us/library/cc770883.aspx.

FIGURE 8.93
Creating an OU using the command line.

Delete an Organizational Unit

Scenario/Problem: Your company has an empty OU that is no longer required.

Solution: Delete an OU by using the Windows interface or the command line.

Delete an Organizational Unit by Using the Windows Interface

To delete an OU by using the Windows interface, perform the following steps:

1. Log on to a domain controller or a member computer that has Windows Server 2008 RSAT installed.

2. Click Start, click Administrative Tools, and then click Active Directory Users and Computers.

3. In the console tree, right-click the OU you want to delete and select Delete.

4. On the confirmation screen to delete the OU, shown in Figure 8.94, click Yes.

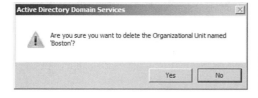

FIGURE 8.94
Deleting an OU using the Windows interface.

Deleting OUs in Windows Server 2008

In Windows Server 2008, the option to protect an OU from accidental deletion is selected by default when the OU is created using Active Directory Users and Computers. If you need to delete an OU, you must ensure that the object is not protected from accidental deletion before it can be deleted.

Delete an Organizational Unit by Using the Command Line

To delete an OU by using the command line, perform the following steps:

1. Log on to a domain controller.

2. Click Start, and click Command Prompt.

3. In the Command Prompt window, type the following command and press Enter:

   `Dsrm "OU=Boston,DC=WS08DOMAIN01,DC=local"`

   (where `"OU=Boston,DC=WS08DOMAIN01,DC=local"` is the distinguished name of the OU you want to delete).

4. Type **Y** on the confirmation to delete the OU and press Enter.

5. Verify that the results of the dsrm command entered above returns dsrm succeeded, as shown in Figure 8.95.

FIGURE 8.95
Deleting an OU using the command line.

TIP   For a full list of dsrm OU parameters, go to http://technet.microsoft.com/en-us/library/cc731865.aspx.

Rename an Organizational Unit

Scenario/Problem: Your company has an OU that was named incorrectly.

Solution: Rename the OU by using the Windows Interface or the command line.

Rename an Organizational Unit by Using the Windows Interface

To rename an OU by using the Windows interface, perform the following steps:

1. Log on to a domain controller or a member computer that has Windows Server 2008 RSAT installed.

2. Click Start, click Administrative Tools, and then click Active Directory Users and Computers.

3. In the console tree, right-click the OU you want to rename and click Rename.

4. Type the new OU name and press Enter.

Rename an Organizational Unit by Using the Command Line

To rename an OU by using the command line, perform the following steps:

1. Log on to a domain controller.

2. Click Start, and click Command Prompt.

3. In the Command Prompt window, type the following command and press Enter:

   `Dsmove  "OU=Boston,DC=WS08DOMAIN01,DC=LOCAL" -newname "Boston Users"`

   (where `"OU=Boston,DC=WS08DOMAIN01,DC=LOCAL"` is the distinguished name of the OU and `"Boston Users"` is the new OU name).

4. Verify that the results of the dsmove command entered above returns dsmove succeeded, as shown in Figure 8.96.

TIP For a full list of dsmove parameters, go to http://technet.microsoft.com/en-us/library/cc731094.aspx.

FIGURE 8.96
Renaming an OU using the command line.

Move an Organizational Unit

Scenario/Problem: Your company is restructuring its AD DS logical design and requires OUs to be nested under other OUs.

Solution: Move an OU by using the Windows interface or the command line.

Move an Organizational Unit by Using the Windows Interface

To move an OU by using the Windows interface, perform the following steps:

1. Log on to a domain controller or a member computer that has Windows Server 2008 RSAT installed.

2. Click Start, click Administrative Tools, and then click Active Directory Users and Computers.

3. In the console tree, right-click the OU you want to move and click Move.

4. On the Move window, select the location where you want to move the OU object; then click OK, shown in Figure 8.97

Move an Organizational Unit Object by Using the Command Line

1. Log on to a domain controller.

2. Click Start, and click Command Prompt.

FIGURE 8.97
The Move window.

3. In the Command Prompt window, type the following command and press Enter:

Dsmove "OU=Boston,DC=WS08DOMAIN01,DC=LOCAL" -newparent
"OU=US,DC=WS08DOMAIN01,DC=LOCAL"

(where *"OU=Boston,DC=WS08DOMAIN01,DC=LOCAL"* is the distinguished name
of the OU to move and *"OU=US,DC=WS08DOMAIN01,DC=LOCAL"* is the location
to which you want to move the OU).

4. Verify that the results of the dsmove command entered above returns dsmove
succeeded, as shown in Figure 8.98

TIP   For a full list of dsmove parameters, go to http://technet.microsoft.com/
en-us/library/cc731094.aspx.

FIGURE 8.98
Moving an OU using the command line.

Modify an Organizational Unit's General Properties

Scenario/Problem: Your company uses the description field on AD DS OUs to identify to which business unit an OU belongs.

Solution: Modify the general properties on an OU.

To modify an OU's general properties, perform the following steps:

1. Log on to a domain controller or a member computer that has Windows Server 2008 RSAT installed.

2. Click Start, click Administrative Tools, and then click Active Directory Users and Computers.

3. In the console tree, right-click the OU account you want to modify and click Properties.

4. Click the General tab, shown in Figure 8.99.

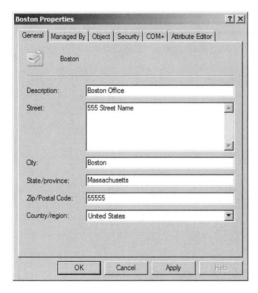

FIGURE 8.99
Modifying an OU's general properties.

5. Modify the applicable properties, and then click OK.

Modify an Organizational Unit's Managed By Properties

Scenario/Problem: Your company needs to record which IT administrator is responsible for the support of a particular OU.

Solution: Modify the Managed By properties on an OU.

To modify an OU's Managed By properties, perform the following steps:

1. Log on to a domain controller or a member computer that has Windows Server 2008 RSAT installed.

2. Click Start, click Administrative Tools, and then click Active Directory Users and Computers.

3. In the console tree, right-click the OU you want to modify and click Properties.

4. Click the Managed By tab.

5. Click Change.

6. On the Select User, Contact, or Group window, shown in Figure 8.100, type the name of the object you want to assign as the manager; then click OK.

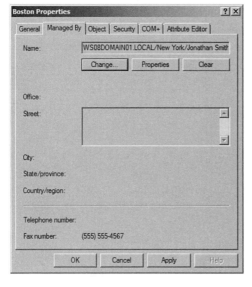

FIGURE 8.100
Modifying an OU's Managed By properties.

Modify an Organizational Unit's COM+ Properties

Scenario/Problem: Your company has a COM+ partition set in AD DS. You need to associate OUs with a COM+ partition set.

Solution: Modify the COM+ properties on an OU.

To modify an OU's COM+ properties, perform the following steps:

1. Log on to a domain controller or a member computer that has Windows Server 2008 RSAT installed.

2. Click Start, click Administrative Tools, and then click Active Directory Users and Computers.

3. In the console tree, right-click the OU you want to modify and click Properties.

4. Click the COM+ tab, as shown in Figure 8.101.

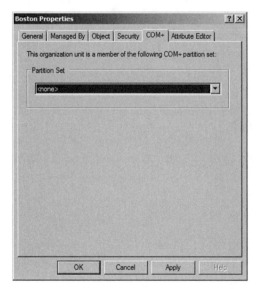

FIGURE 8.101
Modifying an OU's COM+ properties.

5. Modify the applicable properties, and then click OK.

Modify an Organizational Unit's Protection from Deletion

Scenario/Problem: You need to prevent OUs from being accidently deleted from AD DS.

Solution: Modify the accidental deletion properties on an OU.

To modify an OU's protection from deletion properties, perform the following steps:

1. Log on to a domain controller or a member computer that has Windows Server 2008 RSAT installed.

2. Click Start, click Administrative Tools, and then click Active Directory Users and Computers.

3. Ensure that Advanced Features is selected in the View menu.

4. In the console tree, right-click the OU you want to modify and click Properties.

5. Click the Object tab, shown in Figure 8.102.

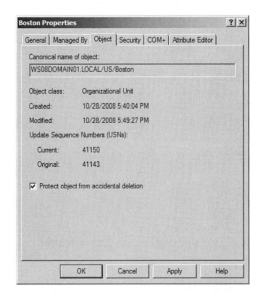

FIGURE 8.102

Modifying an OU's protection from deletion properties.

6. To protect an OU from accidental deletion, select Protect Object from Accidental Deletion.

7. To unprotect an OU from accidental deletion, deselect Protect Object from Accidental Deletion.

8. Click OK to save the changes.

Modify an Organizational Unit's Custom Attributes

Scenario/Problem: Your company has a number of custom attributes in its AD DS forest. You need to edit these attributes for a particular OU.

Solution: Modify custom attributes on an OU.

To modify an OU's custom attributes, perform the following steps:

1. Log on to a domain controller or a member computer that has Windows Server 2008 RSAT installed.

2. Click Start, click Administrative Tools, and then click Active Directory Users and Computers.

3. Ensure that Advanced Features is selected in the View menu.

4. In the console tree, right-click the computer account you want to modify and click Properties.

5. Click the Attribute Editor tab, shown in Figure 8.103.

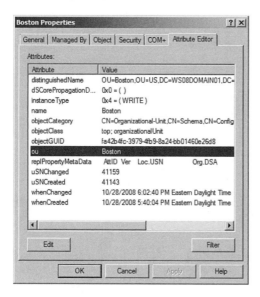

FIGURE 8.103
Modifying an OU's custom attributes.

6. Modify the applicable attributes, and then click OK.

CHAPTER 9

Manage Group Policy

▶ Change the Order of Group Policy Object Links

▶ Filter Group Policy Object Scope by Using Security Groups

▶ Disable User Settings in a Group Policy Object

▶ Disable Computer Settings in a Group Policy Object

▶ Create a WMI Filter

▶ Import a WMI Filter

▶ Export a WMI Filter

▶ Copy a WMI Filter

▶ Link a WMI Filter to a Group Policy Object

▶ Determine a Resultant Set of Policy

▶ Simulate a Resultant Set of Policy Using Group Policy Modeling

▶ Delegate Permissions on a Group Policy Object

▶ Modify Delegated Permissions on a Group Policy Object

▶ Remove Delegated Permissions on a Group Policy Object

▶ Delegate Permissions to Link Group Policy Objects

▶ Modify Delegated Permissions to Link Group Policy Objects

▶ Remove Delegated Permissions to Link Group Policy Objects

▶ Delegate Permissions for Generating Group Policy Modeling Data

▶ Modify Delegated Permissions for Generating Group Policy Modeling Data

▶ Remove Delegated Permissions for Generating Group Policy Modeling Data

▶ Delegate Permissions for Generating Group Policy Results

▶ Modify Delegated Permissions for Generating Group Policy Results

▶ Remove Delegated Permissions for Generating Group Policy Results

▶ Delegate Permissions for WMI Filters

▶ Modify Delegated Permissions for WMI Filters

▶ Remove Delegated Permissions for WMI Filters

Group policy, when used in conjunction with Active Directory Domain Services (AD DS), enables automated management of multiple computers and users. Group policy can be applied to an AD DS site, a domain, or a range of organizational units (OUs). Group policy can be used to implement security settings, enforce IT policies, and implement software distribution.

This chapter describes the steps required to manage group policy.

Create Group Policy Objects

Scenario/Problem: You need to enforce consistent security settings across a number of member servers.

Solution: Create a group policy object (GPO).

To create a group policy object, perform the following steps:

1. Log on to a domain controller or a member computer that has Windows Server 2008 Remote Server Administration Tools (RSAT) installed.

2. Click Start, click Administrative Tools, and then click Group Policy Management.

3. In the console tree, navigate to the domain where you want to create the GPO, right-click the Group Policy Objects node, and click New.

4. In the New GPO window, shown in Figure 9.1, type a name for the GPO in the Name field and click OK.

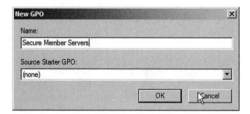

FIGURE 9.1
The New GPO window.

Delete Group Policy Objects

Scenario/Problem: You previously used a GPO to apply security settings. The GPO is no longer required.

Solution: Delete a GPO.

To delete a group policy object, perform the following steps:

1. Log on to a domain controller or a member computer that has Windows Server 2008 RSAT installed.

2. Click Start, click Administrative Tools, and then click Group Policy Management.

3. In the console tree, navigate to the domain that contains the GPO to delete; then select Group Policy Objects.

4. Right-click the GPO you want to delete, and select Delete.

5. Select Yes to confirm the deletion of the GPO on the confirmation window shown in Figure 9.2.

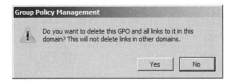

Group Policy Management

Do you want to delete this GPO and all links to it in this domain? This will not delete links in other domains.

Yes   No

FIGURE 9.2
The confirmation to delete a GPO.

Create Starter GPOs

Scenario/Problem: Your company needs a baseline GPO that can be used to create incremental GPOs in your forest.

Solution: Create a starter GPO.

To create a starter GPO, perform the following steps:

1. Log on to a domain controller or a member computer that has Windows Server 2008 RSAT installed.

2. Click Start, click Administrative Tools, and then click Group Policy Management.

3. In the console tree, navigate to the domain in which you want to create the starter GPO, and select the Starter GPOs node.

4. If you have not previously created starter GPOs in this domain, you need to first create the Starter GPOs folder in the domain. In the details pane, click Create Starter GPOs Folder, shown in Figure 9.3.

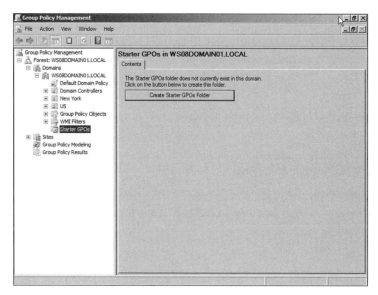

FIGURE 9.3
The Create Starter GPOs Folder button.

5. Right-click the Starter GPOs node in the console tree, and select New.

6. In the New Starter GPO window, shown in Figure 9.4, type a name for the starter GPO in the Name field; then click OK.

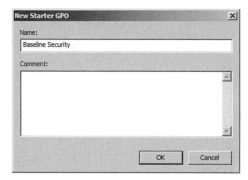

FIGURE 9.4
The New Starter GPO window.

Delete Starter GPOs

Scenario/Problem: Your company previously created a starter GPO that is no longer required.

Solution: Delete a starter GPO.

To delete a starter GPO, perform the following steps:

1. Log on to a domain controller or a member computer that has Windows Server 2008 RSAT installed.

2. Click Start, click Administrative Tools, and then click Group Policy Management.

3. In the console tree, navigate to the domain in which you want to delete the starter GPO, and select the Starter GPOs node.

4. Right-click the starter GPOs you want to delete, and click Delete.

5. Click OK to confirm the deletion of the GPO, shown in Figure 9.5.

FIGURE 9.5
Deleting a starter GPO.

Create a New Group Policy Object from a Starter GPO

Scenario/Problem: Your company has a number of starter GPOs. You need to create a new GPO that is derived from a starter GPO.

Solution: Create a new GPO from a starter GPO.

To create a new GPO from a starter GPO, perform the following steps:

1. Log on to a domain controller or a member computer that has Windows Server 2008 RSAT installed.

2. Click Start, click Administrative Tools, and then click Group Policy Management.

3. In the console tree, navigate to the domain where you want to create the GPO, right-click the Group Policy Objects node, and click New.

4. In the New GPO window, shown in Figure 9.6, type a name for the GPO in the Name field.

5. In the Source Starter GPO field, select the Starter GPO you want to use from the drop-down list and click OK.

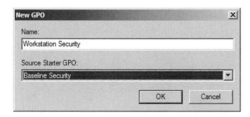

FIGURE 9.6
Creating a new GPO from a starter GPO.

Edit Group Policy Objects and Starter GPOs

Scenario/Problem: You created a new GPO and need to use it to apply security settings to users.

Solution: Edit a GPO.

To edit a GPO, perform the following steps:

TIP These steps can be applied to a GPO and a starter GPO.

1. Log on to a domain controller or a member computer that has Windows Server 2008 RSAT installed.

2. Click Start, click Administrative Tools, and then click Group Policy Management.

3. In the console tree, navigate to the domain that contains the GPO or starter GPO you want to edit.

4. If you want to edit a GPO, select the Group Policy Objects node. If you want to edit a starter GPO, select the Starter GPOs node.

5. Right-click the GPO you want to edit, and select Edit.

6. In the Group Policy Management Editor, shown in Figure 9.7, modify the settings accordingly and then close the Group Policy Management Editor.

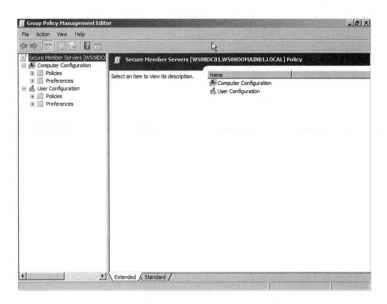

FIGURE 9.7
Editing a GPO.

NOTE The majority of group policy settings are configured in one of two states: Not Defined or Defined. When a group policy setting is configured as Not Defined, the setting is not applied via the GPO. When a group policy setting is configured as Defined, it is applied via the GPO.

Furthermore, when a group policy setting is configured as defined, the way in which the setting is edited varies depending on the setting in question. For example, certain group policy settings can be set to be enabled or disabled, such as the Administrator Account Status. Certain group policy settings can be set to numerical values, such as the Password Policies. Some group policy settings can be set to security principals, such as User Rights Assignments.

Copy Group Policy Objects and Starter GPOs

Scenario/Problem: You have an existing GPO and want to create a new GPO that has the exact same settings, but that you can alter independently.

Solution: Copy a GPO.

To copy a GPO or a starter GPO, perform the following tasks:

TIP These steps can be applied to a GPO and a starter GPO.

1. Log on to a domain controller or a member computer that has Windows Server 2008 RSAT installed.

2. Click Start, click Administrative Tools, and then click Group Policy Management.

3. In the console tree, navigate to the domain that contains the GPO or starter GPO you want to copy.

4. If you want to copy a GPO, select the Group Policy Objects node. If you want to copy a starter GPO, select the Starter GPOs node.

5. Right-click the GPO you want to copy, and select Copy.

6. If you are copying a GPO, right-click the Group Policy Objects node and click Paste. On the Copy GPO window, select how you want permissions for the new GPO to be handled, as shown in Figure 9.8, and click OK.

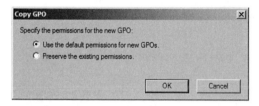

FIGURE 9.8
Copying GPO permissions.

7. If you are copying a starter GPO, right-click the Starter GPOs node and click Paste.

8. Verify that the copy progress succeeded, as shown in Figure 9.9, and click OK.

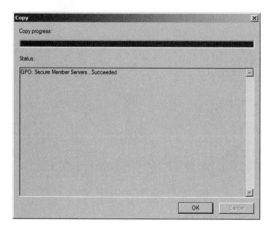

FIGURE 9.9
Verifying the progress of copying the GPO.

9. Rename the GPO accordingly.

Comment Group Policy Objects and Starter GPOs

Scenario/Problem: You need to add text to GPOs so that other administrators know who needs to approve changes to each GPO.

Solution: Comment a GPO.

To comment a GPO or a starter GPO, perform the following tasks:

TIP These steps can be applied to a GPO and a starter GPO.

1. Log on to a domain controller or a member computer that has Windows Server 2008 RSAT installed.

2. Click Start, click Administrative Tools, and then click Group Policy Management.

3. In the console tree, navigate to the domain that contains the GPO or starter GPO you want to comment.

4. If you want to comment a GPO, select the Group Policy Objects node. If you want to comment a starter GPO, select the Starter GPOs node.

5. Right-click the GPO you want to comment, and select Edit.

6. In the Group Policy Management Editor, right-click the name of the GPO or starter GPO in the console tree; then select Properties.

7. On the properties page for the GPO or starter GPO, click the Comment tab, shown in Figure 9.10.

8. Type a comment in the Comment field, and then click OK.

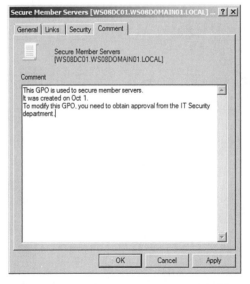

FIGURE 9.10
Commenting a GPO.

View, Print, and Save a Report for Group Policy Objects

Scenario/Problem: You need to produce a report of the settings defined by a GPO.

Solution: View a report for a GPO and save the report.

To view, print, and save a report for a GPO or a starter GPO, perform the following tasks:

TIP These steps can be applied to a GPO and a starter GPO.

1. Log on to a domain controller or a member computer that has Windows Server 2008 RSAT installed.
2. Click Start, click Administrative Tools, and then click Group Policy Management.
3. In the console tree, navigate to the domain that contains the GPO or starter GPO you want to produce the report for.
4. If you want to produce a report for a GPO, select the Group Policy Objects node. If you want to produce a report for a starter GPO, select the Starter GPOs node.
5. Click the GPO or starter GPO for which you want to produce a report, and click the Settings tab. If you are presented with an Internet Explorer Enhanced Security Configuration Error, click Add.
6. To save the report, right-click the details pane, select Save Report, and browse to the location in which you want to store the saved report, as shown in Figure 9.11.

FIGURE 9.11
Saving a GPO report.

7. To print the report, right-click the details pane and select Print.

Back Up Group Policy Objects and Starter GPOs

Scenario/Problem: You plan to modify the settings in a GPO. You want to ensure you can reverse the changes you make in case something goes wrong.

Solution: Back up a GPO.

To backup a GPO or a starter GPO, perform the following steps:

TIP These steps can be applied to a GPO and a starter GPO.

1. Log on to a domain controller or a member computer that has Windows Server 2008 RSAT installed.

2. Click Start, click Administrative Tools, and then click Group Policy Management.

3. In the console tree, navigate to the domain that contains the GPO or starter GPO you want to back up.

4. If you want to back up all GPOs, right-click the Group Policy Objects node and then select Back Up All. If you want to back up all starter GPOs, right-click the Starter GPOs node and then select Back Up All. Proceed to Step 7.

5. If you want to back up a single GPO, select the Group Policy Objects node. If you want to back up a single starter GPO, select the Starter GPOs node.

6. Right-click the GPO you want to back up, and select Backup.

7. On the Back Up Group Policy Object window, shown in Figure 9.12, type or browse to a location to which you want to store the backup in the Location field, enter a description for the backup, and click Back Up.

8. Verify that the backup progress bar shows that it succeeded, as shown in Figure 9.13, and click OK.

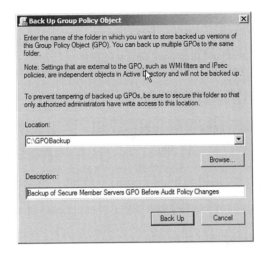

FIGURE 9.12
The Back Up Group Policy Object window.

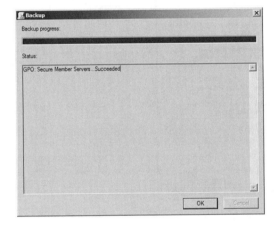

FIGURE 9.13
Backing up a GPO.

Restore Group Policy Objects and Starter GPOs

Scenario/Problem: You modified the settings in a GPO. The new settings had a negative impact on your environment. You need to reverse the changes made to the GPO.

Solution: Restore a GPO.

To restore a GPO or a starter GPO, perform the following steps:

TIP These steps can be applied to a GPO and a starter GPO.

1. Log on to a domain controller or a member computer that has Windows Server 2008 RSAT installed.

2. Click Start, click Administrative Tools, and then click Group Policy Management.

3. In the console tree, navigate to the domain that contains the GPO or starter GPO you want to restore.

4. If you want to restore a GPO, select the Group Policy Objects node. If you want to restore a starter GPO, select the Starter GPOs node.

5. Right-click the GPO you want to restore, and select Restore from Backup.

6. Click Next on the Restore Group Policy Object Wizard window, shown in Figure 9.14.

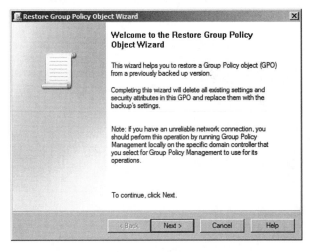

FIGURE 9.14
The Restore Group Policy Object Wizard.

7. On the Backup Location page, shown in Figure 9.15, type or browse to the location of the backup files.

8. On the Source GPO page, shown in Figure 9.16, select the GPO or starter GPO you want to restore and click Next.

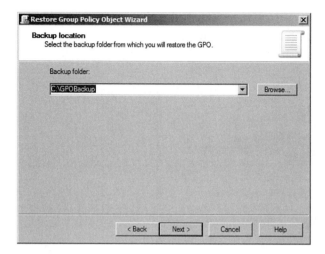

FIGURE 9.15
The Backup Location page.

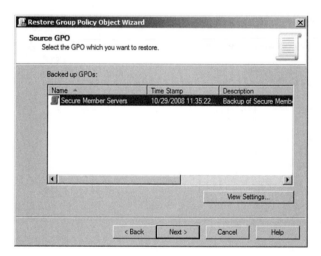

FIGURE 9.16
The Source GPO page.

9. On the Completing the Restore Group Policy Object Wizard page, shown in Figure 9.17, click Finish.

10. Verify that the restore progress bar shows it succeeded, as shown in Figure 9.18; then click OK.

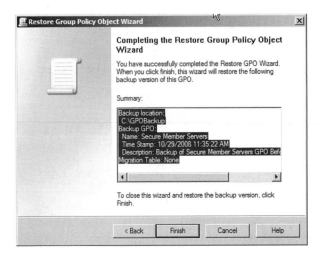

FIGURE 9.17
The Completing the Restore Group Policy Object Wizard page.

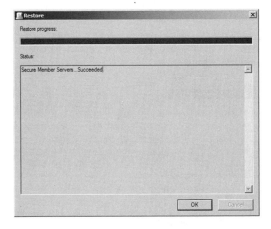

FIGURE 9.18
The progress bar for restoring a GPO.

Export a Starter GPO

Scenario/Problem: You have a number of starter GPOs in your AD DS domain. You need to copy one of these starter GPOs to a domain in another AD DS forest.

Solution: Export the starter GPO.

To export a starter GPO, perform the following steps:

1. Log on to a domain controller or a member computer that has Windows Server 2008 RSAT installed.

2. Click Start, click Administrative Tools, and then click Group Policy Management.

3. In the console tree, navigate to the domain that contains the starter GPO you want to export.

4. Select the Starter GPOs node.

5. In the details pane, shown in Figure 9.19, select the starter GPO you want to export and click Save as Cabinet.

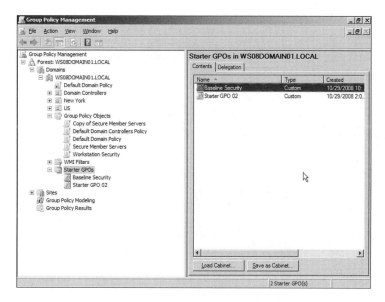

FIGURE 9.19
Exporting a starter GPO.

6. In the Save Starter GPO as Cabinet window, type the name and location to which to export the starter GPO; then click Save.

Import a Starter GPO

Scenario/Problem: You have an export of a starter GPO that you need to import into your AD DS domain.

Solution: Import the starter GPO.

To import a starter GPO, perform the following steps:

1. Log on to a domain controller or a member computer that has Windows Server 2008 RSAT installed.

2. Click Start, click Administrative Tools, and then click Group Policy Management.

3. In the console tree, navigate to the domain that contains the starter GPO you want to import.

4. Select the Starter GPOs node.

5. In the details pane, select Load Cabinet.

6. In the Load Starter GPO Wizard, shown in Figure 9.20, click Browse for CAB.

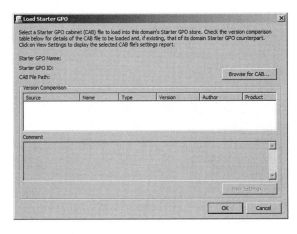

FIGURE 9.20
The Load Starter GPO Wizard.

7. Type the name and location of the starter GPO cabinet file you want to import, and click Open.

8. Click OK to import the starter GPO, as shown in Figure 9.21.

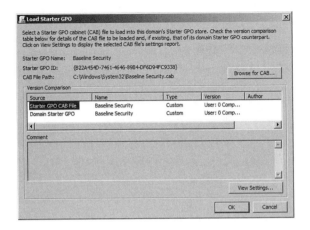

FIGURE 9.21
Importing a starter GPO.

NOTE If you have an existing starter GPO that has the same name as the starter GPO you are importing, you will receive a message that the existing starter GPO will be overwritten.

Search Group Policy Objects

Scenario/Problem: You have a number of GPOs in your AD DS forest. You need to determine which GPOs have computer scripts defined.

Solution: Search a GPO.

To search GPOs, perform the following steps:

1. Log on to a domain controller or a member computer that has Windows Server 2008 RSAT installed.

2. Click Start, click Administrative Tools, and then click Group Policy Management.

3. Right-click the forest node and select Search.

4. In the Search for Group Policy Objects window, shown in Figure 9.22, select the scope of your search by choosing a particular domain or the all domains shown in this forest option in the Search for GPOs in this domain field.

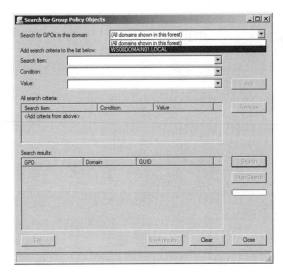

FIGURE 9.22
Selecting the search scope.

5. Select the item you want to search using the Search Item drop down. You can search the following items, as shown in Figure 9.23:

   ▶ GPO Name

   ▶ GPO-links

   ▶ Security Group

   ▶ Linked WMI Filter

   ▶ User Configuration

   ▶ Computer Configuration

   ▶ GUID

6. In the Conditions field, select Contains or Does not Contain.

7. In the Value field, shown in Figure 9.24, select the value you want the condition to match.

8. Click Add.

9. If you want to add more criteria, repeat steps 5–8.

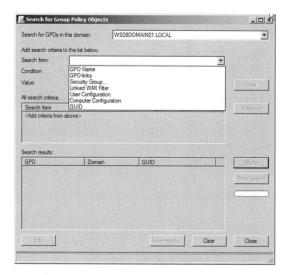

FIGURE 9.23
Selecting the search item.

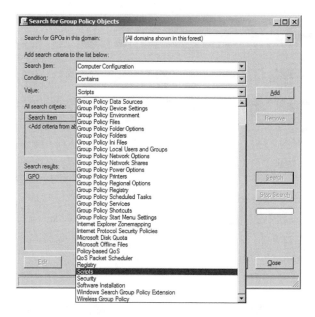

FIGURE 9.24
Selecting a value to search.

10. To open the GPOs that matched your search criteria, click Edit, as shown in Figure 9.25.

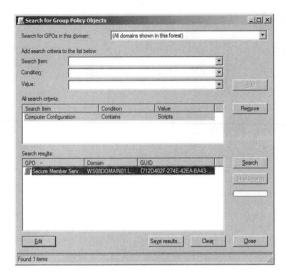

FIGURE 9.25
Opening a GPO.

Create a Migration Table

Scenario/Problem: You have a GPO in your forest that you need to migrate to another forest. The GPO assigns a number of user rights assignments to a group in your forest. You need to ensure that these user rights assignments are migrated to a group in the other forest.

Solution: Create a migration table.

To create a migration table, perform the following steps:

1. Log on to a domain controller or a member computer that has Windows Server 2008 RSAT installed.

2. Click Start, click Administrative Tools, and then click Group Policy Management.

3. In the console tree, right-click the domains node and click Open Migration Table Editor. The Migration Table Editor, shown in Figure 9.26, will open.

4. Right-click the cell below the Source Name column and click Browse.

5. On the Select User, Computer, or Group window, shown in Figure 9.27, type the name of the user, computer, or group in the source domain; then click OK.

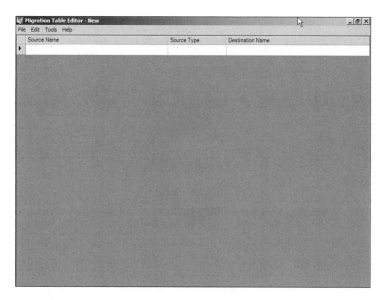

FIGURE 9.26
The Migration Table Editor.

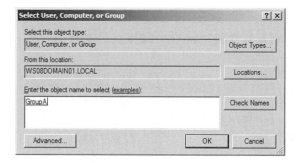

FIGURE 9.27
The Select User, Computer, or
Group window.

6. If required, modify the type of object by using the drop-down list in the Source
   Type column.

7. Type the name of the destination object in the Destination Name column, as
   shown in Figure 9.28.

8. Select File from the menu, and click Save.

9. Enter a name to use to save the migration table, and click Save.

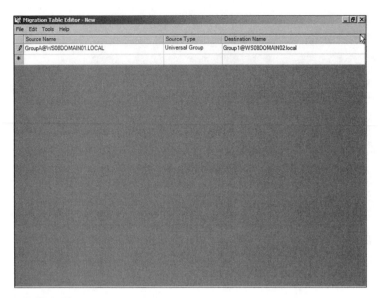

FIGURE 9.28
The Migration Table.

Automatically Populate a Migration Table from a Group Policy Object

Scenario/Problem: You have a GPO in your forest that you need to migrate to another forest. The GPO assigns a number of user rights assignments to groups in your forest. You are unsure which groups are used in the GPO. You need to ensure that these user rights assignments are migrated to a group in the other forest.

Solution: Automatically populate a migration table from a GPO.

To automatically populate a migration table from a GPO, perform the following steps:

1. Log on to a domain controller or a member computer that has Windows Server 2008 RSAT installed.

2. Click Start, click Administrative Tools, and then click Group Policy Management.

3. In the console tree, right-click the domains node and click, Open Migration Table Editor.

4. Select Tools from the menu, and click Populate from GPO.

5. On the Select GPO window, shown in Figure 9.29, select the GPO you want to use to populate the migration and click OK.

FIGURE 9.29
Selecting a GPO.

6. In the Destination Name column, shown in Figure 9.30, type the name of each group in the destination forest.

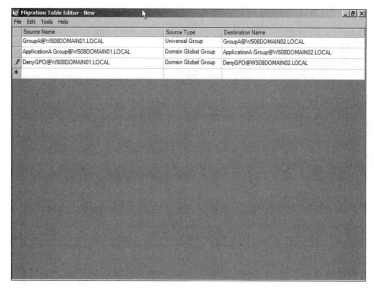

FIGURE 9.30
Automatically populating a migration table from a GPO.

7. Select File from the menu, and click Save.

8. Enter a name to use to save the migration table, and click Save.

Link a Group Policy Object

Scenario/Problem: You recently created a GPO and modified the settings based on your needs. You need to ensure that this GPO is applied to objects in an OU.

Solution: Link the GPO.

To link a GPO, perform the following steps:

1. Log on to a domain controller or a member computer that has Windows Server 2008 RSAT installed.

2. Click Start, click Administrative Tools, and then click Group Policy Management.

3. In the console tree, right-click the site, domain, or OU you want to link the GPO to and click Link an Existing GPO.

4. On the Select GPO window, shown in Figure 9.31, select the GPO you want to link and click OK.

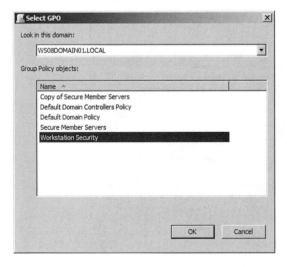

FIGURE 9.31
Selecting a GPO.

Remove a Group Policy Object Link

Scenario/Problem: You accidently linked a GPO to the wrong OU.

Solution: Remove the GPO link.

To remove a GPO link, perform the following steps:

1. Log on to a domain controller or a member computer that has Windows Server 2008 RSAT installed.

2. Click Start, click Administrative Tools, and then click Group Policy Management.

3. In the console tree, expand the site, domain, or OU from which you want to remove the GPO link.

4. Right-click the GPO for which you want to remove the link, and click Delete.

5. Select OK on the confirmation screen, shown in Figure 9.32, to delete the GPO link.

FIGURE 9.32
Removing a GPO link.

Disable a Group Policy Object Link

Scenario/Problem: You have a GPO that is linked to an OU. You suspect the GPO might be causing an issue to computers located in the OU. You need to temporarily prevent the GPO settings from being applied to computers in the OU.

Solution: Disable a GPO link.

To disable a GPO link, perform the following steps:

1. Log on to a domain controller or a member computer that has Windows Server 2008 RSAT installed.

2. Click Start, click Administrative Tools, and then click Group Policy Management.

3. In the console tree, expand the site, domain, or OU for which you want to disable the GPO link.

4. Right-click the GPO for which you want to disable the link, and click Link Enabled.

5. Ensure there is not a check next to Link Enabled, as shown in Figure 9.33.

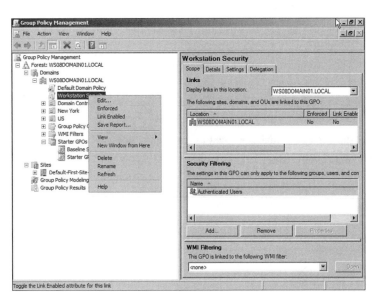

FIGURE 9.33
Disabling a GPO link.

Enable a Group Policy Object Link

Scenario/Problem: You previously disabled a GPO link and need to reenable it.

Solution: Enable a GPO link.

To enable a GPO link, perform the following steps:

1. Log on to a domain controller or a member computer that has Windows Server 2008 RSAT installed.

2. Click Start, click Administrative Tools, and then click Group Policy Management.

3. In the console tree, expand the site, domain, or OU for which you want to enable the GPO link.

4. Right-click the GPO for which you want to enable the link, and click Link Enabled.

5. Ensure there is a check next to Link Enabled, as shown in Figure 9.34.

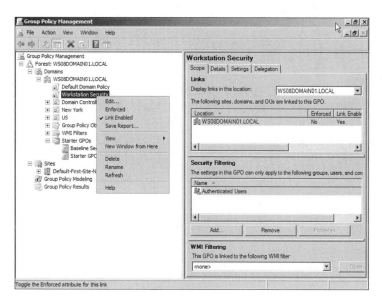

FIGURE 9.34
Enabling a GPO link.

Enforce a Group Policy Object Link

Scenario/Problem: You need to ensure the settings that are in a GPO that is linked to a parent OU are not overwritten by settings in GPOs linked to child OUs.

Solution: Enforce a GPO link.

To enforce a GPO link, perform the following steps:

1. Log on to a domain controller or a member computer that has Windows Server 2008 RSAT installed.

2. Click Start, click Administrative Tools, and then click Group Policy Management.

3. In the console tree, expand the site, domain, or OU for which you want to enforce the GPO link.

4. Right-click the GPO for which you want to enforce the link, and click Enforced.

5. Ensure there is a check next to Enforced, as shown in Figure 9.35.

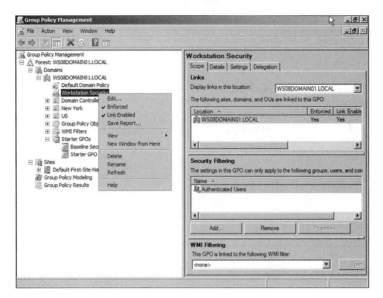

FIGURE 9.35
Enforcing a GPO link.

Remove the Enforcement of a Group Policy Object Link

Scenario/Problem: You previously enabled the enforcement of a GPO link. You no longer require this GPO link to be enforced.

Solution: Remove the enforcement of a GPO link.

To remove the enforcement of a GPO link, perform the following steps:

1. Log on to a domain controller or a member computer that has Windows Server 2008 RSAT installed.

2. Click Start, click Administrative Tools, and then click Group Policy Management.

3. In the console tree, expand the site, domain, or OU for which you want to remove the GPO link enforcement.

4. Right-click the GPO for which you want to remove the GPO link enforcement, and click Enforced.

5. Ensure there is not a check next to Enforced, as shown in Figure 9.36.

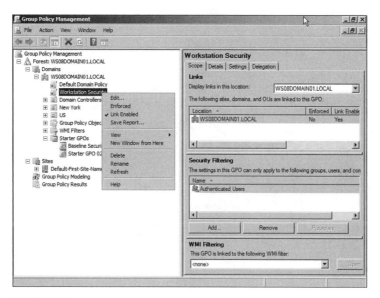

FIGURE 9.36
Removing the enforcement of a GPO link.

Block Inheritance of Group Policy Objects

Scenario/Problem: You need to prevent GPO settings defined in a GPO linked to the parent OU from being inherited to servers in a child OU.

Solution: Block inheritance of GPOs.

To block inheritance of a GPO, perform the following steps:

1. Log on to a domain controller or a member computer that has Windows Server 2008 RSAT installed.

2. Click Start, click Administrative Tools, and then click Group Policy Management.

3. In the console tree, select the site, domain, or OU on which you want to block inheritance, and click Block Inheritance.

4. Ensure there is a check next to Block Inheritance, as shown in Figure 9.37.

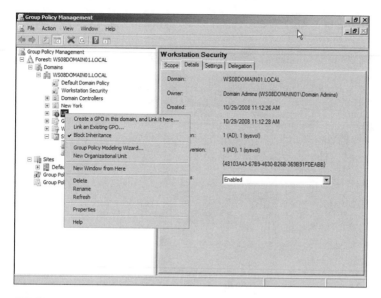

FIGURE 9.37
Blocking the inheritance of GPOs.

Remove Block Inheritance of Group Policy Objects

Scenario/Problem: You previously enabled block inheritance of GPOs. You no longer require this.

Solution: Remove block inheritance of GPOs.

To remove block inheritance of a GPO, perform the following steps:

1. Log on to a domain controller or a member computer that has Windows Server 2008 RSAT installed.

2. Click Start, click Administrative Tools, and then click Group Policy Management.

3. In the console tree, select the site, domain, or OU from which you want to remove block inheritance, and click Block Inheritance.

4. Ensure there is not a check next to Block Inheritance, as shown in Figure 9.38.

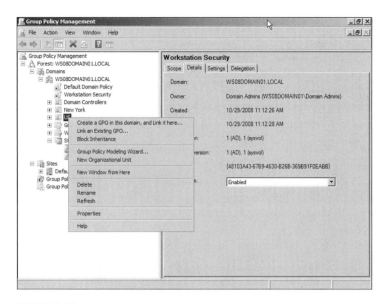

FIGURE 9.38
Removing the block inheritance of GPOs.

Change the Order of Group Policy Object Links

Scenario/Problem: You have multiple GPOs that are linked to an OU. You need to ensure one of these GPOs is applied last.

Solution: Change the link order of GPO links.

To change the order of GPO links, perform the following steps:

1. Log on to a domain controller or a member computer that has Windows Server 2008 RSAT installed.

2. Click Start, click Administrative Tools, and then click Group Policy Management.

3. In the console tree, select the site, domain, or OU for which you want to change the link order.

4. In the details pane, select the GPO for which you want to change the link order and use the arrows on the left side of the details pane to move the GPO higher or lower in order, as shown in Figure 9.39.

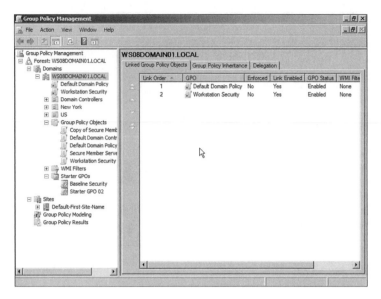

FIGURE 9.39
Changing the order of GPO links.

Filter Group Policy Object Scope by Using Security Groups

Scenario/Problem: You have a GPO linked to an OU. The OU contains user accounts. You need to limit the GPO to be applied only to a subset of the user accounts located in the OU.

Solution: Create an AD DS group. Place the user accounts in the AD DS group. Filter the GPO scope by the AD DS group.

To filter group policy scope by using security groups, perform the following steps:

1. Log on to a domain controller or a member computer that has Windows Server 2008 RSAT installed.

2. Click Start, click Administrative Tools, and then click Group Policy Management.

3. In the console tree, select the Group Policy Objects node.

4. In the details pane, select the GPO on which you want to use group filtering.

5. On the Scope tab, shown in Figure 9.40, click Add.

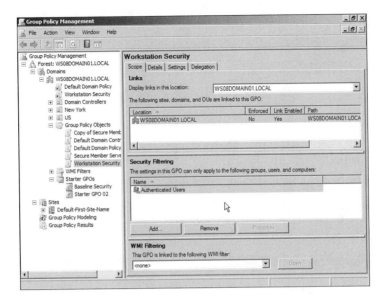

FIGURE 9.40
The GPO Scope tab.

6. On the Select User, Computer, or Group window, type the name of the group with which you want to filter the GPO scope; then click OK.

7. Select Authenticated Users under the Security Filtering section of the Scope tab, and click Remove.

8. Click OK on the remove delegation privilege confirmation screen, as shown in Figure 9.41.

FIGURE 9.41
The confirmation page for removing delegation privilege.

Disable User Settings in a Group Policy Object

Scenario/Problem: You have a GPO linked to an OU. The GPO is used to apply computer configuration. You want to prevent user configuration from being read during group policy processing.

Solution: Disable user settings in a GPO.

To disable user settings in a GPO, perform the following steps:

1. Log on to a domain controller or a member computer that has Windows Server 2008 RSAT installed.

2. Click Start, click Administrative Tools, and then click Group Policy Management.

3. In the console tree, select the Group Policy Objects node.

4. Right-click the GPO on which you want to disable user settings, select GPO Status, and click User Configuration Settings Disabled, as shown in Figure 9.42.

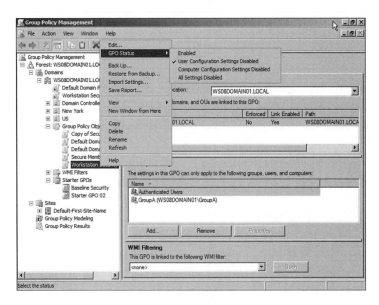

FIGURE 9.42
The User Configuration Settings Disabled option.

Disable Computer Settings in a Group Policy Object

Scenario/Problem: You have a GPO linked to an OU. The GPO is used to apply user configuration. You want to prevent computer configuration from being read during group policy processing.

Solution: Disable computer settings in a GPO.

To disable computer settings in a GPO, perform the following steps:

1. Log on to a domain controller or a member computer that has Windows Server 2008 RSAT installed.

2. Click Start, click Administrative Tools, and then click Group Policy Management.

3. In the console tree, select the Group Policy Objects node.

4. Right-click the GPO on which you want to disable computer settings, select GPO Status, and click Computer Configuration Settings Disabled, as shown in Figure 9.43.

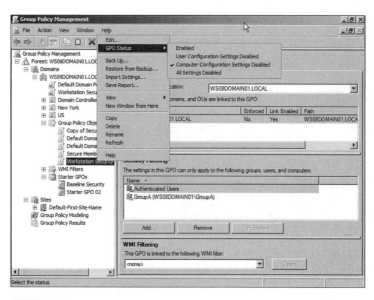

FIGURE 9.43
The Computer Configuration Settings Disabled option.

Create a WMI Filter

Scenario/Problem: You have a GPO in your domain. You want to ensure that the GPO is applied only to computers that have Microsoft Windows XP Professional with Service Pack 2 installed.

Solution: Create a WMI filter.

To create a WMI filter, perform the following steps:

1. Log on to a domain controller or a member computer that has Windows Server 2008 RSAT installed.

2. Click Start, click Administrative Tools, and then click Group Policy Management.

3. In the console tree, expand the domains node, right-click the WMI Filters node and click New.

4. In the New WMI Filter window, shown in Figure 9.44, enter a name for the WMI filter in the Name field and click Add.

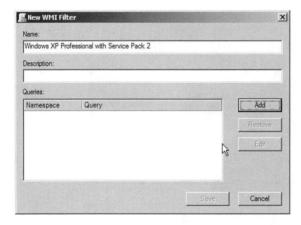

FIGURE 9.44
The New WMI Filter window.

5. On the WMI Query window, shown in Figure 9.45, use the default namespace or type a new one. Type your WMI query into the Query field, and click OK.

6. Click Save on the New WMI Filter window to save the WMI filter, as shown in Figure 9.46.

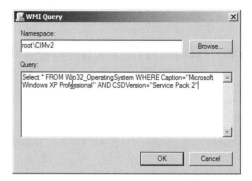

FIGURE 9.45
The WMI Query window.

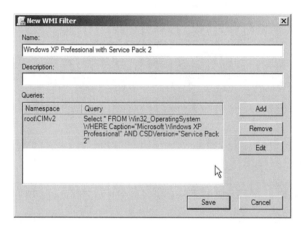

FIGURE 9.46
Creating a WMI filter.

Import a WMI Filter

Scenario/Problem: You created a WMI filter in your test AD DS environment. You want to import this WMI filter into your production environment.

Solution: Import a WMI filter.

To import a WMI filter, perform the following steps:

1. Log on to a domain controller or a member computer that has Windows Server 2008 RSAT installed.

2. Click Start, click Administrative Tools, and then click Group Policy Management.

3. In the console tree, right-click the WMI Filters node and click Import.

4. On the Import WMI Filter window, type the name and location of the file to import; then click Open.

5. On the Import WMI Filter window, shown in Figure 9.47, verify the settings and click Import.

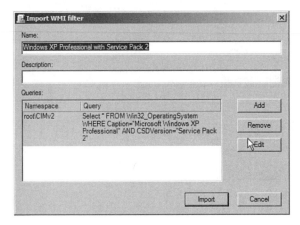

FIGURE 9.47
The Import WMI Filter window.

Export a WMI Filter

Scenario/Problem: You created a WMI filter in your test AD DS environment. You want to export this WMI filter so you can import it into other environments.

Solution: Export a WMI filter.

To export a WMI filter, perform the following steps:

1. Log on to a domain controller or a member computer that has Windows Server 2008 RSAT installed.

2. Click Start, click Administrative Tools, and then click Group Policy Management.

3. In the console tree, expand the WMI Filters node, right-click the WMI filter you want to export, and click Export.

4. On the Export WMI Filter window, type the name and location of the file to export and click Save.

Copy a WMI Filter

Scenario/Problem: You have an existing WMI filter. You want to make a copy of the WMI filter so it can be modified independently of the original.

Solution: Copy a WMI filter.

To copy a WMI filter, perform the following steps:

1. Log on to a domain controller or a member computer that has Windows Server 2008 RSAT installed.

2. Click Start, click Administrative Tools, and then click Group Policy Management.

3. In the console tree, expand the WMI Filters node, right-click the WMI filter you want to copy, and click Copy.

4. Right-click the WMI Filters node and click Paste.

5. Rename the new WMI filter accordingly.

Link a WMI Filter to a Group Policy Object

Scenario/Problem: You created a WMI filter that queries for computers that have Windows XP Professional with Service Pack 2 installed. You need to filter the application of a GPO to computers that have Windows XP Professional with Service Pack 2 installed.

Solution: Link a WMI filter to a GPO.

To link a WMI filter to a GPO, perform the following steps:

1. Log on to a domain controller or a member computer that has Windows Server 2008 RSAT installed.

2. Click Start, click Administrative Tools, and then click Group Policy Management.

3. In the console tree, expand the Group Policy Objects node and select the GPO to which you want to link the WMI filter.

4. In the Scope tab, select the WMI filter from the drop-down list under the WMI Filtering section, as shown in Figure 9.48.

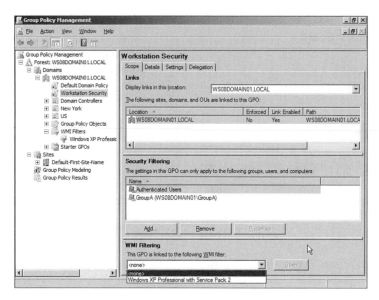

FIGURE 9.48
Linking a WMI filter to a GPO.

Determine a Resultant Set of Policy

Scenario/Problem: You have a computer account that is receiving incorrect settings from group policy. You need to determine which GPO is causing this issue for the computer.

Solution: Determine resultant set of policy.

To determine resultant set of policy, perform the following steps:

1. Log on to a domain controller or a member computer that has Windows Server 2008 RSAT installed.

2. Click Start, click Administrative Tools, and then click Group Policy Management.

3. In the console tree, right-click the Group Policy Results node and click Group Policy Results Wizard.

4. Click Next on the Welcome to the Group Policy Results Wizard page.

5. If you want to determine the resultant set of policy on the local computer, select This Computer on the Computer Selection page and click Next.

6. If you want to determine the resultant set of policy on another computer, select Another Computer on the Computer Selection page, enter the computer name, as shown in Figure 9.49, and click Next.

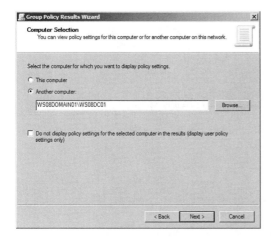

FIGURE 9.49
The Computer Selection page.

7. If you do not want to determine the resultant set of policy for a user account, select Do not display user policy settings in the results on the User Selection page.

8. If you want to determine the resultant set of policy for a user account, select the user on the User Selection page as, shown in Figure 9.50, and click Next.

FIGURE 9.50
The User Selection page.

9. Click Next on the Summary of Selections page.

10. Click Finish on the Completing the Group Policy Results Wizard page.

11. In the details pane, click the Summary tab, shown in Figure 9.51, to view a summary of the Group Policy results, click the Settings tab to view the settings that are applied, or click the Policy Events tab to view any Group Policy related events on the target system.

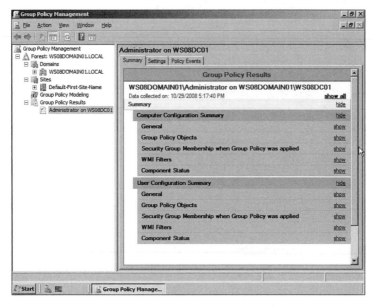

FIGURE 9.51
Group policy results.

Simulate a Resultant Set of Policy Using Group Policy Modeling

Scenario/Problem: You need to assess the group policy impact of moving a computer account to another OU.

Solution: Simulate a resultant set of policy using group policy modeling.

To simulate a resultant set of policy using group policy modeling, perform the following steps:

1. Log on to a domain controller or a member computer that has Windows Server 2008 RSAT installed.

2. Click Start, click Administrative Tools, and then click Group Policy Management.

3. In the console tree, right-click the Group Policy Modeling node and click Group Policy Modeling Wizard.

4. On the Domain Controller Selection page, click Next.

5. On the User and Computer Selection page, shown in Figure 9.52, enter a username and/or computer name; then click Next.

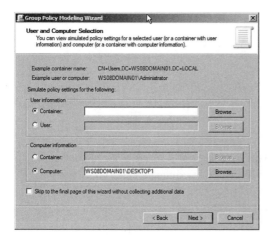

FIGURE 9.52
The User and Computer Selection page.

6. On the Advanced Simulation Options page, shown in Figure 9.53, select the advanced simulation options you desire and click Next.

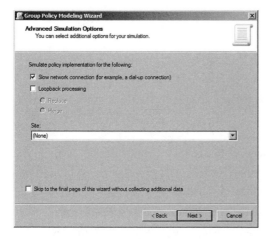

FIGURE 9.53
The Advanced Simulation Options page.

7. On the Alternate Active Directory Paths page, shown in Figure 9.54, enter the new locations to simulate policy settings and click Next.

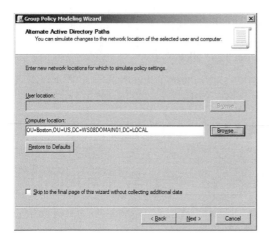

FIGURE 9.54
The Alternate Active Directory Paths page.

8. On the Computer Security Groups page, shown in Figure 9.55, add or remove any security groups you want to include in the simulation and click Next.

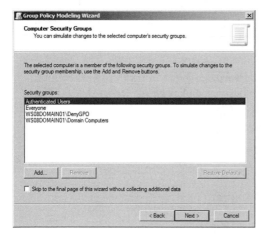

FIGURE 9.55
The Computer Security Groups page.

9. On the WMI Filters for Computers page, shown in Figure 9.56, select All linked filters or Only these filters and click Next.

10. On the Summary of Selections page, click Next.

11. Click Finish on the Completing the Group Policy Modeling Wizard page.

12. In the details pane, click the Summary tab, shown in Figure 9.57, to view a summary of the group policy results, click the Settings tab to view the settings that are applied, or click the Policy Events tab to view any group policy–related events on the target system.

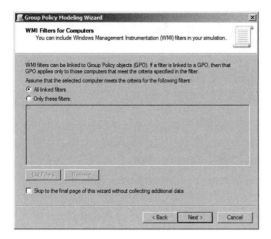

FIGURE 9.56
The WMI Filters for Computers page.

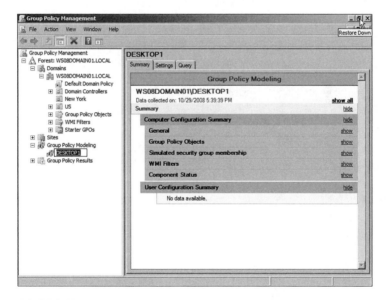

FIGURE 9.57
Group policy modeling.

Delegate Permissions on a Group Policy Object

Scenario/Problem: You created a GPO and linked it to an OU. You need to provide members of a group the capability to edit the settings in the GPO.

Solution: Delegate the permissions on the GPO.

To delegate permissions on a GPO, perform the following steps:

1. Log on to a domain controller or a member computer that has Windows Server 2008 RSAT installed.

2. Click Start, click Administrative Tools, and then click Group Policy Management.

3. In the console tree, expand the Group Policy Objects node and select the GPO on which you want delegate permissions.

4. Click the Delegation tab, shown in Figure 9.58.

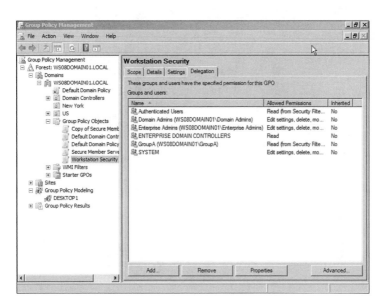

FIGURE 9.58
The Delegation tab.

5. Click Add.

6. In the Select User, Computer, or Group window, type the name of the group to which you want to delegate permissions; then click OK.

7. On the Add Group or User window, shown in Figure 9.59, select the permission you want to delegate and click OK.

FIGURE 9.59
The Add Group or User window.

Modify Delegated Permissions on a Group Policy Object

Scenario/Problem: A group was previously delegated the permission to edit a GPO. You need to also allow the group to modify security on a GPO.

Solution: Modify delegated permissions on a GPO.

To modify delegated permissions on a GPO, perform the following steps:

1. Log on to a domain controller or a member computer that has Windows Server 2008 RSAT installed.

2. Click Start, click Administrative Tools, and then click Group Policy Management.

3. In the console tree, expand the Group Policy Objects node and select the GPO on which you want to modify delegated permissions.

4. Click the Delegation tab.

5. In the details pane, right-click the group for which you want to modify delegated permissions; then select the permission you want to delegate, as shown in Figure 9.60.

6. Click OK on the confirmation to change permissions.

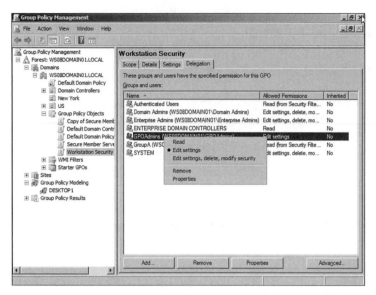

FIGURE 9.60
Selecting the permission to delegate on a GPO.

Remove Delegated Permissions on a Group Policy Object

Scenario/Problem: A group was previously delegated the permission to edit a GPO. This group no longer requires the permissions to edit the GPO.

Solution: Remove delegated permissions on a GPO.

To remove delegated permissions on a GPO, perform the following steps:

1. Log on to a domain controller or a member computer that has Windows Server 2008 RSAT installed.

2. Click Start, click Administrative Tools, and then click Group Policy Management.

3. In the console tree, expand the Group Policy Objects node and select the GPO on which you want remove delegate permissions.

4. Click the Delegation tab.

5. In the details pane, right-click the group for which you want to remove delegated permissions and click Remove.

6. Click OK on the confirmation to remove the delegated permissions, shown in Figure 9.61.

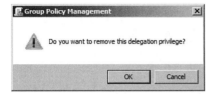

FIGURE 9.61
Removing delegated permissions on a GPO.

Delegate Permissions to Link Group Policy Objects

Scenario/Problem: A team that has the permission to create GPOs requires the capability to link the GPOs to any OU in the domain.

Solution: Delegate the permission to link GPOs.

To delegate permissions to link GPOs, perform the following steps:

1. Log on to a domain controller or a member computer that has Windows Server 2008 RSAT installed.

2. Click Start, click Administrative Tools, and then click Group Policy Management.

3. If you want to delegate the permission to link GPOs on the domain level, select the domain node in the console tree.

4. If you want to delegate the permission to link GPOs on an OU, select the OU in the console tree.

5. Click the Delegation tab. Ensure that the Permission field contains Link GPOs, as shown in Figure 9.62. Click Add.

6. On the Select User, Computer, or Group window, enter the name of the group to which you want to delegate the capability to link GPOs and click OK.

7. On the Add Group or User window, shown in Figure 9.63, select the inheritance settings and click OK.

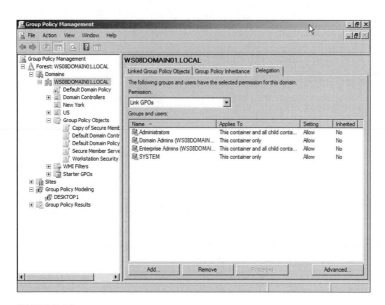

FIGURE 9.62
The Delegation tab.

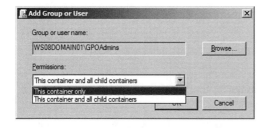

FIGURE 9.63
The Add Group or User window.

Modify Delegated Permissions to Link Group Policy Objects

Scenario/Problem: A team was previously granted the capability to link GPOs at the domain level. They now need this permission at every OU in the domain.

Solution: Modify delegated permissions to link GPOs.

To modify delegated permissions to link GPOs, perform the following steps:

1. Log on to a domain controller or a member computer that has Windows Server 2008 RSAT installed.

2. Click Start, click Administrative Tools, and then click Group Policy Management.

3. If you want to modify delegated permissions to link GPOs on the domain level, select the domain node in the console tree.

4. If you want to modify delegated permissions to link GPOs on an OU, select the OU in the console tree.

5. Click the Delegation tab. Ensure that the Permission field contains Link GPOs.

6. In the details pane, right-click the group for which you want to modify delegated permissions; then select This container only or This container and children.

7. Click OK on the confirmation screen to change inheritance, as shown in Figure 9.64.

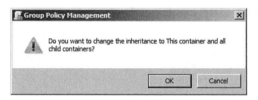

FIGURE 9.64
The confirmation to change inheritance.

Remove Delegated Permissions to Link Group Policy Objects

Scenario/Problem: A team was previously granted the capability to link GPOs at the domain level. They no longer require these permissions.

Solution: Remove delegated permissions to link GPOs.

To remove delegated permissions to link GPOs, perform the following steps:

1. Log on to a domain controller or a member computer that has Windows Server 2008 RSAT installed.

2. Click Start, click Administrative Tools, and then click Group Policy Management.

3. If you want to remove delegated permissions to link GPOs on the domain level, select the domain node in the console tree.

4. If you want to remove delegated permissions to link GPOs on an OU, select the OU in the console tree.

5. Click the Delegation tab. Ensure that the Permission field contains Link GPOs.

6. In the details pane, right-click the group for which you want to remove delegated permissions and select Remove.

7. Click OK on the confirmation screen to remove delegated permissions, as shown in Figure 9.65.

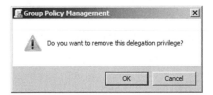

FIGURE 9.65

The confirmation screen to remove delegated permissions.

Delegate Permissions for Generating Group Policy Modeling Data

Scenario/Problem: A team requires the capability to generate group policy modeling data for computers and users located in a particular OU.

Solution: Delegate the permissions to generate group policy modeling data.

To delegate permissions for generating group policy modeling data, perform the following steps:

1. Log on to a domain controller or a member computer that has Windows Server 2008 RSAT installed.

2. Click Start, click Administrative Tools, and then click Group Policy Management.

3. If you want to delegate the permission to generate group policy modeling data on the domain level, select the domain node in the console tree.

4. If you want to delegate the permission to generate group policy modeling data on an OU, select the OU in the console tree.

5. Click the Delegation tab. Ensure that the Permission field contains Perform Group Policy Modeling Analyses, as shown in Figure 9.66. Click Add.

6. On the Select User, Computer, or Group window, enter the name of the group to which you want to delegate the capability to generate group policy modeling data; then click OK.

7. On the Add Group or User window, shown in Figure 9.67, select the inheritance settings and click OK.

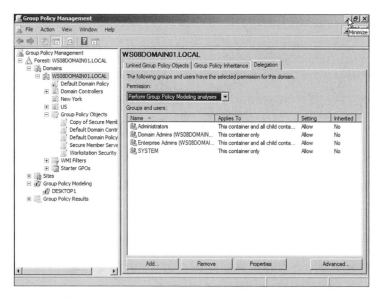

FIGURE 9.66
The Delegation tab.

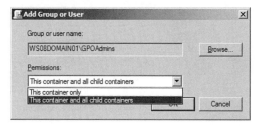

FIGURE 9.67
The Add Group or User page.

Modify Delegated Permissions for Generating Group Policy Modeling Data

Scenario/Problem: A team was previously granted the capability to generate group policy modeling data at the domain level. They now need this permission at every OU in the domain.

Solution: Modify delegated permissions for generating group policy modeling data.

To modify delegated permissions for generating group policy modeling data, perform the following steps:

1. Log on to a domain controller or a member computer that has Windows Server 2008 RSAT installed.

2. Click Start, click Administrative Tools, and then click Group Policy Management.

3. If you want to modify delegated permissions to generate group policy modeling data on the domain level, select the domain node in the console tree.

4. If you want to modify delegated permissions to generate group policy modeling data on an OU, select the OU in the console tree.

5. Click the Delegation tab. Ensure that the Permission field contains Perform Group Policy Modeling Analyses.

6. In the details pane, right-click the group for which you want to modify delegated permissions; then select This container only or This container and children.

7. Click OK on the confirmation to change inheritance.

Remove Delegated Permissions for Generating Group Policy Modeling Data

Scenario/Problem: A team was previously granted the capability to generate group policy modeling data at the domain level. They no longer require this permission.

Solution: Remove delegated permissions for generating group policy modeling data.

To remove delegated permissions for generating group policy modeling data, perform the following steps:

1. Log on to a domain controller or a member computer that has Windows Server 2008 RSAT installed.

2. Click Start, click Administrative Tools, and then click Group Policy Management.

3. If you want to remove delegated permissions to generate group policy modeling data on the domain level, select the domain node in the console tree.

4. If you want to remove delegated permissions to generate group policy modeling data on an OU, select the OU in the console tree.

5. Click the Delegation tab. Ensure that the Permission field contains Perform Group Policy Modeling Analyses.

6. In the details pane, right-click the group for which you want to remove delegated permissions and select Remove.

7. Click OK on the confirmation to remove the delegated permissions.

Delegate Permissions for Generating Group Policy Results

Scenario/Problem: A team requires the capability to generate group policy results data for computers and users located in a particular OU.

Solution: Delegate the permissions to generate group policy results data.

To delegate permissions to generate group policy results data, perform the following steps:

1. Log on to a domain controller or a member computer that has Windows Server 2008 RSAT installed.

2. Click Start, click Administrative Tools, and then click Group Policy Management.

3. If you want to delegate the permission to generate group policy results data on the domain level, select the domain node in the console tree.

4. If you want to delegate the permission to generate group policy results data on an OU, select the OU in the console tree.

5. Click the Delegation tab. Ensure that the Permission field contains Read Group Policy Results data, as shown in Figure 9.68. Click Add.

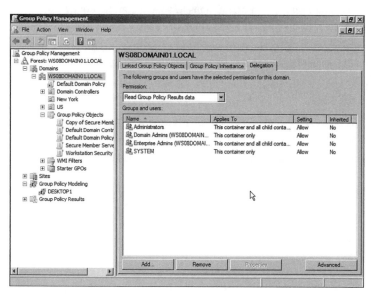

FIGURE 9.68
The Delegation tab.

6. On the Select User, Computer, or Group window, enter the name of the group to which you want to delegate the capability to generate group policy results and click OK.

7. On the Add Group or User window, select the inheritance settings and click OK.

Modify Delegated Permissions for Generating Group Policy Results

Scenario/Problem: A team was previously granted the capability to generate group policy results data at the domain level. They now need this permission at every OU in the domain.

Solution: Modify delegated permissions for generating group policy results data.

To modify delegated permissions for generating group policy results, perform the following steps:

1. Log on to a domain controller or a member computer that has Windows Server 2008 RSAT installed.

2. Click Start, click Administrative Tools, and then click Group Policy Management.

3. If you want to modify delegated permissions to generate group policy results data on the domain level, select the domain node in the console tree.

4. If you want to modify delegated permissions to generate group policy results data on an OU, select the OU in the console tree.

5. Click the Delegation tab. Ensure that the Permission field contains Read Group Policy Results Data.

6. In the details pane, right-click the group for which you want to modify delegated permissions; then select This container only or This container and children.

7. Click OK on the confirmation screen to change inheritance.

Remove Delegated Permissions for Generating Group Policy Results

Scenario/Problem: A team was previously granted the capability to generate group policy results data at the domain level. They no longer require this permission.

Solution: Remove delegated permissions for generating group policy results data.

To remove delegated permissions for generating group policy results, perform the following steps:

1. Log on to a domain controller or a member computer that has Windows Server 2008 RSAT installed.

2. Click Start, click Administrative Tools, and then click Group Policy Management.

3. If you want to remove delegated permissions to generate group policy results data on the domain level, select the domain node in the console tree.

4. If you want to remove delegated permissions to generate group policy results data on an OU, select the OU in the console tree.

5. Click the Delegation tab. Ensure that the Permission field contains Read Group Policy Results Data.

6. In the details pane, right-click the group for which you want to remove delegated permissions and select Remove.

7. Click OK on the confirmation screen to remove the delegated permissions.

Delegate Permissions for WMI Filters

Scenario/Problem: A team requires the capability to create WMI filters, which will be used to filter the application of GPOs.

Solution: Delegate the permissions to create WMI filters.

To delegate permissions for WMI filters, perform the following steps:

1. Log on to a domain controller or a member computer that has Windows Server 2008 RSAT installed.

2. Click Start, click Administrative Tools, and then click Group Policy Management.

3. In the console tree, select the WMI Filters node.

4. In the details pane, click the Delegation tab.

5. Click Add.

6. On the Select User, Computer, or Group window, enter the name of the group to which you want to delegate the capability to create WMI filters and click OK.

7. On the Add Group or User window, select the Full Control or Creator Owner permission and click OK.

Modify Delegated Permissions for WMI Filters

Scenario/Problem: A team was previously granted the Creator Owner permission on WMI filters in your domain. They now need the Full Control permission.

Solution: Modify delegated permissions on WMI filters.

To modify delegated permissions for WMI filters, perform the following steps:

1. Log on to a domain controller or a member computer that has Windows Server 2008 RSAT installed.

2. Click Start, click Administrative Tools, and then click Group Policy Management.

3. In the console tree, select the WMI Filters node.

4. In the details pane, click the Delegation tab.

5. In the details pane, right-click the group for which you want to modify delegated permissions; then select Full Control or Creator Owner.

6. Click OK on the confirmation screen to change inheritance.

Remove Delegated Permissions for WMI Filters

Scenario/Problem: A team was previously granted the capability to create WMI filters. They no longer require this permission.

Solution: Remove delegated permissions for WMI filters.

To remove delegated permissions for WMI filters, perform the following steps:

1. Log on to a domain controller or a member computer that has Windows Server 2008 RSAT installed.

2. Click Start, click Administrative Tools, and then click Group Policy Management.

3. In the console tree, select the WMI Filters node.

4. In the details pane, click the Delegation tab.

5. In the details pane, right-click the group for which you want to remove delegated permissions and select Remove.

6. Click OK on the confirmation screen to remove the delegated permissions.

CHAPTER 10

Manage Password Replication Policies

Password Replication Policies are new in Windows Server 2008. Password Replication Policies define the accounts a read-only domain controller (RODC) is permitted to cache, as well as the accounts it is not permitted to cache. When an RODC is originally deployed, the Password Replication Policy must be configured on the writable domain controller (DC) that will be its replication partner.

In addition to configuring the Password Replication Policy for an RODC, you must perform a number of other tasks for Password Replication Policies. This chapter describes the steps required to manage Password Replication Policies.

Add a User, Group, or Computer to the Password Replication Policy

Scenario/Problem: You recently deployed an RODC in your domain. You need to ensure that the RODC caches passwords for users from your company's New York office.

Solution: Add all New York users to an Active Directory Domain Services (AD DS) group. Add a Password Replication Policy on the RODC to allow passwords to be cached for members of the AD DS group.

To add a user, group, or computer to the password replication policy, perform the following steps:

1. Log on to a domain controller or a member computer that has Windows Server 2008 Remote Server Administration Tools (RSAT) installed.

2. Click Start, click Administrative Tools, and then click Active Directory Users and Computers.

3. Right-click Active Directory Users and Computers in the console tree, and click Change Domain Controller.

4. On the Change Directory Server window, shown in Figure 10.1, select a writable domain controller that has W2K8 in the DC Version column and click OK.

5. In the console tree, expand the domain node and select the Domain Controllers node.

6. In the details pane, right-click the RODC on which you want to configure the password replication policy; then click Properties.

7. On the RODC Properties page, click the Password Replication Policy tab.

> **NOTE** The Password Replication Policy tab will only be presented on the properties page for read-only domain controllers. This tab will not be present for writable domain controllers.

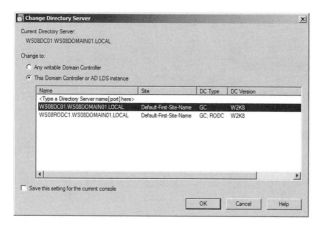

FIGURE 10.1
The Change Directory Server window.

8. Click Add.

9. On the Add Groups, Users and Computers window, shown in Figure 10.2, select Allow passwords for the account to replicate to this RODC or Deny passwords for the account from replicating to this RODC. Then click OK.

FIGURE 10.2
The Add Groups, Users and Computers window.

10. Type the name of the user, group, or computer you want to allow or deny password replication, and click OK. The group, user, or computer will be added to the Password Replication Policy tab, as shown in Figure 10.3.

11. Click OK or Apply to save the changes.

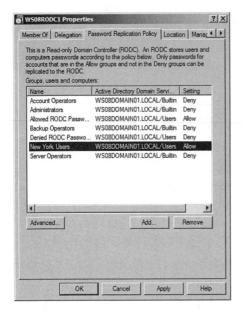

FIGURE 10.3
The Password Replication Policy tab.

Remove a User, Group, or Computer from the Password Replication Policy

Scenario/Problem: A group of employees relocated from your company's New York office to your company's head office. The RODC in the New York office previously cached the password for these employees. These employees no longer need to authenticate against the RODC.

Solution: Remove the group from the Password Replication Policy on the RODC.

To remove a user, group, or computer from the password replication policy, perform the following steps:

1. Log on to a domain controller or a member computer that has Windows Server 2008 RSAT installed.

2. Click Start, click Administrative Tools, and then click Active Directory Users and Computers.

3. Right-click Active Directory Users and Computers in the console tree, and click Change Domain Controller.

4. On the Change Directory Server window, select a writable domain controller that has W2K8 in the DC Version column and click OK.

5. In the console tree, expand the domain node and select the Domain Controllers node.

6. In the details pane, right-click the RODC on which you want to configure the password replication policy; then click Properties.

7. On the RODC Properties page, click the Password Replication Policy tab.

8. Select the user, group, or computer you want to remove from the Password Replication Policy, and click Remove.

9. Select Yes on the confirmation to remove the security principal from the Password Replication Policy, shown in Figure 10.4.

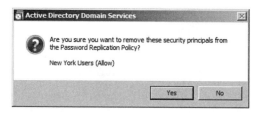

FIGURE 10.4
The confirmation to remove security principal from Password Replication Policy.

View Cached Credentials on a Read-Only Domain Controller

Scenario/Problem: You need to determine which passwords an RODC has cached.

Solution: View the cached credentials on an RODC.

To determine which credentials an RODC has cached, perform the following steps:

1. Log on to a domain controller or a member computer that has Windows Server 2008 RSAT installed.

2. Click Start, click Administrative Tools, and then click Active Directory Users and Computers.

3. Right-click Active Directory Users and Computers in the console tree, and click Change Domain Controller.

4. On the Change Directory Server window, select a writable domain controller that has W2K8 in the DC Version column and click OK.

5. In the console tree, expand the domain node and select the Domain Controllers node.

6. In the details pane, right-click the RODC on which you want to view the cached credentials and click Properties.

7. Click on the Password Replication Policy tab.

8. On the RODC Properties page, click Advanced.

9. On the Advanced Password Replication Policy page, select Accounts whose passwords are stored on this Read-only Domain Controller from the drop-down list, as shown in Figure 10.5.

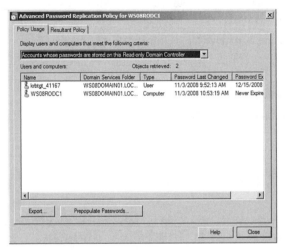

FIGURE 10.5
View cached credentials on an RODC.

10. View the accounts that have been cached by the RODC by reviewing the Users and computers section of the window.

Review Accounts That Have Been Authenticated on a Read-only Domain Controller

Scenario/Problem: You need to determine which users have logged on to AD DS by authenticating against an RODC.

Solution: Review the accounts that have been authenticated on an RODC.

To review the accounts that have been authenticated on an RODC, perform the following steps:

1. Log on to a domain controller or a member computer that has Windows Server 2008 RSAT installed.

2. Click Start, click Administrative Tools, and then click Active Directory Users and Computers.

3. Right-click Active Directory Users and Computers in the console tree, and click Change Domain Controller.

4. On the Change Directory Server window, select a writable domain controller that has W2K8 in the DC Version column and click OK.

5. In the console tree, expand the domain node and select the Domain Controllers node.

6. In the details pane, right-click the RODC on which you want to view the authenticated accounts; then click Properties.

7. Click on the Password Replication Policy tab.

8. On the RODC Properties page, click Advanced.

9. On the Advanced Password Replication Policy page, select Accounts that have been authenticated to this Read-only Domain Controller from the drop-down list, as shown in Figure 10.6.

10. View the accounts that have been authenticated by the RODC by reviewing the Users and computers section of the window.

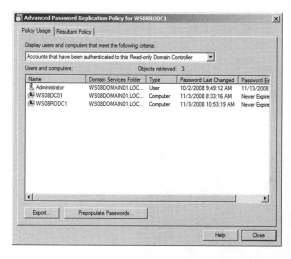

FIGURE 10.6
Viewing authenticated accounts on an RODC.

Automatically Move Accounts That Have Been Authenticated by an RODC to the Allowed List

Scenario/Problem: A number of users have been authenticated by an RODC. You want the RODC to cache the passwords for these accounts.

Solution: Use repadmin /prp to automatically add these accounts to the Allowed List for the Password Replication Policy on the RODC.

To automatically move accounts that have been authenticated by an RODC to the allowed list, perform the following steps:

1. Log on to a writable domain controller that has Windows Server 2008 installed.

2. Click Start, and click Command Prompt.

3. In the Command Prompt window, type the following command and press Enter:

   ```
   repadmin /prp move WS08RODC1.WS08DOMAIN01.local "WS08RODC1
   On-Demand"
   ```

   Table 10.1 lists each parameter used in the previous command.

TIP   For a full list of repadmin /prp parameters, go to http://technet.microsoft.com/en-us/library/cc835090.aspx.

Table 10.1   **Parameters to Automatically Move Accounts That Have Been Authenticated by an RODC to the Allowed List**

Parameter	Meaning
WS08RODC1.WS08DOMAIN01.local	Fully qualified domain name (FQDN) of RODC
"WS08RODC1 On-Demand"	The group name to be created in which to store the accounts

4. On the confirmation to move all security principals from the Auth2 list of the RODC to the Allow list, shown in Figure 10.7, type **Y**.

FIGURE 10.7
Confirmation to move accounts that have been authenticated by an RODC to the Allowed list.

5. On the confirmation page to create the AD DS group, shown in Figure 10.8, type **Y**.

6. Verify the command completed successfully, as shown in Figure 10.9.

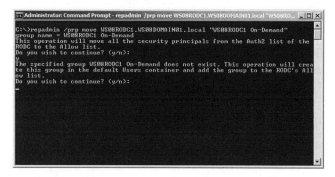

FIGURE 10.8
Confirm group creation.

FIGURE 10.9
Move accounts that have been authenticated by an RODC to the Allowed list.

Pre-populate the Password Cache for Read-only Domain Controller

Scenario/Problem: You want to ensure users can log on to the network in a branch office for the first time, even if the wide area network (WAN) link goes down.

Solution: Pre-populate the password cache for an RODC.

To pre-populate the password cache for an RODC, perform the following steps:

1. Log on to a domain controller or a member computer that has Windows Server 2008 RSAT installed.

2. Click Start, click Administrative Tools, and then click Active Directory Users and Computers.

3. Right-click Active Directory Users and Computers in the console tree, and click Change Domain Controller.

4. On the Change Directory Server window, select a writable domain controller that has W2K8 in the DC Version column and click OK.

5. In the console tree, expand the domain node and select the Domain Controllers node.

6. In the details pane, right-click the RODC on which you want to pre-populate the passwords; then click Properties.

7. Click on the Password Replication Policy tab.

8. On the RODC Properties page, click Advanced.

9. Click Prepopulate Passwords.

10. On the Select Users or Computers window, type the name of the user or computer for which you want to pre-populate the password. Then click OK.

NOTE The accounts for which the password are being pre-populated need to be added to the Allow List in the Password Replication Policy of the RODC. If you try to pre-populate the password for an account that does not belong to the Allow List, you will be presented with an error.

11. On the Prepopulate Passwords window, shown in Figure 10.10, click Yes to send the password to the RODC.

FIGURE 10.10
The Prepopulate Passwords window.

12. Ensure the results shows successful, as shown in Figure 10.11, and click OK.

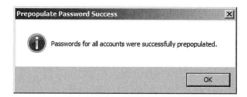

FIGURE 10.11
The pre-populate password results.

Reset the Credentials That Are Cached on a Read-only Domain Controller

Scenario/Problem: An RODC has been compromised. You want to ensure the cached credentials on the RODC cannot be used to compromise your AD DS forest.

Solution: Reset the credentials that are cached on the RODC.

To reset the credentials that are cached on an RODC, perform the following steps:

1. Log on to a domain controller or a member computer that has Windows Server 2008 RSAT installed.

2. Click Start, click Administrative Tools, and then click Active Directory Users and Computers.

3. Right-click Active Directory Users and Computers in the console tree, and click Change Domain Controller.

4. On the Change Directory Server window, select a writable domain controller that has W2K8 in the DC Version column and click OK.

5. In the console tree, expand the domain node and select the Domain Controllers node.

6. In the details pane, right-click the RODC that was compromised; then select Delete.

7. Click Yes to confirm the deletion, shown in Figure 10.12.

FIGURE 10.12
Confirming the RODC deletion.

8. On the Deleting Domain Controller page, select Reset All Passwords for User Accounts That Were Cached on This Read-only Domain Controller, type a location and filename to export the list of accounts that were cached on the RODC in the Location field, and click Delete.

CHAPTER 11

Manage Fine-Grained Password and Account Lockout Policies

Fine-grained password and account lockout policies are a new feature in Windows Server 2008. Fine-grained password policies allow you to define multiple password policies to different sets of users in a domain. Fine-grained account lockout policies allow you to define multiple account lockout policies to different sets of users in a domain.

This chapter describes the steps required to manage fine-grained password and account lockout policies.

> **NOTE** Fine-grained password and account lockout policies require a domain functional level of Windows Server 2008.

Create Password Settings Objects

> **Scenario/Problem:** Your company wants to enforce a stronger password policy for all IT administrators. This policy can apply only to IT administrators.

Solution: Create a password settings object (PSO).

To create a PSO, perform the following steps:

1. Log on to a domain controller (DC) or a member computer that has Windows Server 2008 Remote Server Administration Tools (RSAT) installed.

2. Click Start, click Run, type **adsiedit.msc**, and then click OK.

3. In the ADSI Edit snap-in, right-click ADSI Edit and then click Connect to.

4. On the Connection Settings window, shown in Figure 11.1, in the Name field type the fully qualified domain name (FQDN) of the domain in which you want to create the password settings object (PSO), ensure Default naming context is selected in the Select a well known Naming Context field, and then click OK.

5. In the console tree, expand the domain node; then expand DC=*domainname,* where *domainname* is the name of your domain.

6. Expand CN=System.

7. In the console tree, right-click the CN=Password Settings Container node, select New, and then click Object.

8. On the Create Object window, shown in Figure 11.2, click Next.

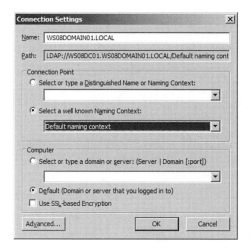

FIGURE 11.1
The ADSI Edit snap-in Connection Settings window.

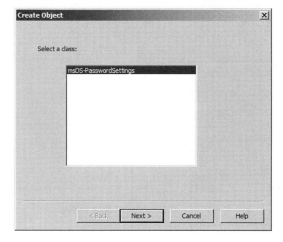

FIGURE 11.2
The Create Object window.

9. For the cn attribute, shown in Figure 11.3, type a name for the PSO in the Value field to set a Common-Name for the PSO; click Next.

10. For the msDS-PasswordSettingsPrecedence attribute, shown in Figure 11.4, type a value for the precedence in the Value field to set a password settings precedence for the PSO. Then click Next.

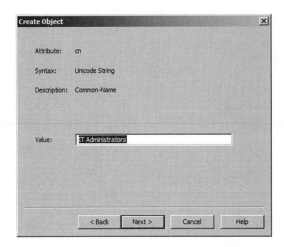

FIGURE 11.3
Creating the PSO's Common-Name.

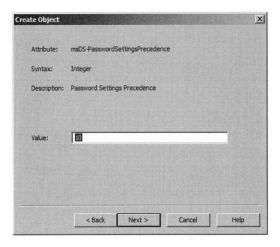

FIGURE 11.4
Creating the PSO's password
settings precedence.

11. For the msDS-PasswordReversibleEncryptionEnabled attribute, shown in
    Figure 11.5, type **TRUE** in the Value field to enable store password using
    reversible encryption or type **FALSE** in the Value field to disable store password
    using reversible encryption. Then click Next.

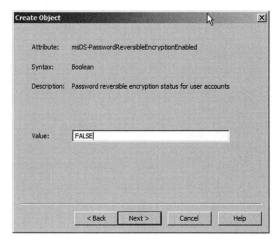

FIGURE 11.5
Creating the PSO's password reversible encryption status for user accounts.

12. For the msDS-PasswordHistoryLength attribute, shown in Figure 11.6, type a value for the password history length in the Value field and click Next.

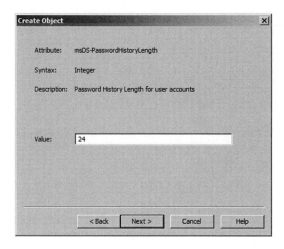

FIGURE 11.6
Creating the PSO's password history length for user accounts.

13. For the msDS-PasswordComplexityEnabled attribute, shown in Figure 11.7, type **TRUE** in the Value field to enable password complexity or type **FALSE** in the Value field to disable password complexity; then click Next.

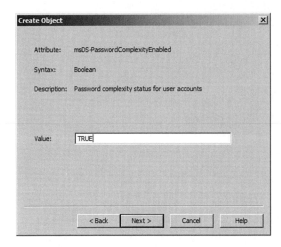

FIGURE 11.7
Creating the PSO's password
complexity status for user
accounts.

14. For the msDS-MinimumPasswordLength attribute, shown in Figure 11.8, type a
value for the minimum password length in the Value field and click Next.

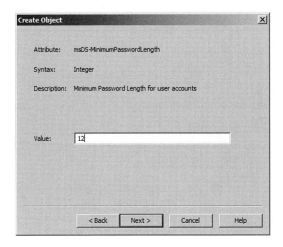

FIGURE 11.8
Creating the PSO's minimum password length for user accounts.

15. For the msDS-MinimumPasswordAge attribute, shown in Figure 11.9, type a
value for the minimum password age in the Value field. Then click Next.

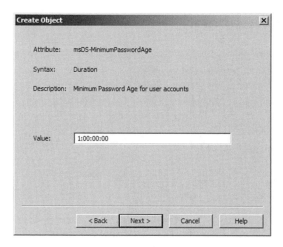

FIGURE 11.9
Creating the PSO's minimum password age for user accounts.

16. For the msDS-MaximumPasswordAge attribute, shown in Figure 11.10, type a value for the maximum password age in the Value field and click Next.

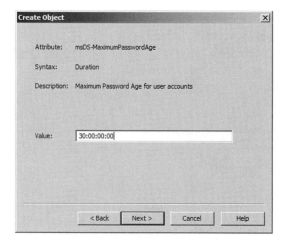

FIGURE 11.10
Creating the PSO's maximum password age for user accounts.

17. For the msDS-LockoutThreshold attribute, shown in Figure 11.11, type a value for the lockout threshold in the Value field; then click Next.

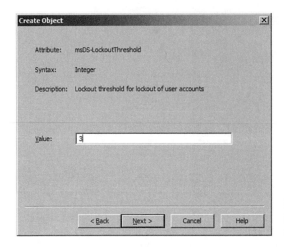

FIGURE 11.11
Creating the PSO's lockout threshold for lockout of user accounts.

18. For the msDS-LockoutObservationWindow attribute, shown in Figure 11.12, type a value for the observation window for lockout of user accounts in the Value field and click Next.

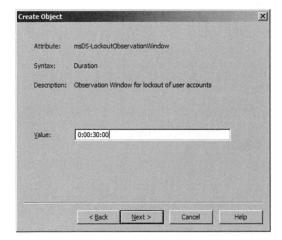

FIGURE 11.12
Creating the PSO's observation window for lockout of user accounts.

19. For the msDS-LockoutDuration attribute, shown in Figure 11.13, type a value for the duration of the lockout of user accounts in the Value field; then click Next.

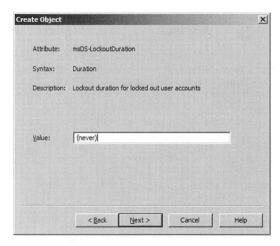

FIGURE 11.13
Creating the PSO's lockout duration for lockout of user accounts.

20. On the Create Object window, shown in Figure 11.14, click Finish to create the PSO.

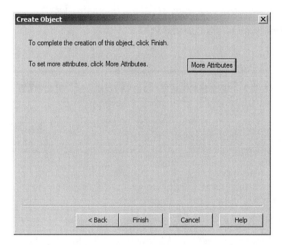

FIGURE 11.14
Completing the Create PSO Wizard.

NOTE The time-related PSO attributes (msDS-MaximumPasswordAge, msDS-MinimumPasswordAge, msDS-LockoutObservationWindow, and msDS-LockoutDuration) must be entered in the d:hh:mm:ss format or the I8 format. The d:hh:mm:ss format is only available in the Windows Server 2008 version of ADSI Edit.

Delete Password Settings Objects

Scenario/Problem: You previously created a PSO in your domain. The PSO is no longer required and you want to prevent it from being used in the future.

Solution: Delete the PSO.

To delete a PSO, perform the following steps:

1. Log on to a DC or a member computer that has Windows Server 2008 RSAT installed.

2. Click Start, click Administrative Tools, and then click Active Directory Users and Computers.

3. On the View menu, ensure Advanced Features is selected.

4. In the console tree, expand the System node and then select the Password Settings Container node.

5. In the details pane, right-click the PSO you want to delete; then click Delete.

6. Select Yes on the confirmation screen to delete the PSO.

View Settings Defined in Password Settings Objects

Scenario/Problem: You need to determine the settings that are applied in a PSO.

Solution: View settings defined in the the PSO.

To view the settings defined in a PSO, perform the following steps:

1. Log on to a DC or a member computer that has Windows Server 2008 RSAT installed.

2. Click Start, click Administrative Tools, and then click Active Directory Users and Computers.

3. On the View menu, ensure Advanced Features is selected.

4. In the console tree, expand the System node and then select the Password Settings Container node.

5. In the details pane, right-click the PSO you want to view; then click Properties.

6. If you do not see attributes whose settings you want to view, click Filter to customize the list of attributes shown on the Attribute Editor tab. The filter dialog box is shown in Figure 11.15.

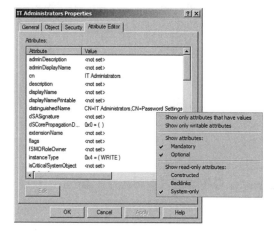

FIGURE 11.15
Customizing the list of attributes shown on the Attribute Editor tab.

7. Scroll the list of attributes to view the settings defined.

Modify Settings Defined in Password Settings Objects

Scenario/Problem: You previously created a PSO. You need to change the minimum password length in this PSO.

Solution: Modify settings defined in a PSO.

To modify the settings defined in a PSO, perform the following steps:

1. Log on to a DC or a member computer that has Windows Server 2008 RSAT installed.

2. Click Start, click Administrative Tools, and then click Active Directory Users and Computers.

3. On the View menu, ensure Advanced Features is selected.

4. In the console tree, expand the System node; then select the Password Settings Container node.

5. In the details pane, right-click the PSO you want to modify and click Properties.

6. If you do not see attributes whose settings you want to view, click Filter to customize the list of attributes shown on the Attribute Editor tab.

7. Select the attribute you want to modify, and click Edit.

8. Modify the value for the attribute, as shown in Figure 11.16, click OK, and then click OK to close the Attribute Editor.

FIGURE 11.16
Modifying the settings defined in a PSO.

Apply a Password Settings Object to Users and Security Groups

Scenario/Problem: You created a new PSO in your domain. You want to ensure the PSO is applied to all IT administrators.

Solution: Apply the PSO to an Active Directory Domain Services (AD DS) group to which all IT administrators belong.

To apply a PSO to a user or group, perform the following steps:

1. Log on to a DC or a member computer that has Windows Server 2008 RSAT installed.

2. Click Start, click Administrative Tools, and then click Active Directory Users and Computers.

3. On the View menu, ensure Advanced Features is selected as shown in Figure 11.17.

4. In the console tree, expand the System node and then select the Password Settings Container node.

5. In the details pane, right-click the PSO you want to configure and select Properties.

6. On the PSO properties page, click the Attribute Editor tab.

7. Click Filter, ensure the Show only attributes that have values option is not checked, as shown in Figure 11.18.

FIGURE 11.17
Advanced features in the Active Directory Users and Computers console.

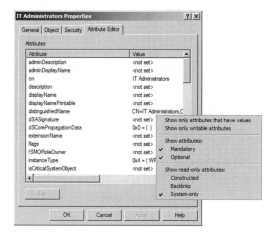

FIGURE 11.18
Filtering attributes in the Attribute Editor.

8. Select the msDS-PsoAppliesTo attribute, and click Edit.

9. On the Multi-valued Distinguished Name with Security Principal Editor window, shown in Figure 11.19, click Add Windows Account.

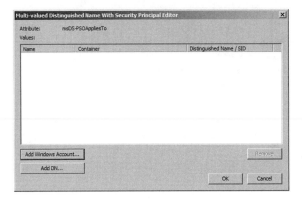

FIGURE 11.19
The Multi-valued Distinguished Name with Security Principal Editor window.

10. In the Select Users, Computers, or Groups window, type the name of the user or global group to which you want to apply the PSO, and click OK.

11. Click OK on the Multi-valued Distinguished Name with Security Principal Editor window; then click OK to close the properties for the PSO.

Modify the Precedence for Password Settings Objects

Scenario/Problem: You have multiple PSOs in your domain that are applied to global security groups. You want to ensure that a particular PSO is always applied to members of the IT Administrators AD DS group.

Solution: Modify the precedence for the PSO.

To modify the precedence for PSOs, perform the following steps:

1. Log on to a DC or a member computer that has Windows Server 2008 RSAT installed.

2. Click Start, click Administrative Tools, and then click Active Directory Users and Computers.

3. On the View menu, ensure Advanced Features is selected.

4. In the console tree, expand the System node and then select the Password Settings Container node.

5. In the details pane, right-click the PSO for which you want to modify the precedence; then select Properties.

6. On the PSO properties page, click the Attribute Editor tab.

7. Select the msDS-PasswordSettingsPrecedence attribute and click Edit.

8. In the Integer Attribute Editor window, shown in Figure 11.20, enter the new value for the PSO Precedence, and then click OK.

> **TIP** When multiple PSOs are applied to users or global groups in AD DS, the PSO with the lowest precedence value wins.

FIGURE 11.20
The Integer Attribute Editor window.

View the Resultant Password Settings Objects for a User or Group

> **Scenario/Problem:** You have multiple PSOs defined in your domain. You need to determine the effective PSO for a user account.

Solution: View the resultant PSOs for a user.

To view the resultant PSO for a user or group, perform the following steps:

1. Log on to a DC or a member computer that has Windows Server 2008 RSAT installed.

2. Click Start, click Administrative Tools, and then click Active Directory Users and Computers.

3. On the View menu, ensure Advanced Features is selected.

4. Locate the user account or group for which you want to view the resultant password settings objects, and click Properties.

5. Click the Attribute Editor tab.

6. Click Filter.

7. Ensure that the Show attributes/Optional check box is selected.

8. Ensure that the Show read-only attributes/Constructed check box is selected.

9. Select the msDS-ResultantPSO attribute and click View.

10. The resultant PSO is listed.

Create Shadow Groups

Scenario/Problem: You recently created a PSO in your domain. You need to apply the PSO to all user accounts located in an organizational unit called New York.

Solution: Create a shadow group in AD DS.

To create a shadow group, perform the following steps:

1. Log on to a DC.
2. Click Start, and click Command Prompt.
3. In the Command Prompt window, type the following command and press Enter:

   ```
   Dsquery user "OU=New York,DC=WS08DOMAIN01,DC=LOCAL" ¦ dsmod group
   "CN=New York Users,OU=New York,DC=WS08DOMAIN01,DC=LOCAL" -chmbr
   ```

   Table 11.1 lists each parameter used in the previous command.

Table 11.1 **Parameters to Create a Shadow Group**

Parameter	Meaning
"OU=New York,DC=WS08DOMAIN01,DC=LOCAL"	The DN of the OU that contains the user accounts.
"CN=New York Users,OU=New York,DC=WS08DOMAIN01,DC=LOCAL"	The DN of the group you want to use as the shadow group.
-chmbr	Replace group membership.

4. Verify that the results of the dsmod command entered above returns dsmod succeeded, shown in Figure 11.21.

FIGURE 11.21
Creating shadow groups.

CHAPTER 12

Manage Active Directory Domain Services Backup and Recovery

Backup and recovery in Windows Server 2008 has changed significantly from previous versions of Windows Server. Microsoft has replaced the NT Backup program with the Windows Server Backup server feature. Windows Server Backup is used to back up and restore Active Directory Domain Services (AD DS).

This chapter describes the steps required to manage AD DS backup and recovery.

Install the Windows Server Backup Server Feature

Scenario/Problem: You need to be able to perform backup and restore tasks on a domain controller.

Solution: Install the Windows Server Backup server feature.

To install the Windows Server Backup server feature, perform the following steps:

1. Log on to a domain controller that you want to back up.

2. Click Start, and then click Server Manager.

3. In the Features Summary section of Server Manager, shown in Figure 12.1, click Add Features.

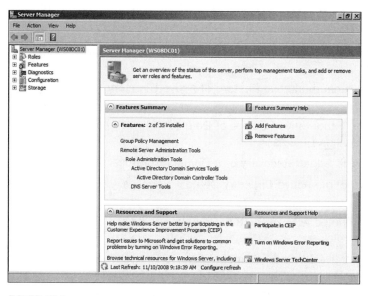

FIGURE 12.1
The Server Manager.

4. On the Select Features page, shown in Figure 12.2, select Windows Server Backup and Command-line Tools under the Windows Server Backup Features node and then click Next.

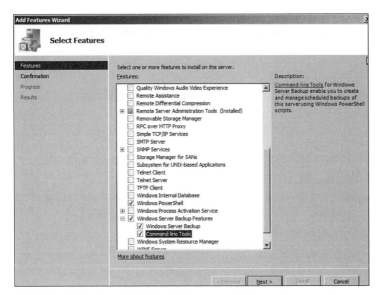

FIGURE 12.2
The Add Windows Server Backup feature.

5. If Windows PowerShell is not installed, you are prompted to install it, as shown in Figure 12.3. Click Add Required Features, and then click Next.

FIGURE 12.3
Adding the required features.

6. On the Confirm Installation Selections page, click Install.

7. Confirm that the installations completed successfully; then click Close.

Perform an Unscheduled Backup of Critical Volumes of a Domain Controller

Scenario/Problem: You are preparing to install new software on a domain controller. You want to be able to recover the domain controller to the state prior to installing the new software in the event of an issue.

Solution: Perform an unscheduled backup of critical volumes of a domain controller.

Perform an Unscheduled Backup of Critical Volumes of a Domain Controller by Using the Windows Interface

To perform an unscheduled backup of critical volumes of a domain controller by using the Windows interface, perform the following tasks:

1. Log on to a domain controller you want to back up.

2. Click Start, click Administrative Tools, and then click Windows Server Backup.

3. On the Action menu in Windows Server Backup, click Backup Once.

4. If you are creating the first backup of the domain controller, click Next to select Different options.

5. On the Backup options page of the Backup Once Wizard, shown in Figure 12.4, click Next.

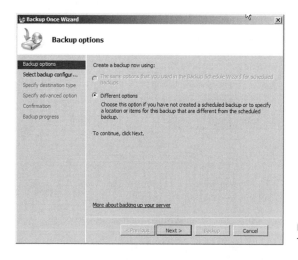

FIGURE 12.4
The Backup options page.

6. On the Select backup configuration page, shown in Figure 12.5, click Custom and then click Next.

FIGURE 12.5
The Select backup configuration page.

7. On the Select backup items page, shown in Figure 12.6, select the Enable system recovery check box to select all critical volumes; then click Next.

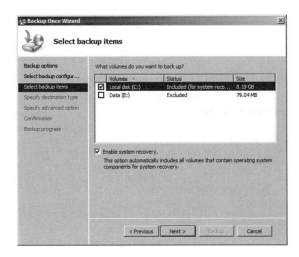

FIGURE 12.6
The Select backup items page.

8. On the Specify destination type page, shown in Figure 12.7, click Local drives or Remote shared folder and click Next.

TIP When a local drive is used as the backup destination, you cannot select a drive that is included in the critical-volume backup.

FIGURE 12.7
The Specify destination type
page.

9. If you are backing up to a local drive, on the Select backup destination page,
   shown in Figure 12.8, in the Backup destination box, select a drive; then click
   Next.

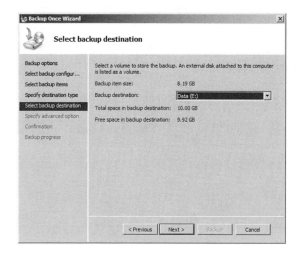

FIGURE 12.8
The Select Backup Destination
page.

10. If you are backing up to a remote shared folder, on the Specify remote folder
    page, shown in Figure 12.9, type the path to the shared folder, select Do not
    inherit under the Access Control section, and click Next.

11. On the Specify advanced option page, shown in Figure 12.10, select VSS copy
    backup and click Next.

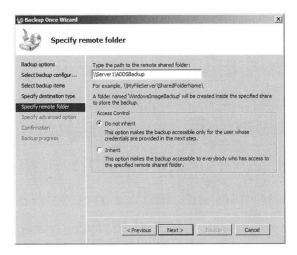

FIGURE 12.9
The Specify remote folder page.

FIGURE 12.10
The Specify advanced option page.

12. On the Confirmation page, shown in Figure 12.11, confirm your selections and click Backup.

TIP After the Backup Once Wizard begins the backup, you can click Close at any time. The backup runs in the background and you can view backup progress at any time during the process. The wizard closes automatically when the backup is complete.

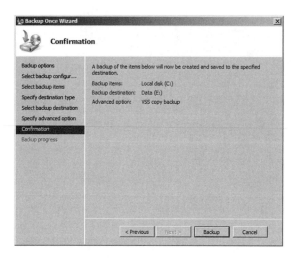

FIGURE 12.11
The Confirmation page.

Perform an Unscheduled Backup of Critical Volumes of a Domain Controller by Using the Command Line

To perform an unscheduled backup of critical volumes of a domain controller by using the command line, perform the following tasks:

1. Log on to the domain controller you want to back up.

2. Click Start, and click Command Prompt.

3. In the Command Prompt window, type the following command and press Enter:

   wbadmin start backup -backupTarget:E: -allCritical -quiet

   Table 12.1 lists each parameter used in the previous command.

Table 12.1   **Parameters to Perform an Unscheduled Backup of Critical Volumes of a Domain Controller by Using the Command Line**

Parameter	Meaning
start backup	Run a one-time backup.
-backupTarget	The storage location of the backup.
-allCritical	Include all critical volumes.
-quiet	Do not prompt to proceed with the backup operation.

TIP When a local drive is used as the backup target, you cannot select a drive that is included in the critical-volume backup.

4. The status and results of the backup are written to the command prompt window, as shown in Figure 12.12.

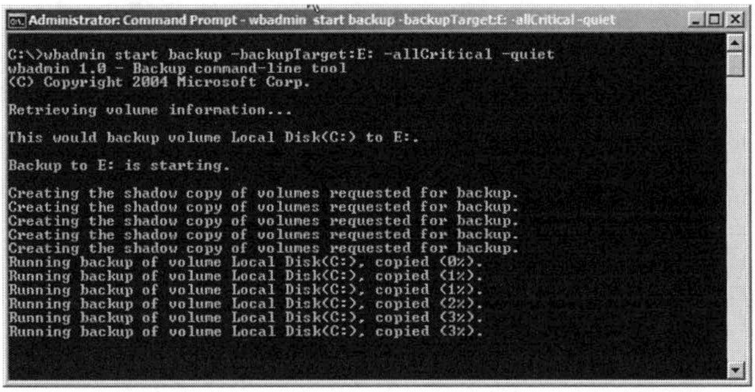

FIGURE 12.12
The critical-volume backup status and results shown in the command prompt window.

TIP For a full list of wbadmin start backup parameters, go to
http://technet.microsoft.com/en-us/library/cc742083.aspx.

Perform an Unscheduled System State Backup of a Domain Controller

Scenario/Problem: You are preparing to make a change to your AD DS database. You want to be able to recover AD DS data in the event that the change is problematic.

Solution: Perform an unscheduled system state backup of a domain controller.

To perform an unscheduled system backup of a domain controller, perform the following steps:

1. Log on to the domain controller you want to back up.

2. Click Start, and click Command Prompt.

3. In the Command Prompt window, type the following command and press Enter:

   wbadmin start systemstatebackup -backupTarget:E: -quiet

   Table 12.2 lists each parameter used in the previous command.

Table 12.2   **Parameters to Perform an Unscheduled System State Backup of a Domain Controller by Using the Command Line**

Parameter	Meaning
start systemstatebackup	Run a system state backup.
-backupTarget	The storage location of the backup.
-quiet	Do not prompt to proceed with the backup operation.

TIP   You cannot store a system state backup on a network shared drive.

4. The status and results of the backup are written to the command prompt window, as shown in Figure 12.13.

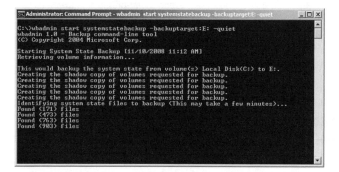

FIGURE 12.13
The system state backup status and results shown in the command prompt window.

NOTE   For a full list of wbadmin start systemstatebackup parameters, go to http://technet.microsoft.com/en-us/library/cc742124.aspx.

Perform an Unscheduled Full Server Backup of a Domain Controller

Scenario/Problem: You are making a configuration change to a domain controller. You want to ensure that data from all volumes can be restored.

Solution: Perform an unscheduled full server backup of a domain controller.

Perform an Unscheduled Full Server Backup of a Domain Controller by Using the Windows Interface

To perform an unscheduled full server backup of a domain controller by using the Windows interface, perform the following steps:

1. Log on to a domain controller you want to back up.

2. Click Start, click Administrative Tools, and then click Windows Server Backup.

3. On the Action menu in Windows Server Backup, click Backup Once.

4. If you are creating the first backup of the domain controller, click Next to select Different options.

5. On the Backup Options page of the Backup Once Wizard, click Next.

6. On the Select backup configuration page, shown in Figure 12.14, click Full server (recommended); then click Next.

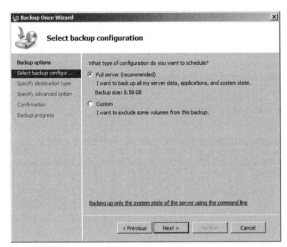

FIGURE 12.14
The Select backup configuration page.

7. On the Specify destination type page, click Local drives or Remote shared folder and click Next.

> **NOTE** When a local drive is used as the backup destination, you cannot select a drive that is included in the critical-volume backup.

8. If you are backing up to a local drive, on the Select backup destination page, in the Backup destination box, select a drive; then click Next.

9. If you are backing up to a remote shared folder, on the Specify Remote folder page, type the path to the shared folder, select Inherit under the Access Control section, and click Next.

10. On the Specify advanced option page, select VSS copy backup and then click Next.

11. On the Confirmation page, confirm your selections and click Backup.

> **TIP** After the Backup Once Wizard begins the backup, you can click Close at any time. The backup runs in the background, and you can view backup progress at any time during the process. The wizard closes automatically when the backup is complete.

Perform an Unscheduled Full Server Backup of a Domain Controller by Using the Command Line

To perform an unscheduled full server backup of a domain controller by using the command line, perform the following steps:

1. Log on to the domain controller you want to back up.

2. Click Start, and click Command Prompt.

3. In the Command Prompt window, type the following command and press Enter:

   `wbadmin start backup -include:C:,D:,F: -backuptarget:E: -quiet`

   Table 12.3 lists each parameter used in the previous command.

Table 12.3   **Parameters to Perform an Unscheduled Full Server Backup of a Domain Controller by Using the Command Line**

Parameter	Meaning
start backup	Run a one-time backup.
-include	The volumes to backup.
-backupTarget	The storage location of the backup.
-quiet	Do not prompt to proceed with the backup operation.

> **TIP** When a local drive is used as the backup target, you cannot select a drive that is included in the full backup.

4. The status and results of the backup are written to the command prompt window.

> **NOTE** For a full list of wbadmin start systemstatebackup parameters, go to http://technet.microsoft.com/en-us/library/cc742124.aspx.

Schedule Regular Full Server Backups of a Domain Controller

Scenario/Problem: You want to ensure that you can restore your domain controller to a previous date.

Solution: Schedule a regular full server backup of the domain controller.

Schedule Regular Full Server Backups of a Domain Controller by Using the Windows Interface

To schedule a regular full server backup of a domain controller by using the Windows interface, perform the following steps:

1. Log on to a domain controller you want to back up.

2. Click Start, click Administrative Tools, and then click Windows Server Backup.

3. On the Action menu in Windows Server Backup, click Backup Schedule.

4. On the Getting Started page, click Next.

5. On the Select backup configuration page, click Full server (recommended) and click Next.

6. If you want to schedule the backup to run once daily, on the Specify backup time page, shown in Figure 12.15, select Once a day, and select the time of day you want the backup to run, and click Next.

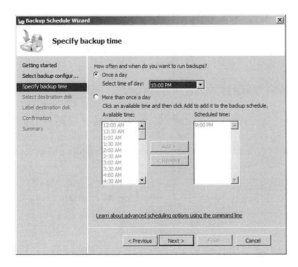

FIGURE 12.15
Scheduling a full server backup to run once a day.

7. If you want to schedule the backup to run more than once a day, on the Specify backup time page, shown in Figure 12.16, select More than once a day, select the times of day from the Available time section, click Add, and then click Next.

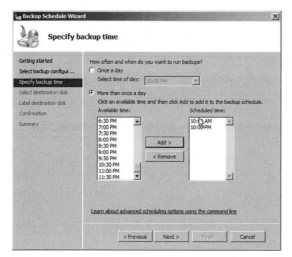

FIGURE 12.16
Scheduling a full server backup to run more than once a day.

8. On the Select destination disk page, click Show All Available Disks.

9. On the Show All Available Disks page, shown in Figure 12.17, select the disk on which you want to store the backups; then click OK.

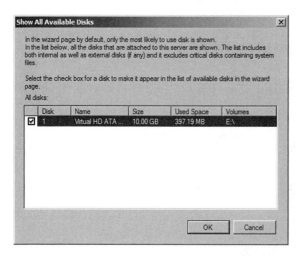

FIGURE 12.17
The Show All Available Disks page.

10. On the Select destination disk page, shown in Figure 12.18, select the disk on which you want to store the backups and click Next.

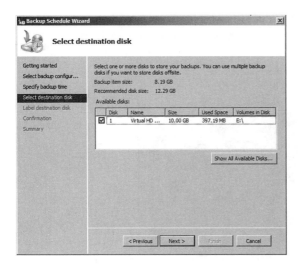

FIGURE 12.18
The Select destination disk page.

11. On the confirmation page to proceed, shown in Figure 12.19, click Yes.

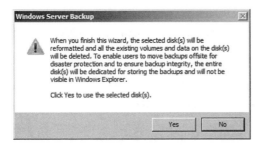

FIGURE 12.19
The page to confirm to proceed.

> **TIP**   When scheduling backups using Windows Server Backup, the destination disk is reformatted and data on that disk is lost.

12. On the Label destination disk page, click Next.

13. On the Confirmation page, click Finish.

Schedule Regular Full Server Backups of a Domain Controller by Using the Command Line

To schedule a regular full server backup of a domain controller by using the command line, perform the following steps:

1. Log on to the domain controller you want to back up.

2. Click Start, and click Command Prompt.

3. To obtain the Disk Identifier value to use for the backup target, type the following command into the Command Prompt window, as shown in Figure 12.20, and then press Enter:

    wbadmin get disks

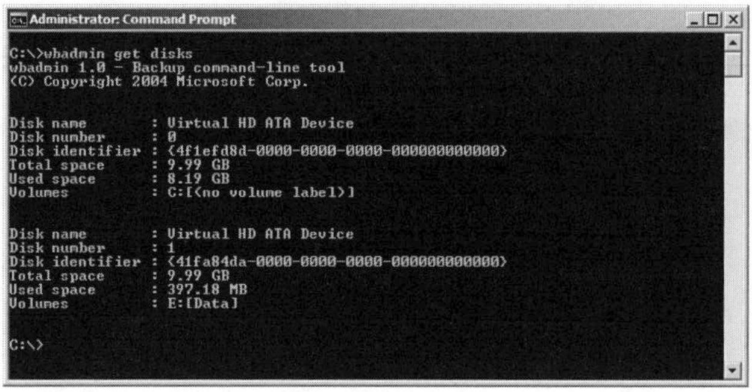

FIGURE 12.20
Obtaining a disk identifier.

4. Copy the value Disk Identifier value.

5. In the Command Prompt window, type the following command and press Enter:

    **wbadmin enable backup -addtarget:{41fa84da-0000-0000-0000-
    000000000000} -schedule:21:00 -include:C: -quiet**

    Table 12.4 lists each parameter used in the previous command.

Table 12.4   **Parameters to Schedule Regular Full Server Backups of a Domain Controller by Using the Command Line**

Parameter	Meaning
enable backup	Configure and enable a daily backup.
-addtarget:	The storage location of the backups.
	{41fa84da-0000-0000-0000-000000000000} represents the object identifier retrieved in Step 3.
-schedule	The schedule of the daily backups.
-include	The disks to include in the backups.
-quiet	Do not prompt to proceed with the backup operation.

TIP   When a local drive is used as the backup target, you cannot select a drive that is included in the full backup.

6. The status and results of the backup are written to the command prompt window, as shown in Figure 12.21.

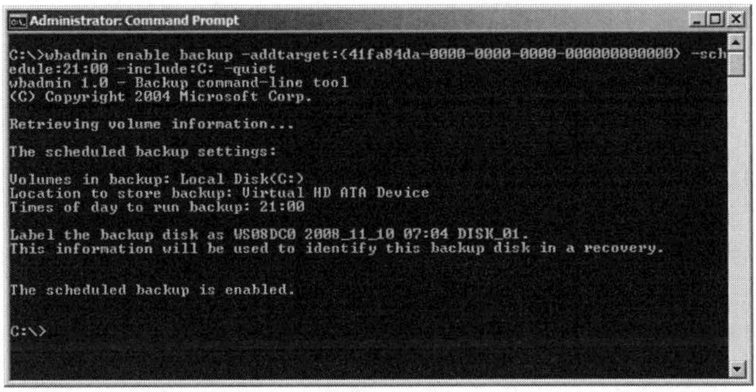

FIGURE 12.21
Scheduling a full backup status and results in the command prompt window.

> **TIP** For a full list of wbadmin enable backup parameters, go to
> http://technet.microsoft.com/en-us/library/cc742130.aspx.

Perform a Nonauthoritative Restore of Active Directory Domain Services

Scenario/Problem: A domain controller experienced a hardware failure that corrupted the AD DS database on this domain controller. The hardware failure has been resolved, and you need to restore the domain controller.

Solution: Perform a nonauthoritative restore of AD DS on the domain controller.

To perform an nonauthoritative restore of AD DS, perform the following steps:

1. Restart the domain controller you want to restore into Directory Services Restore Mode (DSRM).

> **TIP** To restart a domain controller in DSRM, you can use the following command
> before restarting the server: bcdedit /set safeboot dsrepair. After you
> completed your tasks, type the following command to ensure the domain controller
> restarts normally thereafter: **bcdedit /deletevalue safeboot**.

2. At the Windows logon screen, click Switch User and then click Other User.

3. Type .\administrator as the user name, type the DSRM password for the server, and then press Enter.

4. Click Start, and then click Command Prompt.

5. In the Command Prompt window, type the following command and then press Enter:

```
wbadmin get versions -backuptarget:E: -machine:WS08DC01
```

Table 12.5 lists each parameter used in the previous command.

Table 12.5 **Parameters to Get Backup Versions by Using Wbadmin**

Parameter	Meaning
get versions	Lists details of recoverable backups.
-backupTarget	The storage location that contains the backups.
-machine	The computer for which you want the backup details.

> **TIP** For a full list of wbadmin get versions parameters, go to http://technet.microsoft.com/en-us/library/cc742116.aspx.

6. Copy the version of the backup you want to restore, shown in Figure 12.22.

FIGURE 12.22
Getting a backup version identifier.

7. In the Command Prompt window, type the following command and then press Enter:

```
wbadmin start systemstaterecovery -version:11/10/2008-20:17
-backupTarget:E: -machine:WS08DC01 -quiet
```

Table 12.6 lists each parameter used in the previous command.

Table 12.6   Parameters to Get Backup Versions by Using Wbadmin

Parameter	Meaning
`start systemstaterecovery`	Run a system state recovery.
`-version`	The version identifier for the backup you want to restore. `"11/10/2008-20:17"` represents the version identifier retrieved in Step 6.
`-backupTarget`	The storage location of the backup.
`-machine`	The computer for which you want the backup details.
`-quiet`	Do not prompt to proceed with the restore operation.

> **TIP**   For a full list of wbadmin `start systemstaterecovery` parameters, go to http://technet.microsoft.com/en-us/library/cc742035.aspx.

8. The system state recovery process begins, and the status updates in the Command Prompt window, as shown in Figure 12.23.

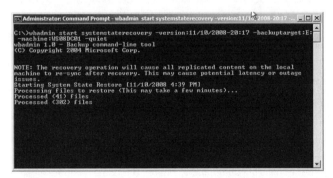

FIGURE 12.23
The system state recovery progress.

9. When the system state recovery is complete, a summary of the recovery operation is written to the Command Prompt window, as shown in Figure 12.24.

10. Ensure the recovery was successful, and restart the domain controller.

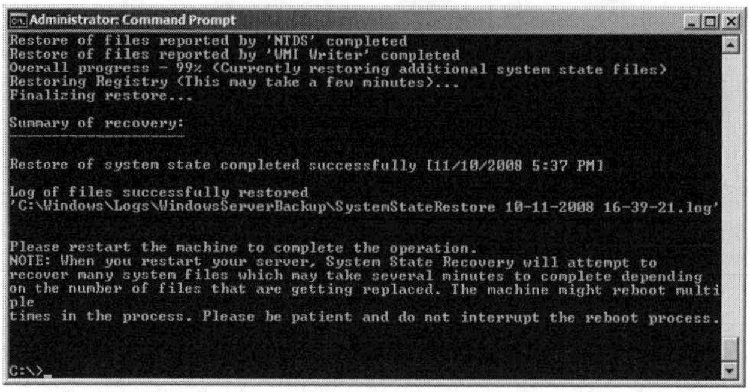

FIGURE 12.24
The summary report for system state recovery.

Perform an Authoritative Restore of Deleted Active Directory Domain Services Objects

Scenario/Problem: An organizational unit (OU) was accidently deleted from your domain. You need to restore the OU and the objects that were located in the OU.

Solution: Perform an authoritative restore of AD DS on the domain controller.

To perform an authoritative restore of AD DS, perform the following steps:

1. Restart the domain controller you want to restore into DSRM.

> **TIP** To restart a domain controller in DSRM, you can use the following command before restarting the server: `bcdedit /set safeboot dsrepair`. After you completed your tasks, type the following command to ensure the domain controller restarts normally thereafter: **bcdedit /deletevalue safeboot**.

2. At the Windows logon screen, click Switch User and then click Other User.
3. Type **.\administrator** as the user name, type the DSRM password for the server, and then press Enter.
4. Click Start, and then click Command Prompt.
5. In the Command Prompt window, type the following command and then press Enter:

   `wbadmin get versions -backupTarget:E: -machine:WS08DC01`

   Table 12.7 lists each parameter used in the previous command.

Table 12.7   **Parameters to Get Backup Versions by Using Wbadmin**

Parameter	Meaning
get versions	Lists details of recoverable backups.
-backupTarget	The storage location that contains the backups.
-machine	The computer for which you want the backup details.

> **TIP** For a full list of wbadmin get versions parameters, go to
> http://technet.microsoft.com/en-us/library/cc742116.aspx.

6. Copy the version of the backup you want to restore, shown in Figure 12.25.

FIGURE 12.25
Getting the backup version identifier.

7. In the Command Prompt window, type the following command and then press
   Enter:

   **wbadmin start systestaterecovery -version:11/10/2008-20:17
   -backupTarget:E: -machine:WS08DC01 -quiet**

   Table 12.8 lists each parameter used in the previous command.

Table 12.8   **Parameters to Start System State Recovery by Using Wbadmin**

Parameter	Meaning
start systemstaterecovery	Run a system state recovery.
-version	The version identifier for the backup you want to restore. "11/10/2008-20:17" represents the version identifier retrieved in Step 6.
-backupTarget	The storage location of the backup.
-machine	The computer you want restore.
-quiet	Do not prompt to proceed with the restore operation.

> **TIP** For a full list of wbadmin `start systemstaterecovery` parameters, go to
> http://technet.microsoft.com/en-us/library/cc742035.aspx.

8. The system state recovery process begins, and the status updates in the
   Command Prompt window, as shown in Figure 12.26.

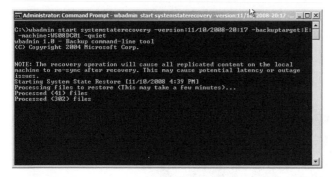

FIGURE 12.26
The progress of the system state recovery.

9. When the system state recovery is complete, a summary of the recovery operation is written to the Command Prompt window, as shown in Figure 12.27.

FIGURE 12.27
The summary report for system state recovery.

10. Ensure the recovery was successful.

11. In the Command Prompt window, type **ntdsutil** and press Enter.

12. At the ntdsutil prompt, type **activate instance NTDS**, as shown in Figure
    12.28, and press Enter.

FIGURE 12.28
The ntdsutil activate instance.

13. At the `ntdsutil:` prompt, type **authoritative restore**, as shown in Figure 12.29, and press Enter.

FIGURE 12.29
The ntdsutil authoritative restore.

14. To restore a subtree, type **restore subtree *DistinguishedName***, where *DistinguishedName* is the distinguished name of the subtree you want to restore.

15. To restore an object, type **restore object *DistinguishedName***, where *DistinguishedName* is the distinguished name of the object you want to restore.

TIP   For a full list of `ntdsutil` parameters, go to http://technet.microsoft.com/en-us/library/cc753343.aspx.

16. On the Authoritative Restore Confirmation Dialog page, shown in Figure 12.30, click Yes.

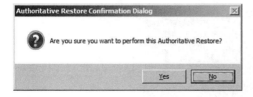

FIGURE 12.30
The Authoritative Restore Confirmation
Dialog page.

17. The status and results of the authoritative restore are written to the Command
    Prompt window, as shown in Figure 12.31.

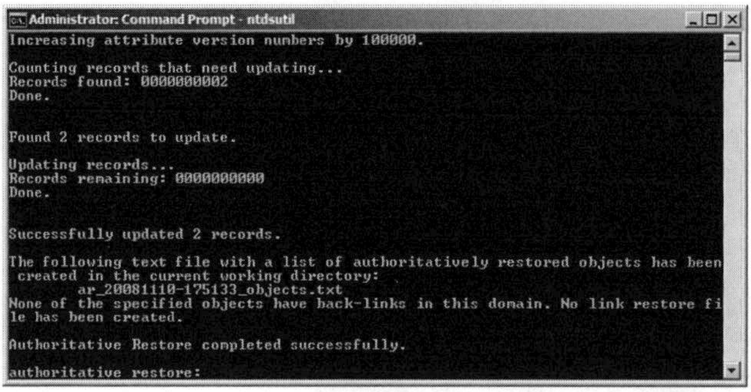

FIGURE 12.31
The authoritative restore results.

18. Ensure the authoritative restore completed successfully.

19. At the authoritative restore: prompt, type **quit**; then press Enter.

20. At the ntdsutil: prompt, type **quit**; then press Enter.

21. Restart the domain controller.

Perform a Full Server Recovery of a Domain Controller

Scenario/Problem: A domain controller experienced a hard drive failure. The faulty hard drive has been replaced. You need to restore the domain controller to a functional state.

Solution: Perform a full server recovery on the domain controller.

Perform a Full Server Recovery of a Domain Controller by Using the Windows Interface

To perform a full server recovery on a domain controller by using the Windows interface, perform the followings steps:

1. Insert the Windows Server 2008 installation DVD into the disk drive, and then restart the domain controller.

2. When you are prompted, press a key to start from the DVD.

3. On the Install Windows screen, shown in Figure 12.32, accept or select language options, the time and currency format, and a keyboard layout; then click Next.

FIGURE 12.32
The Install Windows screen.

4. At the Install Now screen, click Repair your computer.

5. In the System Recovery Options dialog box, shown in Figure 12.33, click anywhere to clear any operating systems that are selected for repair and then click Next.

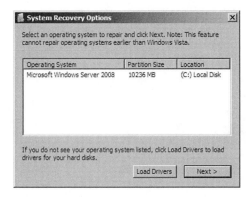

FIGURE 12.33
The System Recovery Options dialog box.

6. Under Choose a recovery tool, shown in Figure 12.34, click Windows Complete PC Restore.

FIGURE 12.34
The System Recovery Options page.

TIP If the backup is stored on a remote server, a message indicates that Windows cannot find a backup on the hard disks or DVDs on this computer. Click Cancel to close the message.

---

7. On the Restore your entire computer from a backup page, shown in Figure 12.35, select Use the latest available backup (recommended); then click Next.

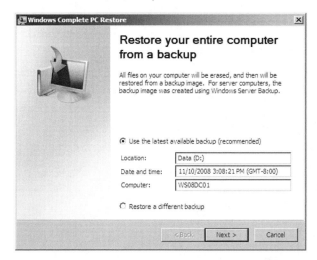

FIGURE 12.35
The Restore your entire computer from a backup page.

8. If you want to replace all data on the volumes, on the Choose how to restore the backup page, select Format and repartition disks; then click Next.

9. To prevent volumes that are not included in the restore from being deleted and re-created, click Exclude Disks, select the check box for the disks you want to exclude, as shown in Figure 12.36, and then click OK.

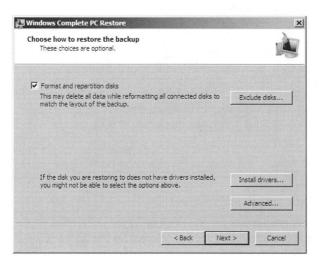

FIGURE 12.36
The Choose how to restore the backup page.

10. Click Next.

11. On the confirmation page, verify the restore settings and click Finish.

12. Select the I confirm that I want to format the disks and restore the backup check box, and then click OK.

Perform a Full Server Recovery of a Domain Controller by Using the Command Line

To perform a full server recovery on a domain controller by using the command line, perform the followings steps:

1. Insert the Windows Server 2008 installation DVD into the disk drive, and then restart the domain controller.

2. When you are prompted, press a key to start from the DVD.

3. On the Install Windows screen, shown in Figure 12.37, accept or select language options, the time and currency format, and a keyboard layout; then click Next.

FIGURE 12.37
The Install Windows screen.

4. At the Install Now screen, click Repair your computer.

5. In the System Recovery Options dialog box, shown in Figure 12.38, click anywhere to clear any operating systems that are selected for repair; then click Next.

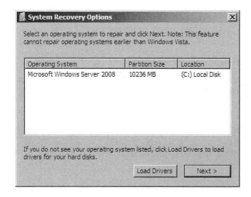

FIGURE 12.38
The System Recovery Options dialog box.

6. Under Choose a recovery tool, click Command Prompt.

7. At the Sources prompt, shown in Figure 12.39, type **diskpart** and then press Enter.

8. At the Diskpart prompt, shown in Figure 12.40, type **list vol** and then press Enter.

FIGURE 12.39
The Sources prompt.

FIGURE 12.40
The list vol Dispart command.

9. Identify the volume from the list that matches the location of the full server backup you want to restore.

10. Type **exit**, and then press Enter.

11. At the Sources prompt, type the following command and then press Enter:

    wbadmin get versions -backupTarget:D: -machine:WS08DC01

    Table 12.9 lists each parameter used in the previous command.

Table 12.9 **Parameters to Get Backup Versions by Using Wbadmin**

Parameter	Meaning
get versions	Lists details of recoverable backups.
-backupTarget	The storage location that contains the backups.
	This is the drive letter retrieved from Step 9.
-machine	The computer for which you want the backup details.

> **TIP** For a full list of wbadmin `get versions` parameters, go to
> http://technet.microsoft.com/en-us/library/cc742116.aspx.

12. Copy the version identifier of the backup you want to restore, as shown in Figure 12.41.

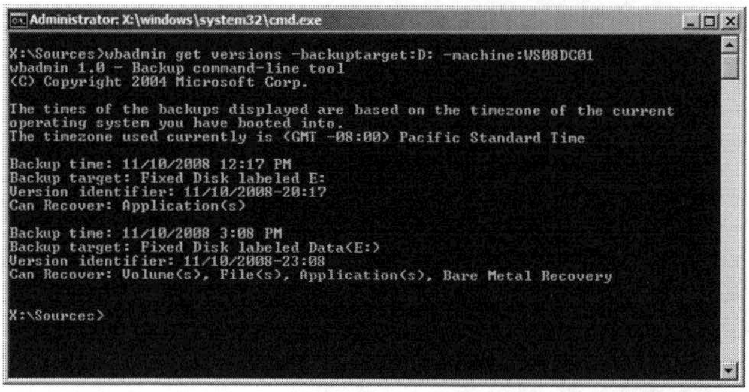

FIGURE 12.41
The backup version identifiers.

13. At the Sources prompt, type the following command and then press Enter:

```
wbadmin start sysrecovery -version:11/10/2008-23:08
-backupTarget:D: -machine:WS08DC01 -restoreAllVolumes
```

Table 12.10 lists each parameter used in the previous command.

Table 12.10   **Parameters to Start Full Server Recovery by Using the Command Line**

Parameter	Meaning
start sysrecovery	Run a system recovery.
-version	The version identifier for the backup you want to restore.
	"11/10/2008-23:08" represents the version identifier retrieved in Step 12.
-backupTarget	The storage location of the backup.
-machine	The computer you want restore.
-restoreAllVolumes	Restores all volumes from the selected backup.

> **TIP** For a full list of wbadmin `start sysrecovery` parameters, go to
> http://technet.microsoft.com/en-us/library/cc742118.aspx.

14. When you are prompted, press **Y** to proceed with the recovery, as shown in Figure 12.42.

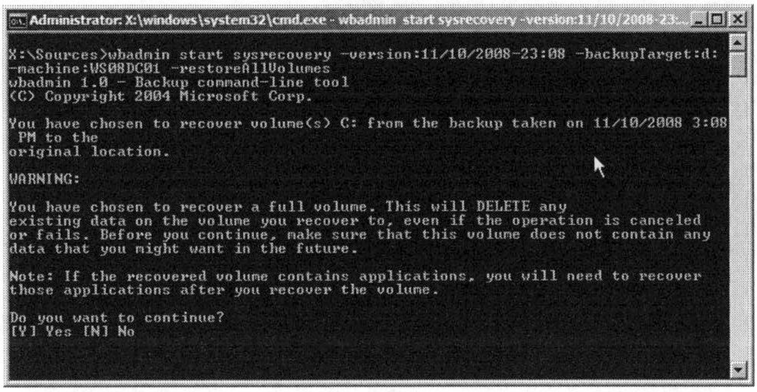

FIGURE 12.42
The confirmation to proceed with the recovery.

15. Restart the domain controller after the recovery operation has completed.

Create a Onetime Active Directory Domain Services Snapshot

Scenario/Problem: You plan to make a bulk change to AD DS data. You want the capability to compare AD DS data after the change against AD DS data before the change.

Solution: Create a onetime AD DS snapshot.

To create a onetime AD DS snapshot, perform the following steps:

1. Log on to a domain controller.

2. Click Start, and then click Command Prompt.

3. In the Command Prompt window, type **ntdsutil** and then press Enter.

4. At the ntdsutil prompt, type **snapshot** and then press Enter.

5. At the snapshot prompt, type **activate instance NTDS** and then press Enter.

6. At the snapshot prompt, type **create** and then press Enter.

7. Record the GUID that is returned by the previous command, as shown in Figure 12.43.

FIGURE 12.43
Creating a snapshot.

8. At the snapshot prompt, type **mount {0ed5ea9a-a3a9-4adc-9b1d-9ccd66048b13}**, where {*0ed5ea9a-a3a9-4adc-9b1d-9ccd66048b13*} is the GUID retrieved from Step 7, as shown in Figure 12.44.

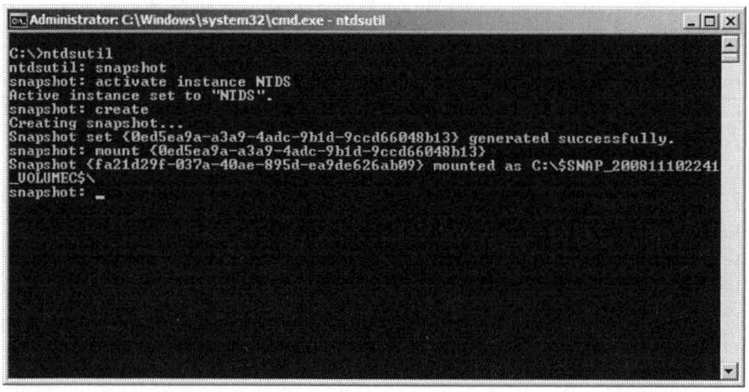

FIGURE 12.44
Mounting a snapshot.

9. Record the path where the snapshot was mounted.

Create Scheduled Active Directory Domain Services Snapshots

Scenario/Problem: You want to be able to compare AD DS data on an ongoing basis.

Solution: Create a scheduled AD DS snapshot.

To create a scheduled AD DS snapshot, perform the following steps:

1. Log on to a domain controller.

2. Click Start, click Administrative Tools, and then click Task Scheduler.

3. On the Action menu in Task Scheduler, click Create Task.

4. On the General tab of the Create Task window, shown in Figure 12.45, type a name for the task in the Name field.

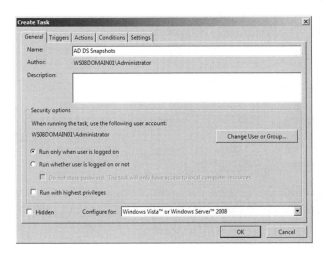

FIGURE 12.45
The General tab of the Create Task Wizard.

5. On the Triggers tab of the Create Task window, click New.

6. On the New Trigger page, define a trigger for the task and click OK, as shown in Figure 12.46.

7. On the Actions tab, click New.

8. On the New Action window, shown in Figure 12.47, ensure Start a program is selected from the drop-down list, type **C:\Windows\System32\ntdsutil.exe** into the Program/Script: field, and type **ntdsutil "activate instance ntds" snapshot create quit quit** into the Add arguments field; then click OK.

9. Click OK on the Create Task Wizard.

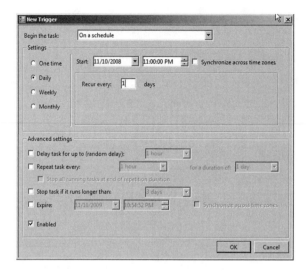

FIGURE 12.46
The New Trigger window.

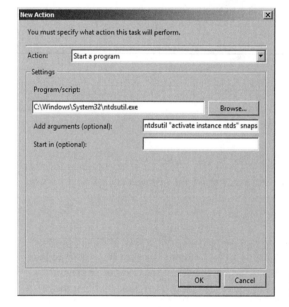

FIGURE 12.47
The New Action window.

Expose an Active Directory Domain Services Snapshot as an LDAP Server

Scenario/Problem: You previously created an AD DS snapshot. You need to be able to view data in the snapshot.

Solution: Expose an AD DS snapshot as an LDAP server.

To expose an AD DS snapshot as an LDAP server, perform the following steps:

1. Log on to a domain controller.

2. Click Start, and then click Command Prompt.

3. In the Command Prompt window, type the following command and press Enter:

   ```
   dsamain /dbpath C:\$SNAP_200811102241_VOLUMEC$\WINDOWS\NTDS\ntds.dit
   /ldapport 51389
   ```

   Table 12.11 lists each parameter used in the previous command.

Table 12.11   **Parameters to Expose an Active Directory Domain Services Snapshot as an LDAP Server**

Parameter	Meaning
/dbpath	Path to database file.
/ldapport	LDAP port number to use.

4. A message indicates that AD DS startup is complete, as shown in Figure 12.48.

FIGURE 12.48
Exposing an AD DS snapshot as an LDAP server.

5. If you plan to access data that is stored in the snapshot, leave the Command Prompt window open.

Access Data Stored in Active Directory Domain Services Snapshots

Scenario/Problem: You previously created an AD DS snapshot. You need to be able to retrieve data from the snapshot.

Solution: Access data stored in an AD DS snapshot.

Access Data Stored in Active Directory Domain Services Snapshots by Using LDP.exe

To access data that is stored in an AD DS snapshot by using LDP.exe, perform the following steps:

1. Log on to a domain controller.

2. Click Start, click Run, type **LDP.exe**, and then press Enter.

3. On the Connection menu, click Connect.

4. On the Connect window, shown in Figure 12.49, type the name of the server or type **localhost** in the Server field, type the port number to use to connect in the Port field, and then click OK.

FIGURE 12.49
The LDP Connect window.

5. On the Connection menu, click Bind.

6. In the Bind type section of the Bind window, click Bind as currently logged on user or click Bind with credentials and type a username, password, and domain for a user account that has permission to access the Active Directory data, as shown in Figure 12.50. Click OK.

7. On the View menu, click Tree.

8. On the Tree View window, shown in Figure 12.51, type the distinguished name of the parent container for the data you want to view; then click OK.

FIGURE 12.50
The LDP Bind window.

FIGURE 12.51
The LDP Tree View window.

9. In the console tree, double-click the container for the object you want to view.

10. The properties of the object appear in the details pane.

Access Data Stored in Active Directory Domain Services Snapshots by Active Directory Users and Computers

To access data that is stored in an AD DS snapshot by using Active Directory Users and Computers, perform the following steps:

1. Log on to a domain controller or a member computer that has Windows Server 2008 Remote Server Administration Tools (RSAT) installed.

2. Click Start, click Administrative Tools, and then click Active Directory Users and Computers.

3. In the console tree, right-click the Active Directory Users and Computers node and click Change Domain Controller.

4. On the Change Directory Server window, shown in Figure 12.52, click <Type a Domain Controller name or an IP Address here>, and type the name and port number of the server on which the snapshot is exposed.

5. Double-click the appropriate containers for the object you want to view, and then double-click that object to view its properties.

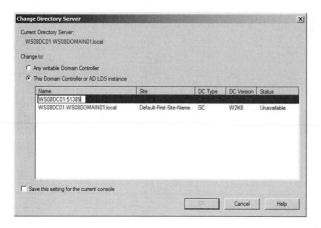

FIGURE 12.52
The Change Directory Server window.

CHAPTER 13

Manage Active Directory Domain Services Auditing

Active Directory Domain Services (AD DS) auditing in Windows Server 2008 has changed significantly from previous versions of Windows Server. Microsoft introduced more granular auditing capabilities in Windows Server 2008. In addition, AD DS auditing in Windows Server 2008 can be configured to log old and new values when changes to objects and their attributes are made.

This chapter describes the steps required to manage AD DS auditing.

Enable the Global Audit Policy

Scenario/Problem: You require the ability to audit access and changes made to AD DS data.

Solution: Enable the global audit policy.

Enable the Global Audit Policy by Using the Windows Interface

To enable the global audit policy by using the Windows interface, perform the following steps:

1. Log on to a domain controller or a member computer that has Windows Server 2008 Remote Server Administration Tools (RSAT) installed.

2. Click Start, click Administrative Tools, and then click Group Policy Management.

3. In the console tree of the Group Policy Management console, expand the Forest node, expand the Domains node, expand the node for the domain in which you want to configure auditing, and then expand the Domain Controllers node.

4. Right-click the Default Domain Controllers Policy, shown in Figure 13.1, and click Edit.

TIP By default, the Default Domain Controllers Policy group policy object (GPO) is linked to the Domain Controllers organizational unit (OU). If you have unlinked this GPO or linked additional GPOs, you need to select the applicable GPO.

5. In the console tree of the Group Policy Management Editor, expand the Computer Configuration node, expand the Policies node, expand the Windows Settings node, expand the Security Settings node, expand the Local Policies node, and select the Audit Policy node.

6. In the details pane, right-click Audit directory service access, shown in Figure 13.2, and click Properties.

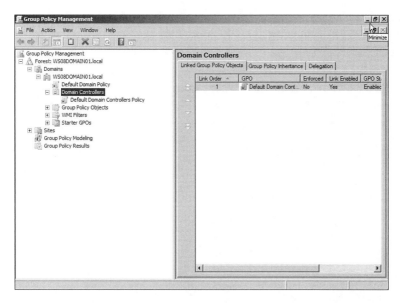

FIGURE 13.1
The Group Policy Management console.

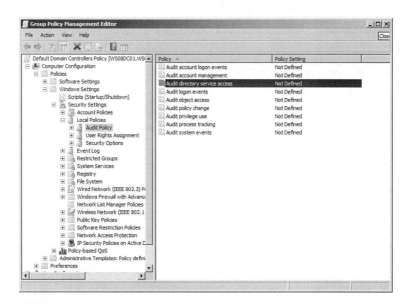

FIGURE 13.2
The Group Policy Management Editor.

7. On the Audit directory service access page, select Define these policy settings.

8. As shown in Figure 13.3, to audit successful directory services access attempts, select Success. To audit failed directory services access attempts, select Failed. Click OK.

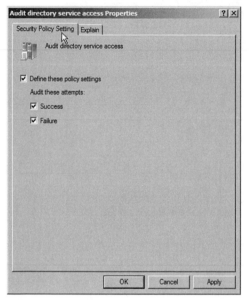

FIGURE 13.3
The Audit directory service access page.

9. Close the Group Policy Object Editor.

TIP Changes to GPOs take effect the next time group policy is applied to a user and/or computer. To force the application of a GPO, type **gpupdate /force** in the command line.

Enable the Global Audit Policy by Using the Command Line

To enable the global audit policy by using the command line, perform the following steps:

1. Log on to a domain controller.

2. Click Start, and then click Command Prompt.

3. To enable the auditing of successful attempts, in the Command Prompt window, type the following command, as shown in Figure 13.4, and then press Enter.

   ```
   auditpol /set /category:"DS Access" /success:enable
   ```

4. To enable the auditing of failed attempts, in the Command Prompt window type the following command, as shown in Figure 13.4, and then press Enter.

   ```
   auditpol /set /category:"DS Access" /failure:enable
   ```

FIGURE 13.4
Enabling the global audit policy using the command line.

5. Close the Command Prompt window.

Disable the Global Audit Policy

Scenario/Problem: You previously required the ability to audit access and changes made to AD DS data. You no longer require this ability.

Solution: Disable the global audit policy.

Disable the Global Audit Policy by Using the Windows Interface

To disable the global audit policy by using the Windows interface, perform the following steps:

1. Log on to a domain controller or a member computer that has Windows Server 2008 RSAT installed.

2. Click Start, click Administrative Tools, and then click Group Policy Management.

3. In the console tree of the Group Policy Management console, expand the forest node, expand the domains node, expand the node for the domain in which you want to configure auditing, and then expand the Domain Controllers node.

4. Right-click the Default Domain Controllers Policy, and click Edit.

TIP By default, the Default Domain Controllers Policy GPO is linked to the Domain Controllers OU. If you have unlinked this GPO or linked additional GPOs, you need to select the applicable GPO.

5. In the console tree of the Group Policy Management Editor, expand the Computer Configuration node, expand the Policies node, expand the Windows Settings node, expand the Security Settings node, expand the Local Policies node, and select the Audit Policy node.

6. In the details pane, right-click Audit directory service access and click Properties.

7. On the Audit directory service access Properties page, shown in Figure 13.5, deselect Define these policy settings.

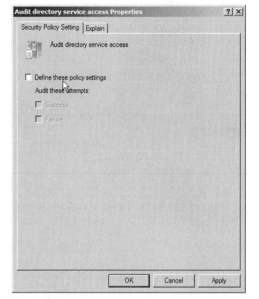

FIGURE 13.5
The Audit directory service access Properties page.

8. Close the Group Policy Object Editor.

> **TIP** Changes to GPOs take effect the next time group policy is applied to a user and/or computer. To force the application of a GPO, type **gpupdate /force** on the command line.

Disable the Global Audit Policy by Using the Command Line

1. Log on to a domain controller.

2. Click Start, and then click Command Prompt.

3. To disable the auditing of successful attempts, in the Command Prompt window, type the following command and then press Enter:

```
auditpol /set /category:"DS Access" /success:disable
```

4. To disable the auditing of failed attempts, in the Command Prompt window type the following command as shown in Figure 13.6, and then press Enter:

```
auditpol /set /category:"DS Access" /failure:disable
```

FIGURE 13.6
Disabling the global audit policy using the command line.

5. Close the Command Prompt window.

Retrieve the State of Directory Service Access Auditing Subcategories

Scenario/Problem: You need to determine the status of directory service access auditing.

Solution: Retrieve the state of the auditing subcategories.

To retrieve the state of Directory Service Access auditing subcategories, perform the following tasks:

1. Log on to a domain controller.

2. Click Start, and then click Command Prompt.

3. In the Command Prompt window, type the following command and then press Enter:

```
auditpol /get /category:"DS Access"
```

4. The status of each subcategory is returned in the Command Prompt window, as shown in Figure 13.7.

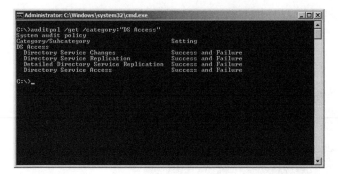

FIGURE 13.7
Retrieving the state of Directory Service Access auditing subcategories.

Enable the Directory Service Access Auditing Subcategory

Scenario/Problem: You need to audit all failed attempts to access AD DS data.

Solution: Enable the Directory Service Access auditing subcategory.

To enable the Directory Service Access auditing subcategory, perform the following steps:

1. Log on to a domain controller.

2. Click Start, and then click Command Prompt.

3. To enable the auditing of successful attempts, in the Command Prompt window, type the following command, as shown in Figure 13.8, and then press Enter:

   ```
   auditpol /set /subcategory:"directory service access"
   /success:enable
   ```

4. To enable the auditing of failed attempts, in the Command Prompt window, type the following command, as shown in Figure 13.8, and then press Enter:

   ```
   auditpol /set /subcategory:"directory service access"
   /failure:enable
   ```

FIGURE 13.8
Enabling the Directory Service Access auditing subcategory.

Disable the Directory Service Access Auditing Subcategory

Scenario/Problem: You do not need to audit all failed attempts to access AD DS data.

Solution: Disable the Directory Service Access auditing subcategory.

To disable the Directory Service Access auditing subcategory, perform the following steps:

1. Log on to a domain controller.

2. Click Start, and then click Command Prompt.

3. To disable the auditing of successful attempts, in the Command Prompt window, type the following command, as shown in Figure 13.9, and then press Enter:

   ```
   auditpol /set /subcategory:"directory service access" /success:
   disable
   ```

4. To disable the auditing of failed attempts, in the Command Prompt window, type the following command, as shown in Figure 13.9, and then press Enter:

   ```
   auditpol /set /subcategory:"directory service access" /failure:
   disable
   ```

FIGURE 13.9
Disabling the Directory Service Access auditing subcategory.

Enable the Directory Service Changes Auditing Subcategory

Scenario/Problem: You need to audit all failed attempts to modify AD DS data.

Solution: Enable the Directory Service Changes auditing subcategory.

To enable the Directory Service Changes auditing subcategory, perform the following steps:

1. Log on to a domain controller.

2. Click Start, and then click Command Prompt.

3. To enable the auditing of successful attempts, in the Command Prompt window, type the following command, as shown in Figure 13.10, and then press Enter:

   ```
   auditpol /set /subcategory:"directory service changes"
   /success:enable
   ```

4. To enable the auditing of failed attempts, in the Command Prompt window, type the following command, as shown in Figure 13.10, and then press Enter:

   ```
   auditpol /set /subcategory:"directory service changes"
   /failure:enable
   ```

FIGURE 13.10
Enabling the Directory Service Changes auditing subcategory.

Disable the Directory Service Changes Auditing Subcategory

Scenario/Problem: You do not need to audit all failed attempts to modify AD DS data.

Solution: Disable the Directory Service Changes auditing subcategory.

To disable the Directory Service Changes auditing subcategory, perform the following steps:

1. Log on to a domain controller.

2. Click Start, and then click Command Prompt.

3. To disable the auditing of successful attempts, in the Command Prompt window, type the following command, as shown in Figure 13.11, and then press Enter:

   ```
   auditpol /set /subcategory:"directory service changes"
   /success:disable
   ```

4. To disable the auditing of failed attempts, in the Command Prompt window, type the following command, as shown in Figure 13.11, and then press Enter:

   ```
   auditpol /set /subcategory:"directory service changes"
   /failure:disable
   ```

FIGURE 13.11
Disabling the Directory Service Changes auditing subcategory.

Enable the Directory Service Replication Auditing Subcategory

Scenario/Problem: You need to audit all failed attempts to replicate AD DS data.

Solution: Enable the Directory Service Replication auditing subcategory.

To enable the Directory Service Replication auditing subcategory, perform the following steps:

1. Log on to a domain controller.

2. Click Start, and then click Command Prompt.

3. To enable the auditing of successful attempts, in the Command Prompt window, type the following command, as shown in Figure 13.12, and then press Enter:

   ```
   auditpol /set /subcategory:"directory service replication"
   /success:enable
   ```

4. To enable the auditing of failed attempts, in the Command Pompt window, type the following command, as shown in Figure 13.12, and then press Enter:

   ```
   auditpol /set /subcategory:"directory service replication"
   /failure:enable
   ```

FIGURE 13.12
Enabling the Directory Service Replication auditing subcategory.

Disable the Directory Service Replication Auditing Subcategory

Scenario/Problem: You do not need to audit all failed attempts to replicate AD DS data.

Solution: Disable the Directory Service Replication auditing subcategory.

To disable the Directory Service Replication auditing subcategory, perform the following steps:

1. Log on to a domain controller.

2. Click Start, and then click Command Prompt.

3. To disable the auditing of successful attempts, in the Command Prompt window, type the following command, as shown in Figure 13.13, and then press Enter:

   ```
   auditpol /set /subcategory:"directory service replication"
   /success:disable
   ```

4. To disable the auditing of failed attempts, in the Command Prompt window, type the following command, as shown in Figure 13.13, and then press Enter:

   ```
   auditpol /set /subcategory:"directory service replication"
   /failure:disable
   ```

FIGURE 13.13
Disabling the Directory Service Replication auditing subcategory.

Enable the Detailed Directory Service Replication Auditing Subcategory

Scenario/Problem: You need to audit detailed replication information.

Solution: Enable the Detailed Directory Service Replication auditing subcategory.

To enable the Detailed Directory Service Replication auditing subcategory, perform the following steps:

1. Log on to a domain controller.

2. Click Start, and then click Command Prompt.

3. To enable the auditing of successful attempts, in the Command Prompt window, type the following command, as shown in Figure 13.14, and then press Enter:

   ```
   auditpol /set /subcategory:"detailed directory service replication"
   /success:enable
   ```

4. To enable the auditing of failed attempts, in the Command Prompt window, type the following command, as shown in Figure 13.14, and then press Enter:

   ```
   auditpol /set /subcategory:"detailed directory service replication"
   /failure:enable
   ```

FIGURE 13.14
Enabling the Detailed Directory Service Replication auditing subcategory.

Disable the Detailed Directory Service Replication Auditing Subcategory

Scenario/Problem: You no longer need to audit detailed replication information.

Solution: Disable the Detailed Directory Service Replication auditing subcategory.

To disable the Detailed Directory Service Replication auditing subcategory, perform the following steps:

1. Log on to a domain controller.

2. Click Start, and then click Command Prompt.

3. To disable the auditing of successful attempts, in the Command Prompt window, type the following command, as shown in Figure 13.15, and then press Enter:

   ```
   auditpol /set /subcategory:"detailed directory service replication"
   /success:disable
   ```

4. To disable the auditing of failed attempts, in the Command Prompt window, type the following command, as shown in Figure 13.15, and then press Enter:

   ```
   auditpol /set /subcategory:"detailed directory service replication"
   /failure:disable
   ```

FIGURE 13.15
Disabling the Detailed Directory Service Replication auditing subcategory.

Configure Auditing on Object Security Access Control Lists

Scenario/Problem: You require the ability to report on changes to user accounts located in a particular OU. You need to report on the value before the change and the value after the change.

Solution: Configure auditing on object security access control lists (SACLs).

To configure auditing on object SACLs, perform the following steps:

1. Log on to a domain controller or a member computer that has Windows Server 2008 RSAT installed.

2. Click Start, Administrative Tools, and then click Active Directory Users and Computers.

3. On the View menu, ensure Advanced Features is selected.

4. Locate the object on which you want to configure auditing; then click Properties.

5. On the object properties page, click the Security tab, shown in Figure 13.16.

6. On the Security tab, click Advanced.

7. On the Advanced Security Settings page, click the Auditing tab.

8. On the Auditing tab, shown in Figure 13.17, click Add.

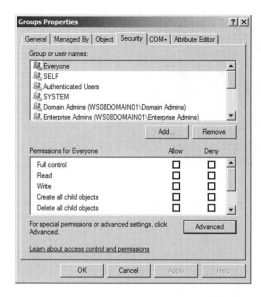

FIGURE 13.16
The object's Security tab.

FIGURE 13.17
The Auditing tab.

9. On the Select User, Computer, or Group page, shown in Figure 13.18, enter the name of the user, computer, or group for which you want to add the auditing entry; then click OK.

10. On the Auditing Entry page, under Apply Onto, select the types of objects to which you want the auditing applied.

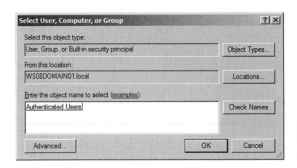

FIGURE 13.18
The Select User, Computer, or
Group page.

11. On the Auditing Entry for Groups, page, under Access, select the Successful and
    Failed actions you want to audit; then click OK.

12. Click OK to close the object properties page.

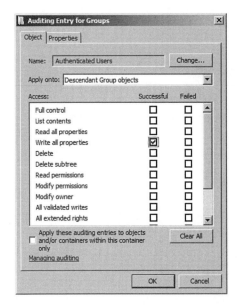

FIGURE 13.19
The Auditing Entry for Groups page.

Exclude an Attribute from Directory Service Auditing

Scenario/Problem: You need the ability to audit changes to user objects.
However, you do not want to audit changes made to the Description attribute.

Solution: Exclude an attribute for directory service auditing.

To exclude an attribute for directory service auditing, perform the following steps:

1. Log on to a domain controller or a member computer that has Windows Server 2008 RSAT installed.

2. Click Start, click Run, type **ADSIEdit.msc**, and then click OK.

3. In the ADSI Edit console, on the Action menu, click Connect To.

4. On the Connection Settings page, shown in Figure 13.20, type **Schema** in the Name field, select Schema from the drop-down list under Select a well known Naming Context, and then click OK.

FIGURE 13.20
The ADSI Edit Connection Settings page.

5. In the console tree, select the Schema node.

6. In the details pane, right-click the attribute you want to exclude from directory service auditing; then click Properties.

7. On the Object Properties page, shown in Figure 13.21, select the searchFlags attribute and then click Edit.

8. On the Integer Attribute Editor page, shown in Figure 13.22, type **0x100** into the Value field and click OK.

9. In the Object Properties page, the value for the searchFlags attribute is changed to 0x100 = (NEVER_AUDIT_VALUE), as shown in Figure 13.23. Click OK to close the Object Properties page.

FIGURE 13.21
The Object Properties page.

FIGURE 13.22
The Integer Attribute Editor page.

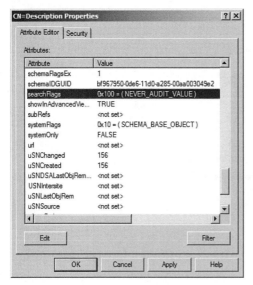

FIGURE 13.23
The Never_Audit_Value.

Index

A

H - I

J - K - L

Q - R

S